Debates in Art and Design Education

Debates in Art and Design Education encourages student and practising teachers to engage with contemporary issues and developments in learning and teaching. It introduces key issues, concepts and tensions in order to help art educators develop a critical approach to their practice in response to the changing fields of education and visual culture.

Accessible, comprehensive chapters are designed to stimulate thinking and understanding in relation to theory and practice, and help art educators to make informed judgements by arguing from a position based on theoretical knowledge and understanding. Contributing artists, lecturers and teachers debate a wide range of issues including:

- the latest policy and initiatives in secondary art education
- the concepts, skills and dispositions that can be developed through art education
- tensions inherent in developing the inclusive Art and Design classroom
- partnerships across the visual arts sector
- creativity in the Art and Design curriculum
- visual art and globalisation
- establishing the significance of 'Design'
- art practice as educational research.

Debates in Art and Design Education is for all student and practising teachers interested in furthering their understanding of an exciting, ever-changing field, and supports art educators in articulating how the subject is a vital, engaging and necessary part of the twenty-first century curriculum. Each chapter points to further reading and each section suggests reflective questions to help shape art educators' teaching. In particular, *Debates in Art and Design Education* encourages art educators to engage in research by providing an essential introduction to critical thinking around contemporary debates.

Nicholas Addison is Visiting Fellow and PhD supervisor in Art, Design and Museology at the Institute of Education, University of London.

Lesley Burgess is Senior Lecturer in Art, Desi........, and PGCE Subject Leader in Art and Desi........ity of London.

Debates in Subject Teaching Series

Series edited by: Susan Capel, Jon Davison, James Arthur, John Moss

The *Debates in Subject Teaching Series* is a sequel to the popular *Issues in Subject Teaching Series*, originally published by Routledge between 1999 and 2003. Each title presents high-quality material, specially commissioned to stimulate teachers engaged in initial training, continuing professional development and Masters level study to think more deeply about their practice, and link research and evidence to what they have observed in schools. By providing up-to-date, comprehensive coverage the titles in the *Debates in Subject Teaching Series* support teachers in reaching their own informed judgements, enabling them to discuss and argue their point of view with deeper theoretical knowledge and understanding.

Titles in the series:

Debates in History Teaching
Edited by Ian Davies

Debates in English Teaching
Edited by Jon Davison, Caroline Daly and John Moss

Debates in Religious Education
Edited by Philip Barnes

Debates in Citizenship Education
Edited by James Arthur and Hilary Cremin

Debates in Art and Design Education
Edited by Lesley Burgess and Nicholas Addison

Debates in Music Teaching
Edited by Chris Philpott and Gary Spruce

Debates in Physical Education
Edited by Susan Capel and Margaret Whitehead

Debates in Art and Design Education

Edited by
Nicholas Addison and Lesley Burgess

Routledge
Taylor & Francis Group

LONDON AND NEW YORK

First published 2013
by Routledge
2 Park Square, Milton Park, Abingdon, Oxon OX14 4RN

Simultaneously published in the USA and Canada
by Routledge
711 Third Avenue, New York, NY 10017

Routledge is an imprint of the Taylor & Francis Group, an informa business

British Library Cataloguing in Publication Data
A catalogue record for this book is available from the British Library

Library of Congress Cataloging in Publication Data
Debates in art and design education / [edited by] Nicholas Addison,
Lesley Burgess.
pages cm—(The debates in subject teaching series)
Includes index.
1. Art—Study and teaching (Secondary)—Great Britain. 2. Design—Study
and teaching (Secondary)—Great Britain. I. Addison, Nicholas, 1954–
editor of compilation. II. Burgess, Lesley, 1952– editor of compilation.
N365.G7D43 2012
707.1—dc23
2012008205

ISBN: 978-0-415-61886-1 (hbk)
ISBN: 978-0-415-61887-8 (pbk)
ISBN: 978-0-203-10071-4 (ebk)

Typeset in Galliard
by Book Now Ltd, London

MIX
Paper from
responsible sources
FSC
www.fsc.org FSC® C004839

Printed and bound in Great Britain by the MPG Books Group

Contents

List of figures

Notes on contributors

Nicholas Addison is a Visiting Fellow in Art, Design and Museology at the Institute of Education, University of London and a PhD supervisor. Until July 2011, Nicholas Addison was a senior lecturer in art, design and museology and programme leader for the MA Art and Design in Education. He has directed research projects investigating the role of critical studies in art and design and, more recently, pedagogic collaborations in contemporary art galleries. His research interests include: art practice as a mode of research within education, critical studies, intercultural education, sexualities and identity politics.

Rasheed Araeen is an artist, writer and the founder of both *Third Text* (London) and *Third Text Asia* (Karachi). He left Karachi for London in 1964 and has lived there since. In 1965 he pioneered minimalist sculpture in Britain. He began writing in 1975 and then publishing his own art journals: *Black Phoenix* (1978), *Third Text* (1987), *Third Text Asia* (2008). He has curated two important exhibitions: 'The Essential Black Art' (Chisenhale Gallery, 1987) and 'The Other Story' (Hayward Gallery, 1989). He is now directing a project that will produce the most comprehensive and inclusive history of art in post-war Britain, 'The Whole Story: Art in Post-war Britain'.

Dennis Atkinson is Professor of Art and Design Education at Goldsmiths, University of London. He is Director of the Research Centre for the Arts and Learning in the Department of Educational Studies. He was Principal Editor of the *International Journal of Art and Design Education* from 2002 to 2009. He has published in international academic journals since 1991 and his books include: *Art in Education: Identity and Practice* (Kluwer, 2002); *Social and Critical Practice in Art Education* (Trentham, 2005, co-editor with Paul Dash); *Regulatory Discourses in Education: A Lacanian Perspective* (Peter Lang, 2006, with Tony Brown and Janice England); and *Art, Equality and Learning: Pedagogies against the State* (Sense, 2011).

Christine Ballengee Morris is a Professor of Art Education and Founding Director of the Multicultural Center at The Ohio State University. She co-wrote a book, *Interdisciplinary Approaches to Art Education in High School*, published by the National Art Education Association. Her research examines social justice, social reconstructivism and post-colonialism as it relates to arts policy, curricula development, integrated curriculum, pedagogy and identity development. She is past president of the United States Society for Teaching through Art. Professor Ballengee Morris is the recipient of the 2006 J. Eugene Grigsby, Jr Award for her commitment to diversity, the 2007 Ziegfeld Award, for her service to diversity, and the 2008 National Art Education Association Higher Education Award–Western Division.

Lesley Burgess is a Senior Lecturer in Art, Design and Museology, Institute of Education, University of London, PGCE subject leader for the PGCE full-time and part-time courses in Art and Design, and module leader for the MA Contemporary Art and Artists in Education and the Foundation degree module: Creativity in Art Craft and Design. She has directed research projects in gallery and museum education and is a member of the ARTIST ROOMS research partnership. Her research interests include: issues of gender, social class, contemporary art and artists in education, gallery education and the international dimension of teacher education.

Helen Charman is Head of Learning at the Design Museum, London. An education professional with 20 years experience in cultural learning, former positions include Head of Learning and Access at the Museum of Contemporary Art, Sydney and Senior Curator: Education at Tate Modern. Helen is a trustee of Engage, the National Association for Gallery Education, and CET, the Creative Education Trust. Examples of publications and articles include *The Art Gallery Handbook* (Tate, 2006) and 'Designerly Learning at the Design Museum' *Design and Technology Education*, 15(3) (2010). She holds a BA (Hons) English Literature Oxon, MA History of Art (University of London) and a Doctorate in Museum Education (University of London). She is a visiting lecturer on the MA Museums and Galleries at the Institute of Education and the Kings/Southbank MA Education in Cultural Settings.

Gemma Cozens is a primary school teacher who specialises in early years education. She has worked in schools across London for the past eight years and now teaches in West Sussex. In 2009 she completed a Masters degree in Art and Design in Education at The Institute of Education, University of London. She has a background in Theatre Design, which she studied as a Bachelors degree at Central Saint Martins College of Art and Design, University of the Arts, London, graduating in 2004.

Leslie Cunliffe is a research fellow at the Graduate School of Education, University of Exeter. Previously he was a senior lecturer in art and art education. He ran the PGCE secondary art course and taught painting, drawing and art history to BA Ed. students with art as their main subject. His research interests include cognitive and socio-cultural processes and art education, assessment and art education, forms of knowledge and art education, creativity and art education, ethics and art education, and the relevance of Gombrich's, Heidegger's and Wittgenstein's work for art education. His publications have appeared in *Innovations in Education and Teaching International*, the *International Journal of Art and Design Education*, the *International Encyclopaedia of Communication*, the *Oxford Review of Education*, the *Journal of Aesthetic Education*, the *Journal of Cognitive Education and Psychology*, the *Journal of Empirical Aesthetics*, the *International Journal of Education through Art*, and the *Journal of Curriculum Studies*. A new article will be appearing in the *Journal of Aesthetic Education*. He has authored several chapters and exhibited at many venues including the Royal Academy of Art in London. In 2009 he gave a keynote address at the MUSE (Measuring Unique Studies Effectively) conference on assessment and creativity in higher art education in Savannah, USA.

Panagiotis Dafiotis is a visiting research associate at the Institute of Education, University of London. He taught art and design for seven years in Greek secondary schools and he is a practising artist. He gained his practice-led PhD in 2011 from the Institute of Education, investigating art practice as a form of research in art education.

Olivia Gude, a Professor at the University of Illinois at Chicago, was awarded the National Art Education Association's 2009 Lowenfeld Award for significant contributions to the field of art education. She is the Founding Director of the Spiral Workshop, a curriculum research project that provides art classes for urban teens. Her current research focuses on identifying new paradigms for structuring visual art curriculum, including the articles, 'Postmodern Principles' and 'Principles of Possibility' in the journal *Art Education*. She has created over fifty mural and mosaic projects, often in collaboration with inter-generational groups. Professor Gude frequently presents lectures and workshops on transforming art education and on community art practices at universities, school districts, conferences and museums.

Yiannis Hayiannis trained as a painter and taught art and design at primary and secondary level at an international school in London for eight years. His MA degree dissertation in art and design in education addressed the contribution of the artist/painter/educator to the art and design curriculum at Key Stage 3. He is presently engaged in doctoral research at the Institute of Education, University of London. His educational research adopts aspects of hermeneutic theory to investigate the significance of painting practice in secondary schools. His research is also informed by his interest in aesthetics and art history. He is a practising painter.

jan jagodzinski is a Professor in the Department of Secondary Education, University of Alberta in Edmonton, Alberta, Canada, where he teaches visual art and media education. His latest books include *The Deconstruction of the Oral Eye: Art and Its Education in an Era of Designer Capitalism* (Palgrave, 2010); *Arts Based Research: A Critique and Proposal*, with Jason Wallin (Sense Publishers, in progress), *Misreading Postmodern Antigone: Marco Bellocchio's Devil in the Flesh (Diavolo in Corpo)* (Intellect Books, 2011) and *Psychoanalyzing Cinema: A Productive Encounter of Lacan, Deleuze, and Zizek* (in progress, Palgrave).

Pam Meecham is a Reader in Museums and Galleries Education at the Institute of Education, University of London. She is currently course leader for the MA Museums and Galleries in Education and supervises doctoral students. Her research interests include contemporary art and museum history and education. She has lectured and published widely on visual culture, the history of art, the arts and regeneration and museum education. She has directed funded research projects on photography and young people and on the relationship between visual and written literacies. Her most recent publications include *Making American Art* (Routledge, 2009) and *Modern Art: A Critical Introduction* (Routledge, 2005) written in collaboration with Professor Julie Sheldon. They are currently writing *A History of Curating* due to be published 2013.

Emily Pringle trained as a painter and has worked in the field of arts and learning for twenty years, as an artist, gallery education coordinator, researcher, writer and teacher. She has a particular interest in the role of the artist in learning contexts and has worked closely with colleagues to investigate the relationship between artistic practice, research and learning. Her publications include 'We did Stir Things up: The Role of Artists in Sites for Learning' (Arts Council England, 2002) and 'The Gallery as a Site for Creative Learning' in '*The Routledge International Handbook of Creative Learning*' (2011). She is currently Head of Learning Practice, Research and Policy at Tate Gallery in London where she works on strategic programme development.

Claire Robins is a lecturer at the Institute of Education, University of London where she is programme leader for the MA Art and Design in Education, supervises PhD and EdD students, and teaches on the MA Museums and Galleries in Education. Originally trained as a fine artist, she has taught in schools, art colleges and galleries. She is currently completing a monograph, which examines the ways in which museums have deployed 'artists' interventions' to reinterpret and critique collections. She is particularly interested in artists who use 'trickster' tactics to intervene in educational contexts in parodic, ludic and disruptive ways.

John Steers was the General Secretary of the National Society for Art Education for thirty years until his semi-retirement in 2011. He has served on many national committees and as a consultant to government agencies. He has published widely on curriculum, assessment and policy issues. He was the 1993–1996 President of the International Society for Education through Art (InSEA). He was the 1998 recipient of the Edwin Ziegfeld Award of the United States Society for Education through Art and in 2011 he received InSEA's Sir Herbert Read Award for significant lifelong contributions to art education in the United Kingdom and internationally. He is a trustee of the Higher Education in Art and Design Trust and serves on the Advisory Committee of the National Arts Education Archive, Bretton Hall, West Yorkshire. He is currently the Chair of the Council for Subject Associations and a governor of Plymouth College of Art.

Acknowledgements

The editors would like to thank Rasheed Araeen for his permission to reproduce a slightly edited version of his paper 'Cultural Diversity, Creativity and Modernism' originally published in *Beyond Cultural Diversity* (London: Third Text Publications, 2010).

The editors would also like to extend their thanks to the Korean Society for Education through Art (KOSEA) for permission to reproduce a version of Olivia Gude's paper 'Creativity, for whom? Together Reconceptualising the Possibilities of Art Education' given at the KOSEA 2011 conference. The full paper is published in the KOSEA journal, 2012.

Emily Pringle would like to thank Mark Miller, Convenor Young Peoples Programmes, Tate Gallery and Henrietta Hine, Head of Public Programmes, Courtauld Institute of Art for the very useful conversations which have informed her chapter.

Introduction

Nicholas Addison and Lesley Burgess

This book is being published at a critical time for the subject Art and Design. Despite the fact that Ofsted (2009) claim that it is one of the best-taught subjects in the curriculum, as we write, its status as a foundation subject is under threat. By the time this book is published, the decision over whether to deny its statutory status will have been taken. We have recently received positive recommendations from the Expert Panel for the National Curriculum Review (James *et al.* 2011), who not only claim that Art and Design should remain as a foundation subject at Key Stages 1, 2 and 3 but also recommend that it should be an option in the basic curriculum at Key Stage 4; nevertheless, we are still unsure how the government will respond. We hope that sense will prevail. John Steers' chapter in this book gives an account of the negotiations that have been taking place between professional organisations such as NSEAD and the UK coalition government, and here sense does not appear to have been winning the day. Steers demonstrates how fraught the process has proved, irrefutable arguments for the subject being rejected in the coalition government's rush to instigate a so-called English Baccalaureate (EBac). This qualification, in its current form at the beginning of 2012, denies a place for art and design. The EBac replicates, almost exactly, the Victorian 'middle class' curriculum of 1868 and thus regresses to a set of subjects designed to fortify the British Empire and its administrative needs at home and overseas. The absence of art and design demonstrates politicians' reactionary failure to acknowledge the development of one hundred and fifty years of art education (which has had a global reach) while also ignoring the needs of the twenty-first century. In particular they have chosen to overlook the pivotal role of art and the visual more widely within contemporary society, specifically in relation to communications, digital technologies, the built environment and international design and fine art networks.

When the authors for this publication were invited to write chapters this scenario was unimaginable. Contributors in the main therefore speak of potential, imagining a developing and central role for art and design. We hope that the current threat to the subject will be short-lived and so the spirit of the book as a whole is towards what the subject could and should be. It would, however, be negligent to ignore this critical moment, and so in some chapters you may sense a feeling of anxiety. Nonetheless, we should remind you that such threats are not new. In the late 1970s, before the Gulbenkian Report was published (Robinson 1982), the subject was likewise being moved to the margins in the United Kingdom. The Gulbenkian Report convinced the then Conservative government of the necessity for the arts, just as the (National Advisory Committee on Creative and

Cultural Education (NACCE) report (Robinson 1999) convinced New Labour of the need for a creative curriculum, once again bolstering Arts subjects. Governments come and go; but it is vital that art educators recognise the seriousness of the current threat and argue cogently and vociferously for the significance of the subject for young people. Often such arguments focus on instrumental and economic benefits, such as feeding the creative industries. Although these are important, a case also needs to be made for Art and Design as a dynamic, creative and critical subject, one through which young people engage with, contribute to, and help to shape visual and material culture.

It is not our intention to claim that art and design teaching has somehow reached a point of consensus, a resolution of practice in which what it is to learn, in and through art, has been neatly defined and can thus be replicated and reproduced. The subject needs continually to be reassessed so that it addresses both its own internal dynamic as well as social and cultural changes. In agreement with many others we have long argued for art and design as an investigative and critical, as well as a creative, practice (Addison and Burgess 2000, 2003, 2007; Addison et al. 2010). An education through which young people not only engage with the potential of art to transform environments but one where they can explore and construct possible identities, investigate their place within cultural histories, and negotiate with others the role of visual and material culture in developing future communities. This requires both a sense of the centrality of making in contemporary global culture as well as knowledge of the diverse ways in which the visual arts provide evidence of historical cultures. Such knowledge enables young people to cherish the accumulated richness of their multiple heritages but also gives them the ammunition with which to question naturalised assumptions, myths of nationhood and other divisive apparatus that would destabilise the creative energies of developing intercultural formations.

The book is divided into five sections. The opening section (Part I) offers two chapters that constitute a prelude in which the authors provide 'cautionary tales', warnings both of current failures, potential losses and (im)possible futures. The central trio of sections follows a spatial pattern looking at: debates within the classroom (Part II), debates outside the classroom (Part III) and debates between classrooms and external interests (Part IV). This latter space is one where the artist teacher works as both educator and artist, often in the role of educational researcher. Increasingly, teachers in schools are being invited to contribute to educational research because of their grounded knowledge of classroom practices (Eisner 1998, 2004; Hickman 2007). In the field of art this often takes the form of practice-based or practice-led research, in which the artist/teacher presents understandings of art education through modes additional to writing. The book concludes (Part V) with a debate in which two authors contribute chapters about what constitutes knowledge in the constantly changing field of art and design education.

Part I: Cautionary tales

As discussed above, John Steers begins by looking at the recent negotiations between professional art educational organisations and a sceptical UK coalition government and usefully reiterates rationales for the purpose of the subject Art and Design in schools. In many senses he reiterates humanist and liberal beliefs rooted in a principled and pragmatic approach to what has worked within recent history, where reasoned argument backed by empirical research has convinced the political classes of the need for art education. From a different position, jan jagodzinski warns about collusion with neoliberalist agendas, castigating the way in which humanist principles both hide and support rampant capitalism and its 'hijacking of creativity'. Drawing on Deleuze he proposes a less reasoned, more vital approach, in which creativity becomes a matter of life rather than personal or national success. At the same time he notes that practices within the subject must acknowledge the primary means of visual communication/creativity in circulation, thus underlining the necessity for working with moving image and multimodal, digital technologies.

Part II: Debates within the classroom

Olivia Gude, revisits the idea that creativity is not a given for art and design but needs to be rethought and won in each new social situation. Like jagodzinski she bemoans the way that the rhetoric of creativity has been subsumed within economic and managerial discourses. She references a set of principles she designed to meet the emerging needs of twenty-first century art education. Although she often teaches outside the official curriculum, indeed with young people for whom school has proved alienating, these principles, co-formed with her students through practice, provide insights about what works, particularly in urban environments in the USA. She therefore adds a series of questions that can help art and design teachers to rethink the curriculum in relation to students' lived experiences and possible futures.

Christine Ballengee Morris looks at the state of race relations in the USA and shows how some artists are working with emergent identities and cultural formations. Taking a personal position, Ballengee Morris discusses what it is to be between races and ethnicities drawing on Critical Race Theory. In this way she navigates the permeable borders of a new identity politics which recognises the diasporic nature of most people's heritages. Although the debates in the United Kingdom follow slightly different trajectories, her insights provide useful strategies for engaging young people in their histories and in the co-construction of identities.

Gemma Cozens visits an early years setting to investigate the way in which children make visual representations. She uses Vygotskian theory on creativity and the imagination to argue a case for the process of making as an embodied experience, one in which the child produces a sequence of signs (akin to a narrative) that gradually unfolds, a process of becoming rather than a simple realisation of ideas. In this sense she critiques the rush towards preconceived learning objectives in which the teacher determines outcomes, even prototypes for replication. Instead she shows how children use available resources inventively to construct their own representations. The implications of this are that art teachers should recognise children's art practice as both temporal and social events, particularly when it comes to assessment (we would argue that this applies equally to students in secondary schools). In response to Cozens, Yiannis Hayiannis revisits the idea of embodiment and demonstrates how her arguments are equally pertinent for secondary schools. He locates his reflections within painting, reflecting on a practice that is sometimes seen as outmoded, but which he argues has much still to offer. He brings further insights on what an embodied practice means for learning with reference to the phenomenological theories of Merleau-Ponty.

Pam Meecham has long argued for critical approaches within art education (Meecham 1996, 2007) encouraging teachers to draw on recent art historical approaches as a resource. Here she looks at how art and design teachers might fruitfully engage with popular culture as a source for investigation. She does so not only as a means to answer the need for relevance and child-centred pedagogies, but rather as a source for engaging young people with history. Taking the current obsession with pirates as her starting point, she investigates historical documents about renowned seafarers, and by looking at illustrations of their time, unearths personas that question normative assumptions about pirate life and, simultaneously, naturalised views on sexuality and gender. She demonstrates that such widely accessible images can counter the reliance on fine art to open up for study the way images are constructed, revised and circulated so as to produce and sustain mythologies. Such investigations are an exercise in understanding power relations and the ways in which subjectivities and identities are formed.

Part III: Beyond the classroom

The debates beyond the classroom focus on the relationship between schools, galleries and history.

Rasheed Araeen has been at the forefront in the debates about what constitutes British art and British identity both as an artist and as a writer. Noted for his polemical writing, here he examines the history of modern art in Britain (and more widely) and reasserts the necessarily dialogic nature of its origins. He sees European modernity as a consequence of the colonial encounter, one in which art had a central educational as well as symbolic role and he unearths the two-facedness of so-called 'benevolent colonialism'. He cites cases in which contributions to the history of modernism by 'black artists' remain unrecognised. In this way he provides teachers in schools with an alternative narrative with which they can begin to rewrite the history of British art to demonstrate its intercultural basis.

Emily Pringle's ideas about learning in galleries resonate closely to those affective experiences theorised by Hargreaves (1983) and Taylor (1986: 18–34), respectively, the 'conversive/traumatic experience' and the 'illuminating experience', in which the person engaging with a work of art finds it disturbing and/or revelatory. Elsewhere we have critiqued the educational benefits of these ideas within formal education, arguing that it is difficult to engineer such experiences through organised gallery visits (Addison and Burgess 2007: 39–40). However, Pringle reconceives Hargreaves' ideas through the lens of Badiou via Atkinson, so that the humanist perspectives of Hargreaves and Taylor are tempered by the anti-pedagogies of Atkinson. However, Pringle also approaches education in galleries from a pragmatic point of view, adopting the principles promoted by Willis (1990) by embracing the 'multiple cultural practices beyond fine art' that constitute young people's entry into and ownership of cultural production. She feels that these everyday, youth practices, indicative of what she calls 'learner intelligence', can be married with the authoritative knowledge of the gallery to form interchanges that challenge both parties and thus reconfigure knowledge. In many ways Pringle's approach is eclectic, synthesising the numerous attempts by theorists since Kant to understand the power of the aesthetic in terms of reception.

Helen Charman looks at a somewhat neglected aspect of art and design, design education itself. In particular, she explores school students' engagement with design in the museum/gallery setting, advocating a critical approach to design history. Not long ago Steers (in Addison *et al*. 2010) provided a useful account of the changing fortunes of design within the secondary curriculum, where it is uncomfortably divided between design and technology and art and design. Here, Charman assumes a firm position for design practice wherever it is placed. She encourages art educators to always ask: where is design in my department's programmes of study? By design do I mean a process common to all making, or a specific field of production? Charman suggests that design is an inchoate field but provides definitions and resources to assist educators to navigate its borders. She also proffers Poynor's (2005) menu of key ingredients for cultural criticism as a vehicle to interrogate design in its many manifestations.

Part IV: Debates in-between

Both Claire Robins and Panagiotis Dafiotis demonstrate approaches to the emergent field of practice-as-research in education, one that has developed significantly since we edited the predecessor to this book, *Issues in Art and Design Teaching* (2003).

Dafiotis talks about the 'teaching artist' (collapsing the separation between activities implicit within the artist/teacher coupling) as an agent who researches by doing things, making art/events, affecting life. He contrasts this with the more usual educational researcher who tends to analyse and reflect on learning after the event, whether as an insider action researcher or an outsider ethnographer. Along with jagodinski he draws on Deleuze to propose a radical undoing of humanist agendas to conceive of more collaborative, open environments than schools usually allow. The examples he explores construct fluid, social environments, a hybrid between the art installation and the art classroom in which all participants can be seen as producers, both of affects and embodied thoughts.

Robins looks at the ways in which the privileging of word, particularly in educational contexts, has affected art and design. She works to further undermine unhelpful oppositions between word and image, demonstrating through specific instances, how art and design teachers reflect on their experience of education through practice-led research. She argues that the different registers of artworks enable artist/teachers to navigate affective territories that within other disciplines, particularly the social sciences, are often found unintelligible. She places this practice-based turn in educational research within the context of the wider critique of fine art practice that artists themselves have been conducting.

Part V: Forever changes

The book ends with two views on the possible future of art education. Both Dennis Atkinson and Leslie Cunliffe promote the study of art as an ethical pursuit: Atkinson in relation to 'the public good', Cunliffe to 'future flourishing'. Both critique those forms of instrumental education that would reduce learning to an apparatus ensuring economic growth. However, Atkinson, drawing on Badiou and Rancière, sees the need for a rupturing of existing knowledge in order that 'real learning' can take place, whereas Cunliffe, with reference to Gombrich and Steiner, extols the virtues of continuity. In this respect Atkinson discusses a 'third way' beyond economic and humanist principles, while Cunliffe sees the humanist project as an unfinished quest worth revitalising. It might be noted that Rancière himself, decidedly on the side of radical rather than humanist politics, argues that: 'the space of these clashes and that of the continuum can even bear the same name: History. History can indeed be two contradictory things: the discontinuous line of revealing clashes and the continuum of co-presence' (2007: 60). This suggests a coexistent and dialectical relationship ensuring 'forever changes'.

We hope the debates aired in this book will enable art educators to articulate a case for the school subject Art and Design as a necessary educational practice, one with a pivotal position within the curriculum. We believe that in the medium to longer term sense will prevail. But in the immediate future it is vital that art educators and teachers are proactive rather than defensive in their pedagogic practice.

References

Addison, N. and Burgess, L. (eds) (2000) *Learning to Teach Art and Design in the Secondary School*, 1st edn, London: Routledge.

Addison, N. and Burgess, L. (eds) (2003) *Issues in Art and Design Teaching*, London: Routledge.

Addison, N. and Burgess, L. (eds) (2007) *Learning to Teach Art and Design in the Secondary School*, 2nd edn, London: Routledge.

Addison, N., Burgess, L., Steers, J. and Trowell, J. (2010) *Understanding Art Education: Engaging Reflexively with Practice*, London: Routledge.

Eisner, E. (1998) *The Kind of Schools We Need*, Portsmouth, NH: Heinemann.

Eisner, E. (2004) 'What Can Education Learn from the Arts about the Practice of Education?', *International Journal of Education & the Arts*, 5 (4). Online. Available at: http://www.ijea.org/v5n4/index.html (accessed 28 January 2012).

Hargreaves, D.H. (1983) 'The Teaching of Art and the Art of Teaching: Towards an Alternative View of Aesthetic Learning', in: M. Hammersley and A. Hargreaves (eds) *Curriculum Practice: Some Sociological Case Studies*, London: Falmer.

Hickman, R. (2007) 'Visual Art as a Vehicle for Educational Research', *International Journal of Art and Design Education*, 26 (3): 314–324.

James, M., Oates, T., Pollard, A. and Wiliam, D. (2011) *The Framework for the National Curriculum: A Report by the Expert Panel for the National Curriculum Review*, London: DfE.

Meecham, P. (1996) 'What's in a National Curriculum', in: L. Dawtrey, T. Jackson, M. Masterton *et al.* (eds) *Critical Studies and Modern Art*, New Haven, CT: Yale University Press.

Meecham, P. (2007) 'Misfits: Technology in Art and Design', in: N. Addison and L. Burgess (eds) *Learning to Teach Art and Design in the Secondary School*, 2nd edn, London: Routledge.

Ofsted (2009) *'Drawing Together: Art Craft and Design in Schools'*, London, HMI/ Ofsted.

Poynor, R. (2005) 'Where Are the Design Critics?'. Online. Available at: http://observatory. designobserver.com/entry.html?entry=3767 (accessed 30 January 2012).

Rancière, J. (2007) *The Future of the Image*, London: Verso.

Robinson, K. (ed.) (1982) *The Arts in Schools: Principles, Practice and Provision*, London: Calouste Gulbenkian Foundation.

Robinson, K. (ed.) (1999) National Advisory Committee on Creative and Cultural Education (NACCCE), *All Our Futures: Creativity Culture and Education*, London: DfEE Publications.

Taylor, R. (1986) *Educating for Art*, London: Longman.

Willis, P. (1990) *Moving Culture*, London: Calouste Gulbenkian Foundation.

Part I

Cautionary tales

Chapter 1

Art and design education at the crossroads

John Steers

Causes for concern

'The Future of Art and Design in Schools' has been a frequent theme of art and design education conferences and publications for as long as I can remember. The reason is obvious: the subject too often is perceived as under some sort of threat in one way or another. It could be argued that art and design teachers are more paranoid than most, but it is worth remembering that even if they are, nevertheless the threats are sometimes real. Following the election of the coalition government in May 2010, all teachers concerned with creative and cultural education in English schools have very good reason to be more than usually concerned. Arts education is at a crossroads or, just as likely, precariously poised on a cliff edge.

Why? The short answer is the coalition government's education policies, experimental and ideological initiatives driven by Michael Gove, the Secretary of State for Education at the time. These include the introduction of the 'English Baccalaureate', a 'root and branch' review of the National Curriculum, proposed far-reaching changes to initial teacher education and student funding. Further concerns include the possible outcome of a Department of Culture Media and Sport (DCMS) review of 'Cultural Education' and the consequences of the decision by the Department of Business Innovation and Skills (BIS) to stop all money for teaching the arts and humanities in universities and specialist higher education institutions. All this is compounded by little evidence of any joined-up government thinking and a long list of likely unintended – or possibly intended – consequences. Each of these concerns is addressed in turn in this chapter.

The English Baccalaureate

The English Baccalaureate or 'EBac' was the first initiative to have a significant effect on art and design education in secondary schools. The government's White Paper *'The Importance of Teaching'* included an announcement of the introduction of the EBac and the news that it was to be reported in the School Performance Tables in January 2011 as an additional measure of a school's performance. The stated intention was 'to provide a powerful incentive for schools to drive the take up of individual science subjects, humanities such as history and, especially, foreign languages'

(DfE 2010: 44). It was claimed the EBac together with a reformed National Curriculum will give schools 'the freedom and the incentives to provide a rigorous and broad *academic* [my emphasis] education' (DfE 2010: 45).

The widespread concern expressed by schools immediately on the introduction of the EBac was not only because it was applied retrospectively, but because the range of subjects included was felt to be too narrow and not in any way inclusive of all students in the school.

It was immediately apparent that the term 'English Baccalaureate' is a misnomer. As currently adopted it is not a qualification, and the intention expressed in the White Paper that achieving the stated combination of GCSEs 'will entitle the student to a certificate recording their achievement' (DfE 2010: 44) has yet to materialise. No organisation has accepted responsibility for issuing certificates to individual students and, at the time of writing, the websites of the awarding bodies make it clear they have no plans to do so. The House of Commons Education Committee (HCEC) in their critical report on the English Baccalaureate proposed that plans for such certification should be shelved and they pointed out: 'We have not seen any evidence, either, that the cost and logistics of certification have been fully thought through' (HCEC 2011: 36). The Committee commented further:

> We do not believe the EBac – the hybrid of a certificate and a performance measure, named after a qualification – is appropriately labelled: it is not a baccalaureate, and as it stands the name can therefore be misleading to parents, professionals and pupils. The Government should assess the extent to which the name might cause confusion.
>
> (HCEC 2011: 13)

Therefore, as it stands the EBac is a government initiative deliberately privileging specific 'academic' subjects in secondary school and setting additional, arbitrary, standards for measuring the 'success' of the English education system.

The lack of any clear rationale for the academic subjects that have been included or omitted in the English Baccalaureate is curious. For example, many perceive the definition of humanities and languages GCSEs to be arbitrary – why include Ancient Hebrew for example? Why exclude the arts, design and technology, citizenship, religious education? John White observes:

> [Gove's] new English Baccalaureate is virtually a carbon copy of the 1868 Taunton report's curriculum for most middle class schools, as they were then called. The new award will be given to all 16-year-olds who have good exam grades in 'English, mathematics, the sciences, a modern or ancient foreign language and a humanity such as history or geography'. Taunton's list is identical, except that it makes both history and geography compulsory. How is it that a curriculum designed for clerks and shopkeepers in Dickens' England is at the cutting edge in 2010?
>
> (White 2011: 27)

It was immediately evident that many schools would now guide their students towards the named subjects at the expense of a broad and balanced curriculum and experience shows that coaching for GCSE examinations will often start in Year 7. The *Times Educational Supplement* published evidence for how the EBac has skewed the option choices that students are being given in 2011–2012: in 48 per cent of schools the curriculum had already been changed or was due to change to 'suit the demands of the English Baccalaureate' (Exley 2011: 22). Options to study subjects like art and design, music, religious education, drama, technology, business and information and communications technology, as well as vocational subjects, are being much reduced or even removed. An earlier (June 2011) indicative survey carried out by the National Society for Education in Art and Design (NSEAD) showed that teachers expected the numbers of students who opted to study art and design at Key Stage 4 to fall by 50 per cent in 2011–2012. At the same time teachers reported a 39 per cent fall in numbers opting for vocational courses, while 38 per cent expected the number of art and design teachers to decline and 57 per cent reported a cut in the capitation for their department (NSEAD 2011).

I had an early opportunity to question Michael Gove and Schools Minister Nick Gibb about the immediate impact of the EBac at the launch of the National Curriculum Review in January 2011. Ministers repeated that they wished to see a 'broad and balanced curriculum' and Gibb said that it was up to head teachers to choose what they offered. Nevertheless it is obvious that non-EBac subjects are being perceived as less valuable by schools, students and parents as a result of this government initiative. I was drawn to the obvious conclusion that – regardless of the ongoing Curriculum Review – the government is determined to slim down the curriculum and focus on academic subjects, and that the EBac was a pre-emptive and not very subtle lever for achieving this outcome with more or less immediate effect. Inevitably more students will be successful in achieving the English Baccalaureate targets in the next two years – purely because significantly more of them will have been entered for the qualifying examinations. The probable 'improvements' in school performance that thus will appear on paper will not directly reflect better teaching or higher student achievements. It will not provide a true, comparative measure of previous school performance although, doubtless, ministers will claim it as such.

Concern has been expressed that some schools have encouraged students to follow 'easier' courses – those that might have a too highly rated tariff for GCSE equivalence – in order to improve their position in the league tables. While this so-called 'gaming' issue needed to be addressed not all vocational courses should be tarred with the same brush. BTEC (Business and Technology Education Council) diplomas in art and design are rigorous and widely accepted for entrance to university art and design courses. The HCEC commented:

> The Government needs either to remove or revalue qualifications appropriately within the performance tables. We therefore welcome the Government's response to the Wolf review with regard to vocational qualifications and their league table tariffs. However, we remain unconvinced that the EBac is an effective way to

redress the perverse incentives generated by existing performance measures (indeed in some ways it risks generating its own perverse incentives) and we feel that the EBac serves as a distraction rather than a solution in this context.

(HCEC 2011: 35)

Ministers seem obsessed by opening up opportunities for admission to preferred Russell Group universities to the exclusion of other reputable institutions. 'Russell Group' seems to be Nick Gibb's shorthand for excellence. This begs the question 'where do specialist institutions like the independent art colleges, the Royal College of Art or the University of the Arts, as well as the art and design faculties of 80 or more other British universities fit into his world view'? It should be recognised that for those students who wish to pursue a career in the arts, especially art and design, the Russell Group have relatively little to offer.

I concede that a redesigned EBac might conceivably have a role as a 'leaving' certificate for students *if* it recognised student achievement in core skills *and* a range of 'academic' and 'practical' subjects – I dislike this pejorative distinction as I reject the implication that the arts are not cognitive activities and just as intellectually challenging as any other subjects. Wider educational achievements also should be included. It would need to be carefully designed, piloted and reviewed by teachers, academics and employers. There are some existing models on which to build. The Welsh Baccalaureate is a qualification for 14- to 19-year-olds that combines personal development skills with existing qualifications to make a wider award. It aims to help students to develop the knowledge and skills that higher education and employers want school leavers to demonstrate. The well-respected International Baccalaureate also provides a reasonable model from which to start. It has none of the limitations of the EBac that, as it stands, will damage the education of far too many young people and alienate them from school.

There is ample evidence there that the government's preferred choice of subjects is far from being the only route to success in so many fields – just take a look at the many stories on the website 'A Better Baccalaureate' (2011). We know that children learn in different ways, at a different pace and with different interests. Yet we hear Matthew Arnold's dictum on *education* often misquoted as a justification for a narrow academic curriculum. Arnold actually said: '... *culture* [my emphasis], the acquainting ourselves with the best that has been known and said in the world' (Arnold 1873: xxvii). That one word change makes a considerable difference to the meaning. If distant bearded sages are to be relied on for insights into twenty-first century education then it is worth remembering two epithets often attributed to Rabindranath Tagore (1861–1941). First: 'Don't limit a child to your own learning, for she was born in another time'. The second is also worth pondering on in this context:

[A]dults, because they are tyrants, ignore natural gifts and say that children must learn through the same process that they learned by. We insist upon forced mental feeding and our lessons become a form of torture. This is one of man's [*sic*] most cruel and wasteful mistakes.

Let us hope that Mr Gove and Mr Gibb, and any future education ministers, take heed.

It is axiomatic that everyone should have a good basic education in core skills and knowledge. But curriculum breadth is also very important, and all should have an education up to the age of 16 that includes the humanities and languages, creative arts, physical education, mathematics, science and technological study alongside the development of other essential skills and values. Students should be encouraged to keep their options open rather than specialise too early – in reality in many secondary schools preparation for GCSEs begins in Year 7. There should be a focus on what young people need to equip themselves for a future in the twenty-first century – not the nineteenth century.

There is an obvious danger that the EBac will be a disincentive to learning for more students than it will help, if it steers them to study courses which are inappropriate for them. Although I am aware that academies, free schools and independent schools are not required to follow the National Curriculum, I have little doubt that the EBac will be a very real factor in determining the curriculum in many such schools. Nick Gibb told the Select Committee that art and music would be fine because there would be 30 per cent of curriculum time available for such options (or 20 per cent for those who opt for triple science). This all seems highly unlikely and back of an envelope calculations suggest that there will be room for only one option choice for most pupils beyond the EBac subjects, plus statutory religious and physical education.

The Council for Subject Associations in its submission to the Education Select Committee's inquiry into the EBac advised that the government should cease to use the current English Baccalaureate as a performance indicator for schools. Instead, after careful deliberations, it should introduce a carefully planned EBac qualification to assure a broad and rounded education for students up to 16; and provide a leaving certificate that recognises a range of achievements and has currency with employers and for access to future education. This also was broadly the view of the HCEC in the conclusions and recommendations of their report which, despite being couched in parliamentary language, was unequivocal in its criticism (HCEC 2011: 39–42). In one final admonishment the House of Commons Select Committee concluded: 'We would therefore encourage the Government to take seriously the lessons to be learnt from [the introduction of the EBac], especially if, as we hope, the Government is to be successful in building greater respect for front-line professionals' (HCEC 2011: 37).

The curriculum review

The White Paper decreed that a new approach to the curriculum is needed, 'specifying a tighter, more rigorous model of the knowledge that every child should expect to master in core subjects at every key stage' (DfE 2010: 10). A review of the National Curriculum was announced with the aim of 'reducing prescription and allowing schools to decide how to teach, whilst refocusing on the core subject knowledge that every child and young person should gain at each stage of their education' (DfE 2010: 10). Over time it became apparent that this involved 'slimming down' the curriculum – that is removing subjects, and concentrating on 'core knowledge' to the exclusion of all else including any advice or guidance about related pedagogy.

Responses to the Curriculum Review were due by a deadline of 14 April 2011 and to the DfE's apparent surprise over 5,000 were submitted. The Department attributed this to unusual 'interest' but perhaps 'concern' would have been a more appropriate word. An Expert Group was established under the chair of Tim Oates from Cambridge Assessment. Oates (2010) had previously written a pamphlet entitled '*Could Do Better: Using International Comparisons to Refine the National Curriculum in England*, that had sufficiently impressed Michael Gove to persuade him to write the foreword and make this appointment. The pamphlet argued that:

> although the National Curriculum for England has been subjected to a protracted process of revision, the latest round of revisions failed adequately to draw from emerging analysis of high-performing systems around the globe.
>
> By taking a wrong turn in revision strategy, accumulated problems were not confronted and new problems were introduced. The paper outlines both the strengths and the weaknesses of current arrangements in England. It argues that a National Curriculum is extremely important, and that stability in arrangements is of considerable advantage to all. It draws from transnational analysis some key concepts – including 'curriculum coherence' and 'curriculum control' – to under-stand the operation of other nation systems and establish what we can learn from them, and identify what we can promote in our own system.
>
> (Oates 2010: 1)

While this sounds fairly innocuous, in reality it was a comprehensive demolition of the rationale and content of the New Secondary Curriculum (NSC) introduced in 2007; Oates argued that the most recent revision was a step backwards from the 1999 specifications and had been disastrous.

Hitherto the primary and secondary curriculum had not been considered together in previous reviews. Subsequent to the introduction of the NSC the former Chief HMI, Sir Jim Rose, was commissioned by the Labour government to undertake an 'independent' review of the primary curriculum. The Tories did not support Rose's final report (DCFS 2009) and on the last day of the parliamentary session before the May 2010 election a motion to introduce Rose's revised primary curriculum was defeated in the Commons. As Mick Waters, one time head of curriculum at the Qualifications and Curriculum Development Agency (QCDA), later admitted it was designed to defuse and undermine the radical overhaul required by Robin Alexander's Cambridge Primary Review (Alexander 2010).

I should probably identify my involvement in these events before I am accused of bias. I was a member of the so-called expert writing group for Jim Rose's report but I was far from happy with the outcome. Rose proposed an 'areas of experience' model that included 'The Arts' and I have argued elsewhere why this seldom works to the advantage of individual arts subjects (Steers 1988). On the other hand the very thor-ough Cambridge Primary Review remains on the table and deserves to be taken very seriously. I was also subject leader for art and design for the introduction of the New Secondary Curriculum in England and involved in its drafting.

From 2007 to 2010 ten subject associations worked with the education charity CfBT over a period of two and a half years to provide professional development for heads of department of their respective subjects. The overwhelming response of thousands of such people to the NSC was strong support. They saw the new curriculum not as over-prescriptive but as liberating. They accepted that they were free to provide a local curriculum tailored to their pupils' needs. Many excellent case studies point to the worthwhile changes taking place. Ofsted, before it seems to have been silenced, recognised it was having a significant impact. It was evident that the NSC was motivating and reinvigorating pupils and teachers alike.

This raises the question of who, apart from Michael Gove and Tim Oates, decided the NSC was a 'disaster'. Where has the evidence been presented? No systematic evaluation has taken place. At the time of writing (Autumn 2011) the first cohort of pupils has yet to take their GCSEs. It may prove somewhat embarrassing if it is seen to be working – or will improved GCSE results in 2012 year be dismissed by ministers as evidence of dumbing down and as the justification for radical change? It could even be claimed as evidence of the success of the EBac. It really is unjustifiable – a positive disgrace – that there has been no proper evaluation of the NSC before launching into yet another major 'review'.

The missing arts

The White Paper makes one solitary reference to the arts in all of its 91 pages. Paragraph 4.31 reads:

> Children should expect to be given a rich menu of cultural experiences. So we have commissioned Darren Henley to explore how we can improve music education and have more children learning to play an instrument. The Henley Review will also inform our broader approach to cultural education. We will support access to live theatre, encourage the appreciation of the visual and plastic arts and work with our great museums and libraries to support their educational mission.
> (DfE 2010: 46)

It will be apparent immediately that the White Paper identifies the government's concern with *appreciation* of the arts and, other than learning to play an instrument, makes no reference to practical creative activity. By the summer of 2011 the promise to support our 'great museums and libraries' began to ring hollow with libraries scheduled for closure across the country and the Museums Association reporting that museum funding was being cut by 25 per cent or more, over 60 per cent of museums having cut back their public events, half having reduced opening hours, and over 85 per cent cutting staff including a 30 per cent cut in education staff (Newman and Tourle 2011). At the same time it was already apparent that many schools will no longer offer the full range of options at Key Stage 4. Arts teachers are being made redundant, departments reduced in size and capitation is being cut. The Curriculum Review asks whether arts subjects should have a place in the curriculum at all. Surely this is philistinism on an unprecedented scale?

Rationales for arts education

There are many justifications for including art and design and arts education as part of general education, some, admittedly, more convincing than others. It has been argued (Kemmis *et al*. 1983) that rationales for art education form three broad categories: Expressionist, Reconstructivist, and Scientific Rationalist. To these categories I might add the pragmatists who would point to the economic value of the arts in society and the growth of the creative industries as a justification for the place of the arts in the curriculum.

Well considered and researched rationales that to a greater or lesser extent embrace all these rationales to emphasise the importance of arts and cultural education include the report of the National Advisory Committee on Creative and Cultural Education (NACCCE) All Our Futures: Creativity Culture and Education (Robinson 1999), the UNESCO Road Map for Arts Education: Building Creative Capacities for the 21st Century (UNESCO 2007), and most recently, the report commissioned by President Obama Reinvesting in Arts Education: Winning America's Future through Creative Schools (PCAH 2011). It seems evident, however, that the British government is either unaware of – or set on ignoring – the wide international consensus on the importance of arts education.

For an even more succinct rationale for the arts in schools I recommend the work of Elliot Eisner. In *The Arts and the Creation of Mind* (Eisner 2002: 75–92) he sets out key arguments for what specifically the arts can teach. In summary he argues that they teach children how to make good judgements and pay attention to qualitative relationships. This is unlike much of the curriculum in which correct answers and rules prevail; in the arts it is nuanced and subtle judgements rather than rules that matter. He quotes John Dewey's idea of 'flexible purposing': that is the ability to shift direction and to show a willingness to surrender to the unanticipated possibilities of a work as it unfolds. In complex forms of problem solving purposes are seldom fixed, but change with circumstance and opportunity. He writes of using materials as a medium: the ability to think through and within a material because all art forms employ some means through which images become real. The arts teach children to shape form to create expressive content: enabling them to have experiences that they can have from no other source and through such experiences to discover the range and variety of what they are capable of feeling. Eisner identifies an important feature of the arts in that they provide permission and encouragement to use the imagination as a source of content. He talks about learning to frame the world from an aesthetic perspective: the arts celebrate multiple perspectives – there are many ways to see and interpret the world. Eisner calls our attention to the way the arts can develop the ability to transform qualities of experience into speech and text. When children are invited to disclose what a work of art helps them feel, they have to reach into their poetic capacities to find the words that will do the job.

Historically the rationale for introducing art education to schools in the mid-nineteenth century was to fulfil two apparently straightforward aims: to provide 'an education of the eye, and of the hand, such as may indeed be the first step in the career of a great artist' (Committee of Council on Education, 1857–1858), but also to meet the economic needs of the country. Both aims remain relevant today although I would add providing the basis for a lifetime's enjoyment of the arts.

If these arguments are insufficiently convincing to the pragmatists then they need only look at today's economic facts. The most up-to-date statistics for the creative industries from the Department of Culture Media and Sport state:

- creative industries contributed 5.6 per cent of the UK's Gross Value Added in 2008;
- exports of services by the creative industries totalled £17.3 billion in 2008, equal-ling 4.1 per cent of all goods and services exported;
- there were an estimated 182,100 businesses in the creative industries on the Inter-Departmental Business Register (IDBR) in 2010, this represents 8.7 per cent of all companies on the IDBR;
- software and electronic publishing make the biggest contribution to GVA of the creative industries, at 2.5 per cent in 2008. They also make up a large number of total creative firms (81,700).

(DCMS 2010)

One in four new jobs in this country is in the creative sector and creative employ-ment provides around two million jobs, in the creative sector itself and in creative roles in other sectors. Employment in the sector has grown at double the rate of the economy as a whole. And yet Secretary of State Michael Gove is on record advocat-ing perspective drawing as the core of the subject, while Schools Minister Nick Gibb complained to me that nobody had taught him how to shade a circle to look like a sphere. (I offered to show him but he did not have time.) These seem extraordinarily limited views of what good art and design education can offer; views reminiscent of nineteenth-century drawing manuals. They both appear content to see the arts – and design and technology – wither in the curriculum without any thought of the eco-nomic realities, let alone less prosaic rationales.

Consequences

What happens to young people who want to pursue creative subjects? Or have more physical or practical leanings... or are less academically inclined? Neuroscientists tell us that not all people learn in the same way and it has long been recognised that some have exceptional ability in certain subjects – maths, music, art for example – that is not matched by all-round academic ability. Will these individuals once again be branded academic failures by the narrow measures of a limited education system? The emphasis on the EBac will have a negative impact on BTEC and other vocational routes, and will affect especially the arts and more practical subjects as students will be drawn into forced study of EBac subjects for GCSE and away from other subjects where their true interests and abilities lie. This clearly is not in their best interests but will be driven by a fear in schools of not meeting the arbitrary targets that have been set. I also think it is unlikely to do much to help the government's ambitions to improve behaviour in schools. The House of Commons Education Committee commented: '[T]he EBac's level of prescrip-tion does not adequately reflect the differences of interest or ability between individual young people, and risks the very shoehorning of pupils into inappropriate courses about which one education minister has expressed concerns' (HCEC 2011: 39).

Is the coalition government's much increased emphasis on academic subjects what employers and industry want? They have long argued that they need people with a range of flexible skills, including: self-reliance; enthusiasm; an aptitude for working as a team; technical skills; versatility; a creative approach to problem solving; creative thinking; ability to innovate; and digital and online creative skills. Surely these are skills that art and design education is especially good at nurturing?

Anyone doubting that many very successful people 'failed' at school should look at the testimonies on the 'A Better Baccalaureate' website. Sadly not all recover from this early set back and much potential talent is wasted. As Ken Robinson has argued there is much more to intelligence than academic ability and much more to education than developing it.

> Academic ability is not the same as intelligence. Academic ability is essentially a capacity for certain sorts of verbal and mathematical reasoning. These are very important, but they are not the whole of human intelligence by a long way. If there were no more to human intelligence than academic ability, most of human culture would not have happened. There would be no practical science or technology, no business, no arts, no music, no dance, drama, architecture, design, cuisine, aesthetics, feelings, relationships, emotions, or love. I think these are large factors to leave out of an account of intelligence. If all you had was academic ability, you wouldn't have been able to get out of bed this morning. In fact there wouldn't have been a bed to get out of. No one could have made one. You could have written about the possibility of one, but not have constructed it. Don't mistake me, I think that academic work – and the disciplines and abilities it can promote – are absolutely vital in education, and to the full development of human intelligence and capacity. But they are not the whole of them. Yet our education systems are completely preoccupied with these abilities to the virtual exclusion of many others that are equally vital – capacities that becoming more important every day.
>
> (Robinson 2001: 81)

The HCEC clearly concurs with this view:

> [A]cademic subjects are not the only path to a successful future, and all young people, regardless of background, must continue to have opportunities to study the subjects in which they are likely to be most successful, and which pupils, parents and schools think will serve them best.
>
> (HCEC 2011: 31)

The government's insistence on a 'slimmed down' curriculum in which the arts are at best marginal and possibly absent sends out a highly misguided and damaging message: it tells children, schools (and too often their parents) very clearly that the arts are unimportant.

An inconclusive and bleak conclusion

It is impossible to predict what might be the outcome of this unprecedented and precarious situation for art and design education. At the time of writing the Education

Bill awaited a full debate in the House of Commons. Despite the criticism of the EBac by the Education Committee, which had received over 300 submissions in response to its call for evidence (only ten of which supported its introduction in the current form), education ministers seem determined not to alter their proposals. In phase one of its work the National Curriculum Expert Committee chaired by Tim Oates focused on English, Maths, Science and Physical Education. Phase one was months behind schedule by Autumn 2011 and phase two had not commenced by this time as planned. No announcement on which subjects would be included in the National Curriculum from 2014 is expected until Spring 2012. Publication of Darren Henley's report on cultural education was also delayed possibly to ensure that it would not conflict with key ministerial decisions. Consultation on the government's strategy for initial teacher education was ongoing although it was becoming clear that neither schools nor universities were happy with the proposals.

These issues were set against mounting teacher unrest about punitive pension proposals, a salary freeze, the promise of more 'accountability measures', more and more schools opting out of local authority control and the abolition of a raft of government agencies including the General Teaching Council for England, and the Qualifications and Curriculum Development Agency. It is abundantly clear that the government has embarked on an unprecedented experiment with the future of education in England and it is impossible to predict what the eventual outcome might be.

However, it seems probable that art and design (and other subjects including music, design and technology, citizenship and religious education) will have a much weaker position in the curriculum and it would be left to the judgement of individual schools whether or not to continue to offer the subject for the foreseeable future. GCSE and GCE A-level entries for art and design could well plummet.

Government policies at both school and university level can be seen to be undermining 150 years steady development of art and design education. This will, I suggest, have a detrimental effect on the British economy and society. Ultimately there is nothing that makes the British inherently more creative than people in other countries: the reason for the United Kingdom's strong creative and design industries and hitherto vibrant arts sector is the education system that drives it. Secretaries of State come and go (they seldom remain in office for more than two years) and sooner or later there will be a U-turn on this issue and the arts and creative and cultural education will again be afforded their rightful place in the curriculum. We can only hope that this occurs before too much irreparable harm has been done.

References

A Better Baccalaureate (2011). Online. Available at: http://abetterbaccalaureate.org/ (accessed 15 July 2011).

Alexander, R. (ed.) (2010) *Children, their World, their Education* (Cambridge Primary Review), London: Routledge.

Arnold, M. (1873) *Literature and Dogma*, New York: Macmillan, Preface, p. xxvii.

Committee of Council on Education (1857–1858), in: S. Macdonald (1970) *The History and Philosophy of Art Education*, London: University of London Press.

DCMS (Department for Culture, Media and Sport) (2010) *Creative Industries Facts and Figures*, London: DCMS. Online. Available at: http://www.culture.gov.uk/what_we_do/ creative_industries/default.aspx (accessed 29 July 2011).

DCSF (Department for Children, Schools and Families) (2009) *Independent Review of the Primary Curriculum: Final Report*, Nottingham: DCSF Publications.

DfE (Department for Education) (2010) *The Importance of Teaching*, London: The Stationery Office.

Eisner, E. (2002) *The Arts and the Creation of Mind*, New Haven, CT: Yale University Press.

Exley, S. (2011) 'A Governor's Lot is Not a Happy One', *Times Educational Supplement*, 15 July, pp. 22–23.

HCEC (House of Commons Education Committee) (2011) *The English Baccalaureate, HCEC*, London: The Stationary Office. Online. Available at: http://www.publications. parliament.uk/pa/cm201012/cmselect/cmeduc/851/851.pdf (accessed 28 July 2011).

Kemmis, S., Cole, P. and Suggett, D. (eds) (1983) *Orientations to Curriculum and Transition: Towards the Socially Critical School*, Melbourne, Australia: Victorian Institute of Secondary Education.

Newman, K. and Tourle, P. (2011) *The Impact of Cuts on UK Museums: A Report for the Museums Association*. Online. Available at: http://www.museumsassociation.org/ download?id=363804 (accessed 20 July 2011).

NSEAD (National Society for Education in Art and Design) (2011) 'Art and Design Teacher Survey #2'. Online. Available at: http://www.nsead.org/Downloads/EBac_ Survey2.pdf (accessed 15 July 2011).

Oates, T. (2010) *Could Do Better: Using International Comparisons to Refine the National Curriculum in England*, Cambridge: Cambridge Assessment.

PCAH (2011) *Reinvesting in Arts Education: Winning America's Future Through Creative Schools*, Washington DC: President's Committee on the Arts and Humanities, May. Online. Available at: http://www.pcah.gov/sites/default/files/photos/PCAH_Reinvesting_ 4web.pdf (accessed 13 July 2011).

Robinson, K. (ed.) (1999) *All Our Futures: Creativity Culture and Education*, London: DfEE Publications.

Robinson, K. (2001) *Out of Our Minds: Learning to Be Creative*, Chichester: Capstone Publishing.

Steers, J. (1988) 'Art and Design in the National Curriculum', *Journal of Art and Design Education*, 7 (3): 303–323.

UNESCO (2007) *Road Map for Arts Education: Building Creative Capacities for the 21st Century.* Online. Available at: http://portal.unesco.org/culture/en/files/40000/125810 58115Road_Map_for_Arts_Education.pdf/Road%2BMap%2Bfor%2BArts%2BEducat ion.pdf (accessed 28 July 2011).

White, J. (2011) 'Gove's on the Bac Foot with a White Paper Stuck in 1868', *Times Education Supplement*, 21 January, p. 27.

Chapter 2

The hijacking of creativity

The dilemma of contemporary art education

jan jagodzinski

It seems globally, art and its education is currently undergoing increasing pressure by state, provincial and national governments to change its 'mindset' as to its place in the school curriculum. This 'mindset' (core belief) has traditionally been a 'humanist' one where expression of the 'self' has dominated the field, and where its so-called 'therapeutic' benefits could be acknowledged in terms of children's mental growth and development. However, the field of art education is undergoing a paradigm shift as screen technologies have encroached into education to the point where they can no longer be ignored. The core 'humanist' studio courses (painting, drawing, printmaking) seem to be almost quaint exercises of bygone years if they are not supplemented by considering the interventions of digitalised photography, the moving image and the architectonics of installation. Ceramics, for example, has continually to justify its existence in relation to its primal material (clay, earth), the chemical experimentation of glazes, and its worth as an activity that does not simply fall into an exercise of 'craft'. I am reminded of Victor Burgin's (1986) comment many years ago when he spoke of the relegation of stained-glass studio, the transcendental art form that 'translated' the light of God in the high Gothic, to the basement of the Royal College of Art (RCA) in London, as perspectival painting became the paradigm art of the Enlightenment.

Art education has been decentred into various issues and interest groups, each vying to maintain its toehold in order to retain its viability as a legitimate and worthwhile activity. The National Art Education Association (NAEA) *Newsletter* in the United States gives a forum for such interests (contributors include: Arts Based Educational Research (ABER); Electronic Media Interest Group (EMIG); Committee on Lifelong Learning (LLL); Lesbian, Gay, and Transgender Issues Caucus (LGBITIC); Caucus on the Spiritual in Art Education (CSAE); Design Issues Group (DIG); Museum Education Division Design, Special Needs (SNAE); Committee on Multiethnic Concerns (COMC); and Caucus for Social Theory in Art Education (CSTAE). But, now it seems that the economic climate of globalisation is forcing governments to harness education for competitive ends as capitalism once again begins to morph into yet another form causing instability and market jitters. Public education has always been used as a state apparatus to steer the institution towards a direction that would satisfy industry and the job market. There is a long tradition in educational critical thought that has charted such an intervention, beginning perhaps with economists Bowles and Gintis (1976) and their now classic study. This is nothing 'new'. Occasionally, the concerns of citizenship, multiculturalism, assimilation, and cultural integration override national economic concerns, especially when a nation finds itself in conflict and turmoil racially, ethnically, or torn apart by class divisions. Public education, under the humanist banner, has had the noble goal to educate 'all' children regardless of class, gender, ethnicity, race, so that their full potential might be reached with the underlying assumption that the greater society will benefit, not only economically, but in terms of psychic health and welfare. In today's global climate, however, something new is afoot that ruins any such idealisations.

Neoconservatives, neoliberals and civil libertarians have managed to spread the perception that government is unable to serve the public; that government is no longer capable of the 'good'. Conservative governments have been elected in most post-industrial societies and these have bought into the neoliberalist agenda by merging their efforts with corporations and big business. Public welfare takes a back seat, while education is once more harnessed to rank up the competiveness of a nation. The World Bank is rather blatantly obvious in this aim. Its Education for the Knowledge Economy (EKE) refers to its work with developing countries 'to cultivate the highly skilled, flexible human capital need to compete in global markets—an endeavor that affects a country's entire educational system' (EKE 2009). The World Bank supports a National Innovation System (NIS), which is a 'well-articulated network of firms, research centers, universities, and think tanks that work together to take advantage of global knowledge' (EKE 2009).

The World Bank initiative echoes throughout the majority of post-industrialised countries. In Britain the coalition government's White Paper *The Importance of Teaching* (DfE 2010) maps out the new agenda for school reform. It begins with a statement by Prime Minister David Cameron who maintains 'what really matters [about education] is how we're doing compared with international competitors. That is what will define our economic growth and country's future. The truth is, at the moment we are standing still while others race past'. Peter Mortimore, of *The Guardian*, who started his career as a London teacher in the early 1960s laments in his very last column that the progressive movements in education have come to a halt and that public education will eventually be privatised (Mortimore 2010). I will come back to this important point latter.

Art education does not escape from this initiative. As a field it must retool itself if it is to be perceived as being 'useful' to the economic cause, otherwise it will be cut as excess, its 'services' to children and students spread throughout the curriculum or rendered as an afterschool activity or become a private undertaking (like piano lessons). It has already begun to retool itself under a signifier that had lost currency for quite some time because 'any' subject could claim it as its own as well: creativity. Art education could not claim exclusive rights, but something has changed. In many respects it is a no-brainer as to why 'creativity' has become the rallying cry to 'save' art education from being rendered obsolete. It has (once more) found its *raison d'être* as it did after the World War 2 period of restoration and recovery. Art education is now placed in the services of the well-known 'creative industries' as first popularised by the conservative economist Richard Florida (2002), who in his latest book maintains that it is even possible to profit from the aftermath of the 2008 global financial crisis (Florida 2010). While the symptoms of this capitalist 'crisis' are seen everywhere globally in the 'Occupy Wall Street' phenomenon, conservative pundits stir up the rhetoric that these protestors are *not* anti-capitalists, they are merely angry that the government is not working in their 'service' and interests but that of the corporations. It is only the excessive greed of capitalism that they are rallying against. To publically link capitalism with the voracity of profitism that simply breeds greed and debt slavery would be to undermine their positions and belief system.

Pimping for capitalism

There are many 'gurus' of creativity. A layer of consultants has sprung up to prep industry about performativity to make them more productive. In education one of the best known is the knighted public speaker, Sir Kenneth Robinson. For anyone who has listened to his entertaining lectures on creativity and the next paradigm shift in education, readily understands that the public system of education, which he rails against, is effectively dead, and has been 'dead' for some time. The competitive edge can be found in such countries as (especially) Finland, Sweden and Norway. Robinson, effectively a 'creative guru' for hire by any institution that will pay him for his 'creative spiel,' calls for the harnessing of each student's potential (the humanist agenda) but now nestled within the emergent technology and entertainment industries. Closely allied with the Technology, Entertainment and Design (TED) lecture series, Robinson popularises what neoliberal educators have been pushing for for quite some time. Work and play become indistinguishable: work is play and play is work. This has become 'artistic creativity', like edutainment, where exploration, freedom and 'learning to learn' appear to open up new vistas for exploitation. One is given as much rope as needed as long as productivity is accounted for. Networking, play and simulation are the new 'order' words. The networker is delivered from direct surveillance and paralysing alienation. This loosens hierarchies so that the worker becomes the manager of his or her own self-gratifying activity, that is, as long as that activity translates at some point into a valuable economic exchange; otherwise you are asked to leave the (symbiotic) network. Julian Dibble (2007) has called this ludocapitalism.

Art education is making its way to realise such a flexible subject. The push towards more 'design education' is one way. Design, as interpreted here, supports a skill set that directly relates to career opportunities in industry and entertainment. The incorporation of digitalised technologies is crucial to such a 'design' agenda. Architectural drawing programs, Photoshop, indesign, Dreamweaver, iweb and so on, open up the world of the 'frameless' image that can be manipulated in any which way. The glut of images, which require constant archiving, documentation and storage, leads to data banks where serialisation, appropriation, layering become the new emergent processes to 'play' with digitalised information. The virtuality of 'game space' has opened up the markets of profitability. Career choices and opportunities by artists now being 'educated' to use these new technological tools as they finish their fine arts programmes in art schools and universities are both carrot and stick for recruitment.

The performativity that flexible capitalism demands to identify those who are the most productive, creative, responsible and diligent requires a curriculum where self-discipline, perseverance, and the ability to sell yourself, or have a representative sell you, are the primary values. An education grounded in self-determination and choice where a student is allowed to explore within a group dynamic that is nestled in a supportive environment, presided over by a teacher who is more of a facilitator in opening up the 'world of information', is what is in order. The teachers and students of the Finnish public school system have a great deal of autonomy, with few tests, non-streaming and no inspection as long as the end goals have been met. This model of educational subjectivisation generates the forms of creativity necessary for the 'creative industries'. Subject areas need to be imploded, divergent thinking 'outside the box', as they say, has to be made room for, and inquiry methods that are self-initiated need to be implemented. The student is 'free' to explore within the limits of the school's (or a company's) game.

The video game environment is indeed the template for such subjectification, which for all intents and purposes is as good as it gets, for it appears that the student is indeed his own interactive learner. Gaming environments are algorithmic designed spaces. This means that such spaces with their predefined levels, directions and controls to move about them, have first to be created *before* a player interacts with them. The inter-actor playing a video game, no matter how interactive it seems, is still controlled by the game's designed space, regardless of its complexity, which makes it appear as if the inter-actor is unable to exhaust its structure. In many respects, gaming space, the space of edutainment, is already here with online courses that will continue to improve their interactive graphics. Desire is carefully staged so that motivation to continue to 'play-learn' is maintained. The consortiums composed of the gaming industry, the government, the university (and the military), as advocated by James Paul Gee (2003), are coming together to continue developing curricula for the emerging screen generation where affect and attention are channelled via carefully structured learning games. It sounds like science fiction, but this realisation is already a possibility.

To enable such a subjectivity to emerge in schools, the current public system of education needs to be broken, and conservative politicians are dismantling public education in every post-industrial country. To return to Peter Mortimore's lament, he specifically mentions Education Minister Michael Gove's 'free schools' that are mentioned 36 times in the White Paper but are never explained. While the concept of privatisation is not discussed in the White Paper, Mortimore detects it as a subtext with the frequent references to 'new providers', 'private sector organisations' and 'a new market of school improved services'. Private companies are waiting in the wings to take over the management of public education to capture a share of taxpayers' money. The free schools that Gove refers to are the charter schools that President Obama's government is championing in the United States in their educational initiative 'Race for the Top'. This initiative parallels what Michael Gove is pushing for in Britain. Charter schools (free schools) occupy the ground between public and private education; they are both private and public in the sense that parents supposedly have more say regarding the curriculum, while a school can design and modify its particular direction of interest without federal approval. They can specialise in technologies for instance. For example, Philadelphia's Charter High School for Architecture and Design developed a curriculum that combined traditional academics with design skills and hands-on training in carpentry, building trades, and structural systems. The Obama administration has been heavily lobbied by two influential philanthropists and billionaire entrepreneurs: Bill Gates and Eli Broad who, through their Broad Grant programme and Gates Foundation, are able to push through neoliberalist educational agendas. Both men have made significant inroads into the Obama's administration's Department of Education. Arne Duncan, Obama's Secretary of Education and Larry Summers, the former economic advisor, are former members of the Broad board of directors. Two of Duncan's top aides, Chief of Staff Margot Rogers and Assistant Deputy Secretary James H. Shelton III came from the Gates Foundation. Teach for America, Inc. requires little teacher training to become a licensed state practitioner.

The clamour to get children into these charter schools by a middle class who see the public school as not providing the kind of curriculum desired so that their children can get jobs, plus the obvious fact that in some states and school districts public education is indeed caught up in an old paradigm, makes the easy turn to eventual privatisation possible. Private schools have always existed in England and the United States. But these have been exclusive institutions for those who could afford them. Charter (free) schools now become a way to get a bit of that same exclusivity by those parents who could pay and think that their children's life chances of getting a job can be improved in such a brutally competitive climate. The documentary *Waiting for Superman* (David Guggenheim 2010) is a heavily biased documentary that claims charter schools are places of achievement while the public school system in the United States is a total disaster because of the power of teachers unions. The film received the US Audience Award for the Best Documentary during the 2010 Sundance Film Festival confirming the investment of desire that the film exposes for the hopes of the liberal middle classes. The illusion of this seems to be working despite the bottleneck of young people qualified with degrees, in serious loan debt, who remain jobless, while those with PhDs are forced into the perennial search for 'post-docs' so that they do not starve, but continue to build their 'performative' profiles.

Creativity unlimited

Creativity is certainly sweeping art education as the new panacea to unite our field from its initial decentring during postmodernism (see Zimmerman 2009). The 'after' postmodern sombreness has led to divisive polarisations as to which way to turn, given that both left and right government political parties in most post-industrial countries are gridlocked, while extreme nationalist parties and libertarian parties form an unnerving alternative. It requires very little research to link creativity with the current global capitalist model that requires 'immaterial labour' (knowledge, information, imagination, ideas) to continue profit through innovative changes and cultural hybridisations. One would have to be blind to miss it. The shift from J.P. Guildford's 1950s research agenda creativity being a form of self-expression and communication to the current link of creativity with successful technological and economic successes is all too obvious (Cropley 1999, 2001; Dacey 1999). John Howkins' *The Creative Economy* (2001) is perhaps the definitive statement in his brazen claims concerning entrepreneurship as being simply a question of individuals having creative ideas and capitalising on them in today's economy. The subtitle of his book could not be made more explicit '*How People Make Money from Ideas*'. In an interview that he gave several years latter (Ghelfi 2005), Howkins articulates how his 'humanism' is manifested in both small and corporate businesses where certain individuals clearly stand out above the rest. 'Creativity is in the individual and it is subjective; innovation is group-based and is objective' (p. 4). He further articulates how the consumer in effect has 'become' the creator. Within the 'creative industrial economy' creativity can occur at any place within the origination, production, distribution and consumption cycle. I think it best to use the neologism 'prosumers' rather than consumers for this development. Within the 'creative industries', most of which are arts based (architecture, design, fashion, software production, video games, marketing, advertising, pop music, the performing arts, publishing and the art market) what is required for creative entrepreneurs are five characteristics: 'vision, focus, financial acumen, pride and urgency' (p. 6). Such intellectual labour is policed by the copyright, patent, trademark and design industries. The division of labour between them is roughly between arts (copyright) and sciences (patents). *Business Week*, in the August 1 edition of 2005 developed a special report dedicated to 'Get Creative: How to Build Innovative Companies'.

Howkins' position is an earlier voice that is added to 'star' authors like Daniel Pink and Richard Florida who equally fuel the 'creative economical argument'. Pink, a keynote speaker at the 2007 NAEA conference was called upon to confirm why it is that 'right-brain' thinkers will rule the future as developed in *A Whole New Mind* (Pink 2005). Artists and art teachers were eager to listen. The ASCD (Association for Supervision and Curriculum Development) called on Pink at their 2010 conference to push 'learning and development' as yet another advantage to foster creativity; he was there to show how behavioural science and motivation would help develop a highly skilled intellectual workforce. Florida's (2007) influential thesis is that the 'new creative class' is made up of intellectuals, artists and designers. This sector surpasses the manufacturing and the service sectors of the economy in terms of earning power. Books such as Eric Jensen's *Arts with the Brain in Mind* (2001) and Patricia Wolfe's *Brain Matters: Translating Research into Classroom Practice* (2001) based on the mind as an 'information-processing model', are two of the many 'brain-related' neurologically informed books that ride the wave of this trend to improve creative learning. Arts education is touted as boosting test scores in other disciplines and shows how learning is enhanced through the use of music, visual and the kinaesthetic arts so that 'thinking' is advanced and there is more positive motivation and inclusivity achieved. It is assumed that a 'clearer' understanding emerges as to 'how' we learn from fMRI (functional magnetic resonance imaging) research and brain development, as if it were possible to see the complexity of the synapses at work. It is yet another form of biopolitics of genetically based research meant to enhance and direct creativity to pimp for global competiveness. While madness has always been associated with creativity, this form of madness is much more annihilating in its alienation; it disregards the caring and cooperative capacities of our species.

Thomas Osborne (2003) offers more insight into this new capitalist mode of 'creative' production by pointing out that psychology as wedded to management – management psychology – has turned creativity into a *techne* so that creativity is 'open' to anyone who can learn to manage it within a personal psychology of life. Such a disposition is not only necessary for a 'flexible' capitalist subject but also necessary as a 'survival' skill where so many social benefits and support systems have been taken away through neoliberalist agendas of privatisation. It seems almost a foregone conclusion that eventually all public education will be privalised as I have argued above. The push towards charter schools and 'free schools' is one step closer in this direction. Charter schools are able to update the curriculum for more 'creative' ends, whereas public schools lag, caught still in the industrial model despite the never-ending critiques of education by critical theorists. The university as a 'knowledge corporation' has already been restructured along corporate ideology. The number of patents applied for by universities has dramatically risen. Few realise that the largest university in the United States is a corporate university: the University of Phoenix (UOP), which boasts 240,000 students around the globe (Breen 2003). It caters to working adults who are employed by transnational corporations (TNCs) such as AT&T, Boeing, IBM, Intel, Lockheed Martin and Motorola offering online degrees. e-Learning is the obvious future here. UOP spans 170 campuses across the USA, Canada, Mexico and Puerto Rico (Araya 2010). What this means is that the old model of universities as some sort of spiritual beacon of learning to guide the national state and its citizenry is effectively dead, a cultural survival that will eventually disappear. 'Learning to learn' is the tautological slogan. Cornell, Massachusetts Institute of Technology, University of Chicago, Stanford, Johns Hopkins, have established experimental programs outside the USA into Eastern Europe, Asia and the Middle East. It is, however, Asia that is pouring money into universities and opening up branch universities (Hvistendalh 2009). The flow of international foreign students into the USA is equally dramatic. As Osborne (2003) puts it: '[T]he creativity explosion is unquestionably variegated and double-edged; it can be captured by business gurus and management writers, California lifestyle sects, new age groups, post-identitarian philosophers, literary critics turned cultural theorists, intellectuals, post-modern geographers, anti-globalization protestors, [*whoever*]' (p. 510, emphasis added). Osborne's own solution to the capitalisation of creativity by business is raised to the status of a doctrine and the discourse of morality (which always shadows creativity in its romantic and heroic forms) and hinges its bets on *inventiveness*. I, however, discuss another flight out.

A flight out: Gilles Deleuze

I am going to switch gears from what has been a more descriptive (some would say polemic) style to a more theoretical one by pondering what 'creativity' may look like from the position of a Deleuzian orientation. I believe Gilles Deleuze shows us the flight out of creativity as it is held hostage by the forces of global capital. While art education is being held hostage to adopt the edutainment creative industries approach to the job market, anyone who has any sort of familiarity with history of (Western) art, knows full well that it has always had its critical, bohemian underbelly providing a critique of the social order. This ability to expose the ills of the social order has become more and more impossible to maintain since there is no higher transcendent moral ground on which to stand. Self-reflexive irony and satire often become just other forms of cynicism, while the art market has become a business in and of itself. Most art criticism has now become a way of promoting particular artists, while artists have to become outrageous performers to compete with the celebrity status of those in popular culture. These forms simply feed into the 'creative entertainment' industries. Shock has become just another selling feature. It is not my intent to pull out a roster of artists whom I think are dodging this particular bullet. I have done that elsewhere (jagodzinski 2010). However, I do wish to raise the spectre of Gilles Deleuze as a thought experiment that might help us to think about art education's 'creative' dilemma in yet another way.

Deleuze puts forward a philosophy of becoming by revolutionising a theory of the 'event', 'line of flight' and 'nomadic thought' and thereby offering a vocabulary that can make 'sense' of complexity and unpredictability in the art making and teaching processes. His critique of metaphysics as based on representation (identity, neurosis, repression), on the nation state as a 'society of control,' and capitalism, which is designed to further this control through commodification, consumption and infantilisation by deference to authority, provides a theory that challenges art and creativity as forms that are subject to easy reification. So, we come to an obvious but absolutely crucial point. Creativity, in and of itself, cannot be defined, a point also made by Zimmerman (2009) in her overview of creativity in art education, but a recurring point stressed again and again throughout the literature on creativity. It is a *virtual* and not an *actual* phenomenon. It can be understood as the striving of *life* itself, or *zoë*, as I have used it elsewhere (jagodzinski 2004). *Zoë* can be thought of as cosmic energy, or life force, as empty chaos and absolute speed movement. Its 'discursive' other-half, *bios*, is 'intelligent' life, but the two cannot be distinguished easily. Both are harnessed by capitalism, but *zoë* is *difference* in and of itself: pure vitality. Simply put, creativity is the processes of differentiation or becoming. It is transversal communication at the *molecular level*.

In the Bergsonian context of 'creative involution', Darwinian *external* 'natural selection' principles are challenged by positing an immanent internal force, or *élan vital* as the force of becoming before it expresses itself as material differentiation; that is, as the actualisation of virtual life into [molar] orgasmic forms. It is here where the processes of actualisation take on ideological ends. Creativity (*zoë*, life, becoming) as captured and harnessed by the capitalist managerial business models, however, can still break free; or, as with Deleuze and Guattari (especially Guattari) the *virtuality* of creative becoming can escape capitalist clutches through forms of deterritorialisation and undoing – what Deleuze (1994) earlier in his work referred to as 'counter-actualization' or 'vice-diction' (pp. 189–191). Such deterritorialisations of molar trappings become Deleuze and Guattari's (1986) form of minoritarian politics. Creativity as a virtual phenomenon, a realm of a multiplicity of differen*t*/*c*iating. Deleuze (1994) explains this double term in *Difference and Repetition* arguing that Hegelian dialectical philosophy relegates difference as a single concept, the negation of the same. Deleuze argues that difference is two concepts: differentiation and differenciation. The second is internal to a body that attributes to its becoming. Transcendental Ideas are then related to a 'body without organs' (BwO) as 'a milieu of experimentation' (as developed in plateau X in their *Thousand Plateaus* book; Deleuze and Guattari 1988). This is the 'environment' from which an organism emerges. The virtual BwO has an indirect impact on the organism as it actualises and forms itself. It also furnishes the material conditions for the organism to undergo (actively or passively) forms of deterritorialisation as well. This provides some agency (as self-autopoetic modification) informed by desire, which affects the wider organismic whole. Symbiosis is therefore a necessary condition for becoming. (No one said this theory was going to be 'easy'.)

Creativity in the broad philosophical sense can be treated along two tendencies: creativity that comes from 'beyond' (transcendentalism) and creativity that comes from within (immanence). Although these are presented dichotomously, we are dealing with tendencies rather than oppositions. Both traditions take Heidegger as the dividing line when it comes to the question of the difference between Being and beings and their relationship to each other. Derrida is an exemplar case of transcendentalism, while Deleuze is the exemplar of immanence (Smith 2003). The one that grips capitalism is the transcendental notion of creativity. What is the significance of this for this discussion? To answer this is to identify how it is that transcendentalism as a philosophy informs capitalism through desire as *lack*. This was the position of Hegel and adopted by Lacan. The Lacanian psychoanalytic position reveals how a transcendental desire circulates in capitalism, as exposed by the oeuvre of Žižek. The lack within desire presents an unobtainable transcendent object as an absolute Idea (the Good Life, Unconditional Power, Wealth, all-Knowing). Such ontological desire is directed at our incompleteness, or our 'lack of being'. Desire then is to fulfil the lack of our being so that it coincides with a more fulfilling life: a healthy beautiful body, the order of the Good, to be number one at one's profession, and so on. Since this is an 'impossible' desire, one is saddled with disappointment, suffering and a 'tragic' vision of life. You never quite 'get there'. What is possible is the pleasure of satisfaction that arrests the desire temporarily before it wells up yet again. One can never 'get enough' satisfaction (like the Rolling Stone song goes). The pursuit of desire is characterised by what Lacan called *jouissance* – the painful pleasure, the twists and turns of achievement and its failure after the impossible object (*objet a*) that characterises capitalism especially in its consumerist phase.

But such transcendentalism goes even further given that desire is infinitely suspended and deferred. For Derrida this presents for us finite creatures (beings) a double bind or *aporia* when confronted with infinitely transcendent Ideas, which we are unable to deconstruct, like justice for instance. The transcendental (pure) Idea of justice will always remain impossible; there are no determinate rules that can give us the certainty of a just decision. We are always struggling with this unknown aspect that is 'beyond' the Law. The law itself is subject to deconstruction and therefore change, but justice remains an absolute Other. Analogously this applies to 'creativity' since it too is a transcendent Idea. There is a 'call' to justice like there is a 'call' to creativity. We recognise 'creativity' always after the fact as the creation of something 'new'. Creativity is thus, in this context, the place for openness and invention. The law books are filled with precedent cases that form the possibility of judgement, as is the history of art. These are all instances of 'satisfactory' pleasurable 'calls' to justice and creativity, but they are not final in any stretch of the term. The 'end of creativity' has not arrived, nor has the end of justice. These are impossible objects, part of the Kantian tradition of *noumena* as opposed to phenomena. But the point to be made here is that there is always judgement (the judge, the art critic, the curator, the teacher, the professor, the paying client, and so on) which then bestows the claim symbolically that 'the child has been born'.

This sounds like a seductive way to proceed. Creativity as an unknowable transcendent Idea is surely a given. However, because of the way such 'transcendence' is put into motion within capitalist forms we end up with the usual set of impossible definitions for its appearance: genius (a transcendental position), unprecedented talent (impossible to define), the new (we grasp only when we are surprised by it), and so on. More to the point perhaps is that creative thinking in this view is caught up to an impossibility that always alludes the artist, an enslavement to the anxiety of 'not making it' in the world, succumbing to the demands of the Other. In the most dramatic sense, to break with such enslavement is characterised by Freud's 'death drive', which Lacan was to develop more fully: if 'pleasure' is the immanent unit of measure as to the success of creative fulfilment then the 'end game' can only be a death drive to free oneself eventually from the impossibility of desire, or to overdose in pleasure – the addictions of drugs. This destructive side of creativity is seldom mentioned in schooling. When living on such an edge, it is difficult to judge if it is productive or destructive. That is the risk. In capitalism such pleasure is transvalued as 'shock' for recognition, to narcissistically stand out and hence (paradoxically) escape from the demand of the Other (the symbolic order). Shock, once a form of avant-garde resistance, has been successfully harnessed by capitalism to promote individualism (Warhol), celebrity (Madonna), brand, logo and label recognition (Fcuk, Benetton), life style (Michael Jackson, sport personalities). These become the exemplars of those who have escaped the demand of the Other: they are their 'own' bosses so to speak, achieving the pinnacle of what fame and money has to offer. They are as 'good' as their publicists and managers and the paying (or voting) public that are caught by their performances performatives.

Desire as lack leads directly into fantasy formations to 'fill in' what is missing, the object of desire 'containing' the *objet a*, that unknowable part that is to restore our sense of completeness (i.e. the rationale for the purchase of weapons which will 'guarantee' our safe-hood). Desire as lack is the key to capitalist expansion and profit. Creativity is always harnessed to the transcendental ideal dream – the Idea of Power, Wealth, Goods as the Good, these are all absences that are lacking. Is there another way? Deleuze also retains 'transcendence' but comes at it from an 'empirical' base; empirical meaning within the lived world, an analysis of the 'state' of things. Why Deleuze departs with transcendentalism when it comes to creativity is that, from the tradition of immanent philosophy he draws on (esp. Spinoza, Nietzsche), values are internal (immanent) standards. To live life creatively and well is to fully express the limits of one's potential and certainly not to be caught in existing standards to measure up to, but also not to be enslaved by impotence to the transcendence of impossibility, which (in a literal sense) one is to 'die' for, the point where one's life can only be counted as either completely powerless or completely heroic. Deleuze and Guattari in contrast look for symbiotic ways to release life, to open up dimensions of psychic freedom with others. Such becoming is always theorised in terms of processes. Deleuze offers a view of creativity for art education that preserves the notion of transcendence but grapples with the 'impossibility' as defined by transcendent philosophies where 'lack' dominates and drives the capitalist machinic impulses. Creation for Deleuze is always a becoming event. There is nothing to die for but everything to live for. As a structure of constant change, becoming always undermines a set of relations that have been actualised by molar forces. A creative act thus affirms the chaos and multiplicity of the virtual. However, it is indeed a *rare* event.

> A creator who isn't seized by the throat by a set of impossibilities is no creator. A creator is someone who creates his own impossibilities, and thereby creates possibilities. It's by banging your head against the wall that you find an answer.

> (Deleuze 1992: 292)

References

Araya, D. (2010) 'Cultural Democracy: Universities in the Creative Economy', *Policy Futures in Education*, 8 (2): 217–231.

Bowles, S. and Gintis, H. (1976) *Schooling in Capitalist America: Educational Reform and the Contradictions of Economic Life*, New York: Basic Books.

Breen, B. (2003) 'The Hard Life and Restless Mind of America's Education Billionaire', *Fast Company*, 28 February. Online. Available at: www.fastcompany.com/magazine/68/sperling.html (accessed 15 July 2011).

Burgin, V. (1986) *The End of Art Theory: Criticism and Post-modernity*, New York: Palgrave Macmillan.

Cropley, A.J. (1999) 'Definitions of Creativity', in: M.A. Runco and S. Prozkers (eds) *Encyclopedia of Creativity*, San Diego, CA: Academic Press.

Cropley, A.J. (2001) *Creativity in Education and Learning: A Guide for Teachers and Educators*, London: Kogan Page.

Dacey, J. (1999) 'Concepts of Creativity: A History', in: M.A. Runco and S. Prozkers (eds) *Encyclopedia of Creativity*, San Diego, CA: Academic Press.

Deleuze, G. (1992) 'Mediators', in: J. Crary and S. Kwinter (eds) *Zone 6: Incorporations*, New York: Zone Books.

Deleuze, G. (1994) *Difference and Repetitions*, Trans. Paul Patton, New York: Columbia University Press.

Deleuze, G. and Guattari, F. (1986) *Kafka: Toward a Minor Literature*, Trans. Dana Polan, Minneapolis: University of Minnesota.

Deleuze, G. and Guattari, F. (1988) *A Thousand Plateaus: Capitalism and Schizophrenia*, London: Athlone Press.

DfE (Department for Education) (2010) *The Importance of Teaching*, London: The Stationery Office.

Dibble, J. (2007) '[iDC] Notes Toward a Theory of Ludocapitalism (O Rly?)'. Online. Available at: https://lists.thing.net/pipermail/idc/2007-September/002833.html (accessed 29 January 2012).

EKE (Education for the Knowledge Economy) (2009). Online. Available at: http://web.worldbank.org/WBSITE/EXTERNAL/TOPICS/EXTEDUCATION/0,,contentMDK:20161496~menuPK:540092~pagePK:148956~piPK:216618~theSitePK:282386,00.html (accessed 29 January 2012).

Florida, R. (2002) *The Rise of the Creative Class, Cities and the Creative Class*, New York: Basic Books.

Florida, R. (2007) *The Flight of the Creative Class: The New Global Competition for Talent*, New York: Harper Collins.

Florida, R. (2010) *The Great Reset: How Ways of Living and Working Drive Post-Crash Prosperity*, New York: Harper.

Gee, J.P. (2003) *What Video Games Have to Teach Us About Learning and Literacy*, New York: Palgrave Macmillan.

Ghelfi, D. (2005) 'Understanding the Engine of Creativity in a Creative Economy: An Interview with John Howkins'. Online. Available at: http://www.wipo.int/export/sites/www/sme/en/documents/pdf/cr_interview_howkins.pdf (accessed 28 January 2012).

Howkins, J. (2001) *The Creative Economy: How People Make Money From Ideas*, London: Penguin.

Hvistendalh, M. (2009) 'Asia Rising: Countries Funnel Billions into Universities', *The Chronicle of Higher Education, Shanghai.* Online. Available at: http://chronicle.com/article/Asia-Rising-Countries-Funn/48682/ (accessed 25 July 2011).

jagodzinski, j. (2004) *Youth Fantasies: The Perverse Landscape of the Media*, New York: Palgrave Macmillan.

jagodzinski, j. (2010) *Visual Art and Education in an Era of Designer Capitalism*, New York: Palgrave Macmillan.

Jensen, E.P. (2001) *Arts With the Brain in Mind*, Alexandria, VA: ASCD EBook

Mortimore, P. (2010) *Markets Are for Commodities, Not Children*, Keynote Lecture Campaign for State Education Conference, 20 November 2010. Online. Available at: http://www.guardian.co.uk/education/2010/dec/07/fight-gove-education-reforms (accessed 29 January 2012).

Osborne, T. (2003) 'Against "Creativity": A Philistine Rant', *Economy and Society*, 32 (4): 707–525.

Pink, D. (2005) *A Whole New Mind: Moving from the Information Age to the Conceptual Age*, New York: Riverhead Books.

Smith, D. (2003) 'Deleuze and Derrida, Immanence and Transcendence: Two Directions in Recent French Thought', in: P. Patton and J. Protevi (eds) *Between Deleuze and Derrida*, New York: Continuum Books.

Wolfe, P. (2001) *Brain Matters: Translating Research into Classroom Practice*, Alexandria, VA: Virginia Association for Supervision and Curriculum Development.

Zimmerman, E. (2009) 'Reconceptualizing the Role of Creativity in Art Education Theory and Practice', *Studies in Art Education*, 50 (4): 382–410.

Part II

Debates within the classroom

Chapter 3

Questioning creativity[1]

Olivia Gude

Many in the field of arts education today proclaim that cultivating creativity ought to be central to the field's goals and outcomes. I am struck by how rarely such proposals grapple with the aesthetic, cultural, and political implications of emphasising creativity in the economic and social climates of today. I have encountered bewildered looks when suggesting to a 'Creativity Advocate' that it might be wise to step back from enthusiastic advocacy for all things new and consider from whence this newly found emphasis on creativity arises and what questions are not being represented in the current creativity discourse.

Could it be said that claiming the centrality of *creativity* for art education is a public relations ploy? In these grim times of economic uncertainty, advocates for arts education, feeling that the field is threatened with huge cuts in resources, often respond by attempting to justify the need for arts education with reasons that they believe will find popular support in today's cultural climate: higher test scores, improved school attendance, creative approaches to learning 'core' academic subjects. The assumption is that philistines, who do not believe in the importance of culture and the arts in the lives of students and their communities, will be controlling education budgets and making cuts (or perceived to be planning to make cuts) to the arts in education. Thus, whatever their actual beliefs, some art education advocates deem it expedient to shift debate from the cultural contributions that the arts make to individual and collective life, to claiming that creativity in itself, in any and all domains, is *the* major aim of art education.

In this public relations discourse, creativity is defined as the ability to freely 'make new' ideas or things on demand. This is a stripped down concept of creativity, a creative capacity unsullied by the messiness of artistic insight, cultural complexity, human need, or ethical considerations. To the extent to which this discourse on the necessity for creativity education originates in the United States, it is important to remember that in the United States today it is controversial in some cities and states to even use the word 'culture' to a Board of Education because of the perceived potential of 'cultural' art investigations to undermine traditional habits of mind and traditional social organisation. The fear is that art has the potential to reveal and disrupt conservative ideologies encoded in representations of such things as gender roles, race, sexuality, patriotism, or what is 'natural'.

Is emphasising teaching *creative process* in art education curriculum a deliberate, ideologically motivated shift away from teaching *artistic process*? Is this current emphasis on teaching creative process a move away from the educational commitment to fostering core artistic behaviours that are associated with the capacity of the arts to re-make perceptions and hence, potentially to re-make human subjects and societies? Individual creativity can be a powerful force of generativity and potential in human life. In many societies, the artist is seen as someone who shifts the perspectives of everyday living by calling attention to other ways of perceiving and being. The artist in modern times extended this role, often functioning as a disruptor, as an iconoclast: smashing the images and styles of the past, inventing new art to stimulate new ways of being, often shining light on what was once only seen in fear-inducing shadows.

In our contemporary, postmodern world, the artist often retains this role of challenger to the status quo, by acting as a bricoleur-leader, not by destroying or disposing of past styles and making totally new ones but by eclecting, selecting, and remixing tropes of meaning making to open up and undermine conventional thinking, to find meaning in the interstices between conventional habits of knowing.

In much current art education the creativity curriculum distances itself from the disruptive or radically inventive potential of the arts, instead urging its applicability for any and all aspects of human life and endeavours in everyday life (as it is currently organised). Such curriculum is often structured to teach steps towards creative work, methods to approach perceived problems. Curriculum focuses on developing such capacities as freely and flexibly ideating, playing with concepts and materials, suspending judgement, brainstorming, working collaboratively, pushing boundaries and other identified methods to stimulate and develop fresh approaches to any given problem.

Certainly, it makes sense for an art education curriculum to help students develop the habits of mind and habits of making that will enable them to freely engage with forms and materials. However, not to focus on understanding the aesthetic methodologies through which actual contemporary artists explore many aspects of inner and outer life greatly truncates the potential for creative endeavours that actually generate new forms of experiencing, thinking and living. Contemporary creativity curriculum touts itself as fulfilling the needs of twenty-first century societies, further described as the needs of twenty-first century economies. It claims that it can foster the creative class needed to fuel economic growth in capitalist societies in which sustaining prosperity must be driven by ever growing consumption.

In a world with rapidly diminishing resources, such creativity curriculum sells itself as a necessary adjunct to making flexible adjustments within the course prescribed by dominant economic models for maximum economic development around the globe. The creative worker of tomorrow is viewed as one who can successfully compete individually (and as a creative collective) in capitalising opportunities created by changing technologies. Rather than emphasising openness to divergent experiences of a satisfying and joyous everyday life – today and in an imagined future – conventional creativity curriculum teaches our students to solve any problem presented by a teacher or, in future, by an employer. Creativity is taught as a set of tools to be deployed to solve problems firmly within boundaries set by conventional social structures.

What are the social and ecological implications of developing in people such a *manic creativity*, always privileging the magic of the new and different? What are the ethical implications of a manic creative capacity, trained to generate 'creative solutions' to problems without first considering whether these problems are poorly formulated to address real needs or desirable outcomes? It is, perhaps, too charged to suggest that in such an unsubtle approach to the human capacity of inventiveness, build-a-better-mousetrap easily morphs into build-a-better-instrument-for-extracting-information-from-a-human-being. However, it is not difficult to foresee the potential harmfulness of promoting the ability to build better ways to entrap people in cycles of unfulfillable desire by inventing increasingly alluring images and products. An almost sure indicator that one is dealing with ungrounded manic creative energy is that, when questioned about the environmental impact of such unrestrained creativity, the creativity promoter blithely asserts that this is the sort of problem that will be solved by creatively inventing sustainable technological solutions. It is virtually never stated that the creative talent will invent new social solutions to the problem of manufactured desire.

Is the renewed emphasis on *creativity* an attempt to revert to an earlier stage in the development of art education curriculum? Is shifting the focus of art teaching to creativity a reinstatement of traditional art education goals of stimulating creative and mental growth through children's free 'creative' self-expression? Voices associated with contemporary, critical approaches to art education, such as those sometimes grouped together under the heading of Visual Culture Art Education (Duncum 2006; Tavin 2003), often decry the renewed focus on creativity as such because this is seen as a regression to a Lowenfeldian, acultural, ahistorical conception of the free child, freely expressing intrinsic creative capacity before being burdened with the strictures of a given culture (Lowenfeld 1952). These perceptive scholars correctly question whether it is possible for humans to make anything (with the exception perhaps of bodily wastes in the very earliest stages of infancy) that is not shaped by culturally determined habits of experiencing and perceiving, available materials, codes for making meaning, means of distribution, and perceptually and conceptually formed spaces of reception. As Arthur Efland, so persuasively argued in 1976 in the article 'The School Art Style: A Functional Analysis' (Efland 1976), creative child art endeavours 'may not be as free as they look', but instead may in actuality be examples of students enacting adult fantasies of child art to affirm that schools are places in which students can freely develop as creative beings. In fact, most schooling has always been designed to enculturate students to fit into current regimes of knowledge and modes of behaving.

Philosophies such as dialogical education, social reconstructionist education, critical pedagogy, feminist pedagogy and resistance theory education have over the past one hundred years articulated many methodologies for re-imagining restrictive educational practices. These models share the desire to develop forms of education that do not merely transmit established knowledge, but that engage students in creating new knowledge. Teaching disciplinary knowledge is thus seen, not as an end in itself, but as the transmission of the tools needed for conducting creative investigations into important themes in the lives of students and their communities.

Can contemporary art educators develop and implement an art education practice in which students are encouraged to pursue individual and collaborative visual and cultural research agendas through creative activities?

The Discipline-Based Art Education movement (Eisner 1987) advocated that art education be based on understanding and emulating professional practices in the arts. Unfortunately, its conceptions of practices of aesthetics, criticism, art history and art making were not based on contemporary professional practice, excluding (at any rate, not incorporating) many of the most important philosophical and artistic ideas developed in the twentieth century. What understanding of the role of artists as twenty-first century cultural researchers would need to be taught today so that students could emulate the serious, engaged cultural practices of professional artists and cultural workers? How can we incorporate critical insights drawn from visual culture theory into the art curriculum while retaining the imaginative and productive potential of arts curriculum?

Can we redefine what it means to 'exercise creativity' in art education settings? All too often, projects taught in K-12 (US) and Key Stage 3 (UK) art education function as recipes – outlining steps to be taken that will reliably deliver attractive products, or as directives – requiring students to illustrate with abstracted or realist symbolic representations that which is already believed and known, or as exercises – encouraging students to play with forms such as elements and principles without any deep intention or belief that something of substance and meaning is at stake. The assumption seems to be that if students are readied to 'jump in and make something' on demand, they will be able to 'jump in and make something' of their lives. Such direction-following conceptions do not account for the importance of experiencing, studying and making art that explores significant content that enlarges and deepens students' understanding of recurring and newly generated problems and opportunities of living.

In 'Principles of Possibilities: Considerations for a 21st Century Art and Culture Curriculum' (Gude 2007), I looked for overlaps in the perspectives of contemporary students and contemporary artists and educators and then articulated important life content to be addressed in a quality art education curriculum. This list of Principles of Possibility is a tentative formulation of some of the important areas of development, learning, and investigation that ought to be included in a quality art education (the article, accompanied by images of student work, is posted on the National Art Education Association website: http://naea.digication.com/omg/Art_Education_Articles.

When a district, school, department or individual teacher designs an art curriculum, it makes sense that planning begins with how content and activities will contribute to the students' capacities to experience, examine and shape various aspects of living. I identify these principles as:

- Playing – as pleasurable investigation and as a means to connect to deeply personal, unarticulated, idiosyncratic aspects of one's being;
- Forming Self – using art to understand the self as a constructed, complex and evolving entity;
- Investigating Community Themes – identifying and inquiring into the problems and potentials of particular times and places;

- Encountering Others – understanding and being ourselves re-shaped and transformed through encounters with other ways of conceiving of the world;
- Attentive Living – in the natural and human-constructed environment;
- Empowered Experiencing and Empowered Making – understanding and enacting the many meaning-making strategies of artists and other cultural workers;
- Deconstructing Culture – using an array of artistic and theoretical tools to perceive and analyse the cultural construction of meanings;
- Reconstructing Social Spaces – forming and participating in physical, virtual, and discursive spaces for social interaction;
- Not Knowing – accepting the open-endedness of complex thinking, not enforcing premature closure because of anxiety when experiencing the uncertainty, liminality, and fluidity of contemporary life.

The core goal of the pedagogical practices of art education ought to be enabling our students' empowered making and empowered experiencing by introducing them to the many practices of making meaning that have been developed by artists throughout the world and throughout the ages. We owe it to our students to teach them about great traditions of art and culture, but even more so to introduce them to the latest contemporary art practices and to contemporary theorising about images, objects, and events so that they will be able to participate in contemporary cultural conversations. In making a curriculum plan, the focus ought not to be on comprehensive coverage, on surveys of 'important' art or on 'fundamental' techniques for making. Rather the principles of selection should be based on such questions as: What aesthetic practices do our students need to know about in order to engage the cultural wealth of our (and other) societies? What knowledge of particular aesthetic practices will enable them to expand their frameworks of experiencing, perceiving and understanding? What aesthetic practices will give them the means to conduct investigations of phenomena and issues of contemporary life?

A quality art education teaches students 'aesthetic codes' that they can adopt and adapt to make their own meanings – as interpreters and as artist makers. Understanding these aesthetic codes gives students the capacity to 'read' and make meaning in styles of brushwork or in the editing choices of a film. Like any language systems, these ways of communicating are unintelligible unless one has been introduced through formal or informal education to the ways in which aesthetic choices generate a series of meaning-laden associations, through contrasts and similarities with other tropes of meaning making.

However, it is important to understand that the experience of making meaning through art as an interpreter/experiencer or as a maker is more than an intellectual exercise in deciphering codes or playing with signifiers. Awareness of a range of aesthetic practices also expands the affective and perceptive range. One literally becomes a different sort of person, experiencing the world differently by virtue of internalised, cultivated ways of being in and with the world.

Imagine a twenty-first century art education in which we teach students that it is through internalising established and evolving artistic-aesthetic practices – that are then appropriated, deconstructed, hybridised, remixed, reassembled, and utilised for one's own ends – that we each have the capacity to function as makers and shapers of culture. Can we together imagine art education practices in which we develop in our students the willingness and capacity to 'enter into' aesthetic practices and the ability to select and shape these practices for use as experience-generating, information-generating, pleasure-generating and purpose-generating vehicles of aesthetic investigation?

Note

1 This is a version of Olivia Gude's paper 'Creativity, for whom? Together Reconceptualising the Possibilities of Art Education' given at the KOSEA 2011 conference.

References

Duncum, P. (2006) *Visual Culture in the Art Class*, Reston, VA: National Art Education Association.

Efland, A. (1976) 'The School Art Style: A Functional Analysis', *Art Education*, 17 (2): 37–44.

Eisner, E. (1987) *The Role of Discipline-Based Art Education in America's Schools*, Santa Monica; CA: Getty Foundation.

Gude, O. (2007) 'Principles of Possibility: Considerations for a 21st Century Art and Culture Curriculum', *Art Education*, 60 (1): 6–17.

Lowenfeld, V. (1952) *Creative and Mental Growth*, 2nd edn, New York: Macmillan.

Tavin, K. (2003) 'Wrestling With Angels, Searching for Ghosts: Towards a Critical Pedagogy of Visual Culture', *Studies in Art Education*, 44 (3): 197–213.

Chapter 4

Critical race, multicultural art education

Christine Ballengee Morris

... meaning happens around how the objects relate to each other... I try to bring the invisible into view...

All these representations that I grew up with are telling me who I am, whether I realize it or not. And so putting them all out and having them talk to each other is my way of taking control of who I am: what is me and what is something that the rest of the world has said that I am.

(Wilson 2005)

I have spent many years contemplating interculturalism, multiculturalism, and multiple identities, long before I was even aware of such terms. I have explored these concepts, terms, and issues with many others, both within and outside my academic life. Here, I offer some of the dialogues which have helped me to understand my identity as a white Appalachian, American Indian, disabled, woman educator, who lives in the United States. A dialogic approach has assisted me to grow in many ways and I suggest this as a tactic for use with one's students when exploring issues of diversity through visual culture. Knowing oneself and culture makes possible an understanding of the construction of identities whereby students can knowingly explore and create art works.

Identification, including cultural and historical frameworks, is how we group and identify ourselves and how others do the same. This process is based on race, gender, sexual orientation, religion, nationality, socio-economic status, art forms, dress, speech, dialect, narratives and history, to name just a few categories. Identity development and understanding are fluid concepts, broad in definition and grounded in fragmentation and dualism. Self-identity is by nature transitory, self-centred thinking and, as such, impacts our perceptions and experiences with the world – beginning locally, and expanding outward, eventually including the nation and the world.

Due to social, political, historical and cultural inequities, many individuals and/or groups are disenfranchised or empowered based on race, gender, class, sexual orientation, religion and geography. These forms of inequity and limited privilege are often influenced and/or communicated by the production of visual culture. A critical analysis of production and consumption of visual culture provides opportunities to investigate relationships between issues of personal, national and global cultural identities construction. Through this experience teachers and students have the opportunity to explore and communicate their learning and development to increase their social justice competency.

Context: multiculturalism in the United States of America

Ladson-Billings and Tate (1995) state that one's social reality is constructed by the formulation and exchange of stories, which, historically, have been a kind of medicine that heals the wounds caused by racial oppression. Ultimately, I hope this reflective exploration encourages readers to go beyond the self and engage with their own identities, power, and how they impact the curricula and methodologies they use in the classroom.

At the Ohio State University in Columbus, Ohio, I knew that there were two professors, Drs Patricia L. Stuhr and Vesta H. Daniel, who would be excellent colleagues with whom to explore multiculturalism. In our collaborations, Patricia, Vesta and I often discussed family issues more than we would write, which enriched my understanding of complex terms and relationships. At one time we agreed that since the turn of the nineteenth century, people have been interpreting multiculturalism through various lenses (e.g. socio-cultural, political, academic and pedagogical), all of which are biased. The evolution of terms, specifically the word *multicultural*, is constantly being questioned as its reality shifts. It is through historical exploration that a foundation can be provided to help define a vocabulary for considering the term multicultural. Historical analysis also provides a focused vision, which, through critical reflection and analysis, reveals the nature of conflicts surrounding the term multicultural. Through this type of analysis, it can be shown that the evolving term *multicultural* now includes intercultural, intracultural, and cross-cultural, and their intersections and complexities. The breadth of the conceptual changes surrounding the term multicultural is profoundly affected by and, in turn, affects visual and kinetic cultures and education as represented through the arts, contemporary media, artefacts and associated narratives.

Although multiculturalism is presented primarily in terms of educational reform, the broader concept of multiculturalism is not new because of our ancestors' nomadic life styles. The *National Geographic*'s 1999 article on 'Global Culture' (Swerdlow 1999) visualised and described the nomadic nature of our predecessors. Nomadic life demanded that humans develop adaptations to the new environments they encountered. These diverse environmental adaptations helped groups of humans to create varied cultural systems.

The complex issues of cultural diversity are often studied as a part of the school reform movement known as Multicultural Education, which is a concept, philosophy and process that originated in the 1960s as part of the Civil Rights Movement to combat racism (Sleeter and Grant 1998). It was then, and still is, an educational process dedicated to providing equitable opportunities in social, political and especially educational arenas for disenfranchised individuals and groups. This is an ideal, like the ideal of democracy, which may never be completely met; however, it is still seen by many as a worthy and necessary educational goal for a more just and equitable society (Sleeter and Grant 1998).

Multiculturalism concepts should be continually subject to the process of revision in order to encourage social justice and thriving, constructive communities. Process rather than product should be the consequence of an art curriculum guided by democratic and social justice goals. These goals are meant to confront the 'racial class, gender, and homophobic biases woven into the fabric of society' (Bigelow *et al.* 2001: 1). This process helps explain and confront those colonialist practices that stem from one group of people having power over another group's 'education, language(s), culture(s), lands and economy' (Ballengee Morris 2000: 102). Moreover, these goals and values provide for classroom practices that are built on democracy and social justice.

Critical Race Theory, which came out of critical legal studies and entered the education fields in the late 1980s, focuses on issues of racism and racial subordination and discrimination, expanding the notion of multicultural education. Ladson-Billings and Tate (1995) suggest three propositions: 1) race is still a significant factor in the United States; 2) property rights determine power; and 3) the intersections of race and property should be analysed as a part of the creation of inequities. Multicultural education theories often focus on learning about 'others' and do not explore property ownership, policies and applications. The practice of storytelling is key because it requires one to name one's reality. Such stories can be healing to the teller and can help listeners realise their own participation in the process of oppression.

Curricula and teaching should connect with students' narratives, needs, experiences and communities. Students need to understand that their identities are constructed by the stories that they tell about themselves and the stories that are told about them (Cohen-Evron, 2005). Teachers and students should:

1 investigate how their lives connect to and are limited by the broader society, and develop critical skills to address social issues;
2 explore how some groups may benefit or suffer from the colonial practices and decisions of other people;
3 recognise their own biases and those of others in order to see the connections between power and wealth and injustice.

The concept of justice and equitable opportunities for all are important goals. To help students in understanding these goals, it is necessary to create opportunities that they can experience first-hand and within which they can actively participate. Examining and producing visual culture imagery and objects that lead to, and end in, an understanding of justice and the complexities of social, political and economic relations are valuable, if challenging, goals for education. I believe that young people are unlikely to understand these issues in the larger world until they have understood them in the smaller world in which they grow and live.

Multiple ethnicities

Before and during the Civil Rights era in the United States in the 1960s, many non-white Americans had been rendered invisible, either through exclusion from majority establishments or through self-invisibility practices. In part this was a survival mechanism afforded to the few whose skin tone and facial features lent themselves to such a practice; many people of colour would render themselves invisible by 'passing' as white (this is discussed in relation to the work of Adrian Piper below). When racial heritage borrows from multiple groups and renders the subject as a biracial, multiracial, mixed blood, Métis, half, hapa, etc., 'other', the process of making invisible is further complicated. Such racial identity affords further opportunities for invisibility, both self-inflicted and externally motivated.

Fifty years ago in the United States, we were in a 'one drop' classification, meaning that if a person had even the smallest trace of non-white ancestry she or he was considered non-white regardless of how their facial features might otherwise qualify them as white. Today, at least in the United States, we embrace a self-classified, one category system of racial identification. While these 'we' positions do not necessarily reflect the entire membership of minority groups in the United States, these positions have, to a great extent, become the assumed positions of members within and external to minority groups. In many cases, mass media, popular sentiment and legislated practices have collectively governed and influenced the limits and extent to which racial and cultural classifications have been defined in the self-called 'greatest country on Earth'.

Personal

Personal identity involves many cultural intersections – race, ethnicity, gender, class, age, ableism, language, sexual orientation, parenthood, religion and spirituality – which bring different experiences to one's development. Personal identity and self-awareness and freedom involve many intersections, compounded by social norms, understandings, perceptions and political movements. Historically, visual identifiers have been the ultimate definers of 'who' one could be and to which group one could belong. As a cognitive-map, identity functions in a multitude of ways to guide and direct exchanges with one's social and material realities (Cross 1995). Racial identity theory draws from the traditional treatment of race as a socio-political and cultural construction (Helms 1995), while ethnic identity defines a segment of a larger society whose members have a common origin, share segments of a common culture and participate in shared activities in which the common origin and culture are significant ingredients. Ethnic identity development (Phinney 1990) focuses on what people learn about themselves from shared religions, languages and geographies, but fails to capture the complexities of multiracialism.

The exploration of identity is educationally significant because research in the areas of biracial identity and multiracial identity development is still relatively young and negative attitudes and prejudicial treatments threaten the self-concept of minority youth. The issue of being assigned an invisible identity as well as construct-ing such an identity for oneself can be examined as a theoretical discourse as much as a lived one.

There is an equal fear of giving biracial, multiracialism visibility due to the long and hard efforts exerted to obtain power and voice through ethnic movements such as Black and Red Power in the 1970s in the United States. The multiracial movement is challenging, as it not only deals with halves and wholes but also the continued recy-cling of previous racial definitions such as the 'one drop' and 'blood quantum'.

The artist Adrian Piper addresses her halves/wholes, identifying as an African American but being viewed white. Her art is narrative, in a style told through black and white images with text, and sometimes, as in *Art for the Art-World Surface Pattern* (exhibited 1977), where the text is indecipherable. This leads one to ask – what is missing? As an artist she narrates her identity journey through emersion, rejection, border-crossing and self-identification (Piper 1996). Her work and process is an example of Critical Race, Multicultural Education and encourages us to examine critically the negative influence of images from a white lens that perpetuates self-hatred. Historical and current media and images that continue stereotypical represen-tations of Blacks, Native Americans, Asians, Southerns, Appalachians and Latino/as need to be analysed. What are the implications?

An approach through stories

Long before people had written language, we told our narratives through stories, poems, song, drawings and dance. What do we learn from stories? Stories not only convey information, but they have the power to change. The exchange of stories from teller to listener can help overcome ethnocentrism. As the story is consumed, the immediate reaction is heartfelt and then, as it proceeds to our intellect, self-reflexive engagement occurs, which can lead to rethinking relations of power (Asher and Crocco 2001). As we explore pedagogical implications, there are several power com-ponents to consider in relation to external and internal positioning: power-over, power-with and power-within.

Nina Asher, an education scholar, proposes to open up educational spaces for the emergence of hybrid identities and cultures by rejecting the 'don't ask, don't tell' and 'see no race, differences of sexuality or relations of power', and embracing the affir-mation of diversity by creating a culture of 'do ask, do tell' (Asher 2007: 71). Sharing stories through text, movies, television programming, visual arts, theatre, dance and music, helps provide social contexts that situate ourselves for others. Telling and shar-ing our own stories also extends ourselves beyond a personal space into a dialogic place that encourages social justice.

The various aspects of personal, cultural identities are in transition and dynamic. Recognising our own socio-cultural identity and biases makes it easier to understand the multifaceted cultural identities of others. It may also help us to understand why and how they respond as they do (Ballengee Morris and Stuhr 2001). Ultimately, all we can ever understand is a part of a cultural group's temporal experience as they report or express it (Scott *et al*. 1995). Because partial, temporal understandings of a group are all that exist, it is not possible to come to a complete understanding of a homogeneous culture. For example, there is no such thing as 'an' African American, Native American or Jewish culture. There is no one representation of a cultural group that can be understood by memorising its characteristics. The more one learns about the narratives of various members of a particular group and its history, heritage, traditions and cultural interactions, the more one comes to understand its richness and complexity (Stuhr 1999).

Students need to understand that their identities are constructed by the stories they tell about themselves and that are told about them (Cohen-Evron 2005). When it is possible to do so, it is important to move students conceptually and physically outside the classroom and link with real-world communities, issues and problems in order to practice these critical skills. This type of critical investigation is not without threat or danger; thus, teachers must be empathetic, practical and cautious in creating mentally and physically safe environments for this learning to occur.

Diversity curriculum development

Concepts of multiculturalism in art education should encourage social justice and thriving, constructive communities. But how do teachers design curricula that work toward these goals? A few years ago I collaborated in the writing of the book *Interdisciplinary Approaches to Teaching Art in High School* (Taylor *et al*. 2006). As we suggested in our book, we believed one way was to begin to consider the following question: Do you as a teacher use a variety of images and diverse artists that represent a wide range of one's community, region, nation and world?

Visual culture includes images from mass media. Images create meaning and a vision of life for our students. An example of this is Abercrombie and Fitch, a clothing chain in the United States that caters to teens. They design T-shirts that display slogans such as 'Wong Brothers Laundry Service: Two Wongs can make it white,' and 'It's all relative in West Virginia'. Both slogans are derogatory to two cultures within the United States. Teachers can stimulate and establish relevancy when they connect socio-cultural issues, question, problems, concepts or topics to students' personal cultural identity. Since visual culture plays a prevalent part in students' lives and is connected to multiple disciplines across the curriculum, it is vital to use it as the centre for curriculum development.

Conclusion

Educators who guide their students to make meaning out of this complex and ambiguous world help them to make sense of their place and space. Learning how to make connections and not see subjects or people in isolated, unrelated ways is a lifelong skill that is vitally important for our students to learn. When a particular concept is addressed in the classroom, it is more meaningful to pose it as an issue or question for students, which becomes the driving force of the curriculum. In exploring concepts such as racism or identity through visual culture, teachers could help students to investigate how events do or do not impact their lives and to deal responsibly with the emotions they engender.

To conclude, a curriculum with the goal of social justice helps students to view images in a thoughtful manner so they develop democratic ways of thinking and become informed consumers. Learning about the ways in which the visual arts influence people, empowers children to decide how they allow themselves to be influenced. They can learn early on how civic leaders use imagery to represent self and influence people's voting choices. To promote social justice, children should begin to learn about the ways in which groups of people are represented in imagery.

Through art education, they can come to understand the damaging effects of visual stereotypes (Freedman and Stuhr 2005). The need to reflect about histories of privilege, prejudice, oppression and actions all become part of this dialogue that often guides people to question their beliefs and behaviours. Diversity is about everything: how we teach, what we teach, who we teach, who we are, the communities we live in, our past, our present, our future, and our students' present and future. It is about our life and the world we live in and the world makers we are teaching.

References

Asher, N. (2007) 'Made in the (Multicultural) USA: Unpacking Tensions of Race, Culture, Gender, and Sexuality in Education', *Educational Researcher*, 36 (2): 65–73.

Asher, N. and Crocco, M.S. (2001) '(En)gendering Multicultural Identities and Representations', *Theory and Research in Social Education*, 29 (1): 129–151.

Ballengee Morris, C. (2000) 'A Sense of Place: Allegheny Echoes', in: K. Congdon, D. Blandy and P. Bolin (eds) *Making Invisible Histories of Art Education Visible*, Reston, VA: National Art Education Association.

Ballengee Morris, C. and Stuhr, P.L. (2001) 'Multicultural Art and Visual Culture Education in a Changing World', *Art Education*, 54 (4): 6–13.

Bigelow, B., Harvey, B., Karp, S. and Miller, L. (2001) *Rethinking Our Classrooms, Volume 2: Teaching for Equity and Justice*, Milwaukee, WI: Rethinking Schools Limited.

Cohen-Evron, N. (2005) 'Students Living Within a Violent Conflict: Should Art Educators "Play it Safe" or Face "Difficult Knowledge"?', *Studies in Art Education*, 46 (4): 309–322.

Cross, N. (1995) 'Discovering Design Ability', in: R. Buchanan and V. Margolin (eds) *Discovering Design*, Chicago, IL: Chicago University Press.

Freedman, K. and Stuhr, P.L. (2005) 'Curriculum and Visual Culture', in: M. Day and E. Eisner (eds) *Handbook of Art Education Research*, Reston, VA: National Art Education Association.

Helms, G. (1995) *Black and White Racial Identity: Theory, Research, and Practice*, New York: Greenwood Press.

Ladson-Billings, G. and Tate, I.V. (1995) 'Toward a Critical Race Theory of Education', *Teachers College Record*, 97 (1): 1–22.

Phinney, J.S. (1990) 'Ethnic Identity in Adolescents and Adults: Review of Research', *Psychological Bulletin*, 10 (3): 499–514.

Piper, A. (1996) *Out of Order, Out of Sight*, Cambridge MA: MIT Press.

Scott, A.P., Krug, D. and Stuhr, P. (1995) 'A Conversation About Translating the Indigenous Story', *Journal of Multicultural and Cross-Cultural Research in Art Education*, 13 (1): 29–45.

Sleeter, C. and Grant, C. (1998) 'An Analysis of Multicultural Research in the United States: A Postmodern Feminist Perspective on Visual Arts in Elementary Education', *Harvard Educational Review*, 57 (4): 421–445.

Stuhr, P.L. (1999) 'Multiculturalism Art Education: Context and Pedagogy', *FATE, Journal of the College Art Association*, 22 (1): 5–12.

Swerdlow, J.L. (1999) 'Global Culture', *National Geographic*, 196 (2): 2–5.

Taylor, P.G., Carpenter II, S.B., Ballengee-Morris, C. and Sessions, B. (2006) *Interdisciplinary Approaches to Teaching Art in High School*, Reston, VA: National Art Education Association.

Wilson, F. (2005) Online. Available at: www.pbs.org/art21/artists/wilson (accessed 4 March 2011).

Chapter 5

Symbolic representational processes

A case for embodied practice

Gemma Cozens

Introduction

As a teacher with a background in theatre design, the first key feature of my research interests is a holistic and interdisciplinary conceptualisation of what art education is, encompassing aspects of performance-based creative disciplines. The second key feature is a concern for developing dialogic and collective practice within the classroom, accommodating notions of co-learning through engaged, critical *dialogue* between teacher and student.

For me, the notion of *dialogue* encompasses three aspects: *internal* dialogue (debating oppositional ideas towards conscientisation); *situated* dialogue (between oneself and the media and environment); and *interpersonal* dialogue (including semiotic exchanges without, before or beyond language). Here, I discuss the educative value of multiple voices in dialogue: *collectivity*. I use this definition to construct a tool for examining the imagination, within the boundaries of making that takes place in social environments.

Symbolic representational processes are conceived of here as encompassing dramatisation, mark-making and imaginative play. The case study discussed within this chapter investigates the value of creative activities that embrace a performance dynamic, encapsulating the pedagogies of experiential learning, learning through play and social interaction. Vygotskian social-constructivist theories on the relationship between learning and development provide a basis for understanding the role of collaborative and participatory action in embodied learning.

The disembodied eye

The current skills-based national curriculum cultivates a representational imperative for visual research and technical mastery. Representation in this context can be understood as 'mirroring': mental constructs visualised without embodied explorations or dialogue with materials and tools. Responding to institutional pressures and a national culture of accountability and culpability, teachers frequently prize realistic products, conforming to adult aesthetic criteria (Atkinson 2008). Such prescribed outcomes are generally most reliably achieved through the use of rigid instructions and templates that limit freedoms and stunt explorative possibilities.

The ethic of *play*, characterised as having no definite objective, rejects the requisite for over-determined representational outcomes. Commitment to the ontological dimension of learning through play reveals its most fundamentally valuable feature. By this, I refer to the nature of play as a process-based, procedural and active form of learning. It possesses a transformative function that is in stark contrast to the epistemological basis for learning, which is concerned with the accrual of non-applied forms of knowledge, characteristic of the national curriculum.

Play can be understood as encompassing imagination, experimentation and dramatisation. Here, these aspects find convergence in the notion of *embodiment*. Recognising visual art as an embodied practice attacks the curricular objective for representation as mirroring by establishing a link between the body and representation. Embodied practice engages with that which is outside language, which exceeds language. It uncovers equivalents for experiences to help develop a repertoire of forms, sympathetic with an affective, emotional motivation and mode of making.

I possess a long held belief that the value of creative activity for children lies in the imaginative process rather than in the end product (Vygotsky 2004; Matthews 2003). Through previous research, I have come to understand children's representational, meaning-making processes as 'live events' in which image, word and gesture are integrated as visual media in union. I consider that the *process* or the 'live event' is, in itself, the meaning, derived from a symbiotic union of representation of past experiences with the temporal aspect of interacting with the media (Atkinson 2002). Though young children's drawings will often not conform to adult perceptions of aesthetics or representations (based on visual realism), Kress and Leeuwen (2006: 7) argue that their multimodal representational processes employ intentional 'signs' for *subjective* and *intersubjective* forms of communication.

Through analysis of an indicative event, I explore the value of multimodal creative processes involving explorative play and embodiment for representational purposes. Specifically, I exemplify the relationship between, and potential influence of, embodied action on subsequent visualisation, in the form of collaborative mark-making. Consideration is also given to the mediating role of materials and tools and to children's selection and deployment of these for symbolic effect.

Play, imagination and creativity: a Vygotskian perspective

It is crucial, when discussing children's representational activities (in play, embodiment and painting), to consider the roles of creativity and imagination. Vygotsky (2004) defines creativity as being 'present… whenever a person imagines, combines, alters, and creates something new' (p. 10). Central to this definition is the notion of *combinatorial* creative activity, which is the operation of the *imagination* (pp. 9, 12 and 13). This notion emphasises the fact that the 'new' product of a creative act is never entirely novel but is rather rooted in prior experiences. It is a reworked and restructured combination of elements of reality.

The most fantastic creations are nothing other than a new combination of elements that have ultimately been extracted from reality and have simply undergone the transformational or distorting action of our imagination.

(Vygotsky 2004: 13)

Vygotsky continues by elaborating on the relationship between imagination and reality by proposing *four* different types of association. The *first* type of association is completely dependent upon *the individual person's amassed experience*, which 'provides the material from which the products of fantasy are constructed' (Vygotsky 2004: 14–15). In this sense, real experiences feed our imaginations and thus enhance our potential for creative activity. The implication of this, which bears significance to educational pedagogy, is that the diversity and wealth of a person's experience directly corresponds with the capacity of their imagination.

Vygotsky states that the *second* connection between imagination and reality occurs when 'the product of imagination, not just its elements, corresponds to some real phenomenon' (2004: 16). This, Vygotsky claims, is dependent upon *social experience*: the experience of someone else (p. 17). He elaborates that the accounts of someone else's experience can be integrated into our own consciousness through the workings of our imaginations. In this way, our own experience is expanded by our imagination of the experience of another (ibid.).

Thus there is a double, mutual dependence between imagination and experience. If, in the first case, imagination is based on experience, in the second case experience itself is based on imagination.

(Vygotsky 2004: 17)

Vygotsky asserts that the *third* connection between imagination and reality is through the factor of *emotion*. This factor seems to possess a dual aspect. First, Vygotsky explains that our internal emotions affect the combinatorial activity of our imaginations: we select and combine elements of reality based on their 'emotional signs' (2004: 18) and the correspondence of these with our internal mood. Such emotional signs of (mental) imagery are thought to be universal in that they evoke a similar emotional response in everyone. While this first aspect of the theory describes the influence of emotion on imagination, the second aspect describes the converse: the influence of imagination on emotion. This is termed the *law of emotional reality of the imagination* (p. 19).

This means that every construct of the imagination has an effect on our feelings, and if this construct does not itself respond to reality, nonetheless the feelings it evokes are real feelings, feelings a person truly experiences.

(Vogotsky 2004: 19–20)

Finally, the *fourth* association between imagination and reality is through the notion of *embodied imagination*. This theory considers that any new product of combinatorial imaginative activity comes into existence in reality once it has been 'crystallized' in external material form (Vygotsky 2004: 20). 'In this way imagination becomes reality' (ibid.). Thus, the relationship between imagination and reality is a cyclical one: reality informs our imaginative capabilities, and in turn, the products of our imaginations become embodied realities.

> It is a fact that precisely when we confront a full circle completed by the imagination is when we find both factors – the intellectual and the emotional – are equally necessary for an act of creation. Feeling as well as thought drives human creativity … [which has] … the power, not of external, but of internal truth.
>
> (Vygotsky 2004: 21)

Imaginative play can be understood as one of the earliest manifestations of combinatorial creativity in childhood. Vygotsky asserts that play begins as an embodied 'recollection' (1978: 103) of real situations based on the child's knowledge of social and cultural rules of behaviour. In accordance with the child's own needs and desires, he/she alters and restructures elements taken from real experiences and observations to create a new reality explored through role-play (Vygotsky 2004: 11 and 29). Describing the process of combinatorial creativity, Vygotsky (2004) explains that perceived *associations* between elements of reality must be broken down and *disassociated* before new imaginary realities can be internally constructed from the parts or 'traces' of external realities (pp. 25–26). Through *distortion*, *exaggeration* and *minimisation*, 'these traces are actually processes, they move, change, live and die, and this dynamism guarantees that they will change under the influence of the imagination' (p. 26). Imagination possesses a transformative function, which enables social processes to be internalised within the consciousness of the individual child. Through imaginative play, the cognitive abilities of the child are thus extended beyond his actual developmental level and play creates a zone of proximal development (ZPD) (Vygotsky 1978: 102). Through a child's interactions with those around him/her (more experienced learners – including adults), he/she will be able to achieve beyond his/her actual developmental level. Once these functions have been 'internalized' and become intrapersonal as opposed to interpersonal, the child will be able to achieve them independently (p. 56).

> From the very first days of the child's development his activities acquire a meaning of their own in a system of social behaviour and, being directed towards a definite purpose, are refracted through the prism of the child's environment. The path from object to child and from child to object passes through another person. This complex human structure is the product of a developmental process deeply rooted in the links between individual and social history.
>
> (Vygotsky 1978: 30)

In alignment with arguments in favour of multimodal creative processes involving explorative play and performance aspects, Vygotsky discusses the creative connection between dramatisation and play (2004: 69–74), citing Petrova who 'consider[s] play to be the primary dramatic form … [through] which children's representations of the world are rooted in action' (cited 2004: 71). Vygotsky advocates educational practice that incorporates drama, reasoning the compatibility of active, embodied representational modes with the child's imagination. He continues his promotion of the dramatic mode of creativity with reference to his notion of the cyclical nature of embodied imagination: 'the dramatic form expresses with greatest clarity the full cycle of imagination … the drive for action, for embodiment, for realisation that is present in the very process of imagination here finds complete fulfilment' (p. 70). Also key to this statement is the phrase, '*process* of imagination'. This also corresponds with a key aspect of my own pedagogical position: that the value of creative activity for young children lies in the imaginative process rather than in the product. In this regard, my own position is in complete alignment with that of Vygotsky who stresses:

> It must not be forgotten that the basic law of children's creativity is that its value lies not in the results, not in the product of creation, but in the process itself. It is not important what children create, but that they do create, that they exercise and implement their creative imagination … the whole production should be organized in such a way that the children feel that they are playing for themselves and are consumed with interest in this, in the process, and not in the final result … and not the success or approval the child receives from adults.
>
> (Vygotsky 2004: 72–73)

We're Going on a Bear Hunt

Vygotsky conceives that imagination, 'like all functions of consciousness, originally arises from action' (1978: 93). Hence, in endeavouring to engage the children in drawing and painting, I felt that it was important to view these processes not as isolated representational actions, but rather as 'members of a family' of representational, imaginative and expressive actions in collaboration with one another (Matthews 2003: 7–16).

The 'case study' involved a series of activities within a nursery setting, which attempted to employ 'art' (within a broader performance context) as a tool for exploration, investigation and interpretation of a given text: the children's picture book, *We're Going on a Bear Hunt* (Rosen and Oxenbury 1989). I intended that these activities would be experiential and performance-based, linking experiences, movement and mark-making in a holistic and interdisciplinary way.

The project took place over five days spread over five consecutive weeks. Over this period, the children listened to and retold the story of *We're Going on a Bear Hunt*, engaged in whole-class movement sessions and free role-play, and latterly, worked in groups to create visualisations of the environments travelled through whilst on the 'bear hunt' (long wavy grass, a deep cold river, thick oozy mud, a big dark forest, a swirling whirling snowstorm and a narrow gloomy cave). Although I was mindful of ensuring that the focus remained on the *process* rather than any prescribed end prod-ucts, in alignment with Vygotsky's educational recommendations, I also recognised that absolute freedom can have the counter effect. I therefore scaffolded the activities by imposing a series of constraints, which, I hoped, would, in fact, cultivate possi-bilities. I selected the story starting point, the times and places for exploratory move-ment sessions, and the available resources for visualisation. Within these parameters, the children were given agency and I reduced my input as the project progressed. During the visualisation sessions, the children worked in self-selected groups and chose their own materials and tools for their chosen representational purposes. Bruner's metaphorical term 'scaffolding' is closely linked to Vygotsky's notion of the ZPD. Central to both theories is a belief in the important influence of social interac-tion on the learning process. However, whereas the ZPD accommodates interactions with 'more capable peers', the notion of 'scaffolding' specifically refers to adult inter-vention and support (which may be in the form of teacher–student dialogue), which can be gradually withdrawn as the child increases in their independence as a learner.

Sign-using activity in embodied practice

I have defined the aspects of *play* as finding convergence in *embodiment*: uncovering equivalents of experiences towards developing a repertoire of forms. Here, I discuss evidence that demonstrates children were learning to create and employ semiotic systems of symbols and signs to communicate meaning, through both the representa-tional modes of embodied action in time and three-dimensional space, and painted action in time and two-dimensional space. For this reason, at this point I refer to Vygotsky's theories concerned with the historical–cultural development of sign-using activity.

Throughout *Mind in Society* (1978), Vygotsky considers a diverse range of sign-using behaviour, including: gesture, speech, drawing and symbolic play (to name those that will be relevant to subsequent analysis of my own research). Vygotsky asserts that 'sign operations are the product of specific conditions of *social* develop-ment' (p. 39). He elaborates that sign-using activity arises as a result of a complex transformative process of developmental events, each of which informs the last. The influential factor on this transformative process is the interrelationship between the individual and the society to which they belong. Sign operations are neither adopted by the child directly from adults, nor independently 'invented' (p. 46) but are the result of a reflexive dialogical relationship between the two.

Vygotsky offers a staged theory of sign development in children, beginning with gesture as the first visual sign and progressing through symbolic play and drawing towards written language. He insists that this developmental process follows a 'uni-fied historical line that leads to the highest forms of written language' (Vygotsky 1978: 116). Matthews (2003), refutes Vygotsky's staged theory of development, believing that it implies a 'deficit model' of development. I question whether the implication of Vygotsky's theory is that children must overcome deficiencies, correct-ing errors as they move from one developmental stage to the next. Instead it seems to me that Vygotsky's staged theory is less about deficiencies and more about a hierarchy of symbolisation, although I would contest this notion of the hegemony of one sign system over another. I feel this argument assigns inadequate value to drawing as a representational, communicative and expressive mode in its own right for both children with little or no written language and adults with advanced written language.

Despite reservations, it is also important to note that I believe Vygotsky's theory also offers insights that remain relevant alongside more contemporary theories surrounding this subject. To support my analysis, I refer to Matthews' notion of 'action representation' (1999, 2003). In fact, the influence of embodiment on painting and drawing is, it seems, a relatively under-explored concept. However, although not accredited by Matthews in his discussion of this, Vygotsky also recognised the relationship through experimentation by which he established 'the kinship between gestural depiction and depiction by drawing, and obtained symbolic and graphic depiction through gestures in five-year-olds' (1978: 108).

During the movement sessions, children explored the imaginary long wavy grass primarily in two ways. Some children used their arms, stretched up above their heads to represent the tall stalks of grass, swaying them gently from side to side to simulate the grass blowing in a breeze. Other children imagined moving through long grass, pushing one palm at a time outwards, away from their torsos as though parting the grass in order to move through it. Transposing these actions onto the paper, children produced a combination of *vertical and horizontal arcs* (Matthews 1999, 2003). Having observed the painting in progress, I sense that the vertical arcs represent the tall spears of grass whilst the horizontal arcs are indicative of the motion of sweeping the grass aside (Figure 5.1). According to Matthews, 'early drawings are about shapes; the shapes on paper and the shapes of the movements which produce them and their relationship to objects and events in the world' (2003: 89).

Marrying visual representation with verbal and kinaesthetic modes, one child spoke the words, 'swishy swashy' from the story repeatedly as he rhythmically stroked and dragged his paint-laden fork (his chosen tool) from side to side, leaving in its wake trails of paint in horizontal arcs. Vygotsky conceives of drawing as 'graphic speech … telling a story' (1978: 112). Although disputing the notion that drawing functions solely as the initial stage in the development of writing, I recognise the interrelationship between the communicative and expressive modes of drawing and speech throughout children's representational processes and the multimodal approach to representation that children adopt in order to make meaning.

Continuing with notions of the interactivity of sign systems, Vygotsky also observed that children often switch from drawing to 'dramatization' (1978: 107). He sensed that the marks produced in drawing were 'supplementary' traces of the children's embodied gestural depictions. In this vein, I observed one child alternating back and forth seamlessly between representational modes: at some moments, swaying and waving his hands freely in the air and at other moments, using his sweeping hand actions to generate marks on the paper. Moving between embodiment and representation, he directly mapped his movements from the three-dimensional space onto the two-dimensional surface (Figure 5.2).

Figure 5.1 Vertical and horizontal arcs. (Photographer: Gemma Cozens)

When imagining being caught in a swirling whirling snowstorm (Figure 5.3), which, in the story, is accompanied by the onomatopoeic words 'hoooo woooo' to echo the sound of a howling wind, children had enacted being blown around uncontrollably by the wind. With their arms stretched out to their sides for balance, children twirled around in spiralling trajectories through the space. Moving to visualisation, it appears that the children possessed an understanding of the shape of the path created

Figure 5.2 Alternating between representational modes. (Photographer: Gemma Cozens)

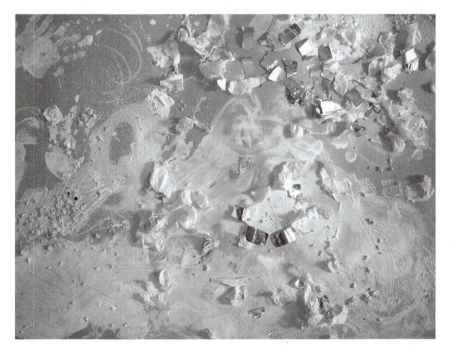

Figure 5.3 'A swirling whirling snowstorm'. (Photographer: Gemma Cozens)

Figure 5.4 Travelling loops. (Photographer: Gemma Cozens)

by such a movement (Figure 5.4). Using their selected tools, children created *travelling loops* of paint on paper (Matthews 2003).

It appears that they had made the complex series of cognitive leaps from experiencing the feeling of an embodied movement through space, to understanding the shape created by this movement as if seen from a bird's-eye view, to finally using smaller hand actions to manipulate tools and materials in order to record this shape/movement as a travelling mark. Matthews (2003) describes this product of action-representation, in which a three-dimensional elevated perspective is mapped on to a two-dimensional surface as a plan view, as a *projected relationship* (pp. 67 and 87). Action representations 'are based on vectors of movement practised with the entire body through space' (Matthews 2003: 86).

In these examples, the outcomes of the visualisation episodes were traces of embodied movement and, in this way, the children were using marks on the paper's surface to stand for previously embodied movements, which in themselves had been generated by the children to represent their physical and emotional understanding of experiences. In this way, the children's representations were semiotic, symbolic processes. There were also notable differences between the pace, pressure and intensity of the children's mark-making processes applied to the visualisations of the different environments. The children approached their visualisation of the grass at a gentle yet rhythmical pace, with a softness of touch and a relaxed demeanour, reflecting the mood of the story at this particular point (when the family are beginning their expedition).

Comparatively, when 'making' the snowstorm, children created their travelling loops frantically, gripping their tools tightly so as to exert a greater pressure onto the paper. This (measured) chaos again reflected the mood of the story as the family neared the fearful conclusion of their hunt. In alignment with Vygotsky's second emotional link between imagination and reality, when emotion influences imagination, it seems that the children's imaginative marks were made in response to their internal mood at the time of creation (based on the internalised mood of the story).

> (Painting) is a rhythmical, patterned dance or play with paint and body actions in space and time ... It is precisely the interrelationships between sensory-perceptual modes which give it its richly layered meaning.
>
> (Matthews 2003: 26–27)

Conversing with materials and tools

As discussed, through modes of action-representation – initially embodiment, followed by dynamic mark-making – children were able to associate and synchronise painting actions with actions created using their whole bodies. In other words, the children were able to use a painting action to represent another bodily action. They were able to translate ideas across from modes of representation, which captured movement in time (embodiment) to modes which captured form in space (painting). 'The dynamic aspects of the schemas has guided and enriched the configurative aspects' (Matthews 2003: 121). Here, the focus turns to examining the children's selection and deployment of materials and tools for representational purposes. I anticipated that the children would make confident colour choices in order to visualise or 'make' the different environments visited on the bear hunt, but in addition, the distinct differences between the processes applied to each visualisation indicate a much deeper understanding of the properties of each of the environments. In alignment with Matthews' analyses of painting and drawing episodes, Vygotsky describes how children depict the 'general qualities' (1978: 108) of objects rather than specific features as they appear from a singular viewpoint. He concludes that this is because they are drawing from memory rather than direct observation. Matthews (1999, 2003) describes this notion as the difference between 'seeing' and 'knowing'. Children draw what they 'know' about an object with less concern for visual realism.

Free from 'preconceptions about boundaries and conventions of representational systems' (Matthews 2003: 121), particularly with regard to the confines of visual realism, the children's visualisations were free-flowing representations of interiorised visual imagery, kinaesthetic experiences and linguistic sounds. Children were able to explore the possibilities (and limitations) afforded by the media and tools available when used in conjunction with movement, a reciprocal dialogue between the thinking, acting child and the evolving visualisation, mediated by media and tools.

Children were provided with the same selection of media (paint in primary colours, plastic bags, foil, cling film, food grains and glue) and tools (paint brushes, plastic forks, drinking straws, sponges, glue spreaders and cotton buds) for each visualisation. These are materials that are readily available within many settings for painting and junk modelling.

Children selected tools to use based on a range of criteria and for a variety of reasons. Some tools were chosen because they, in themselves, bore visual resemblance to aspects of the environment being represented. For example, children chose to use the plastic forks as painting tools to represent grass because of their 'spiky' appearance and feel. In the same way, others chose to use the cotton buds as painting tools to represent the snowstorm because 'they look like snowballs'. Vygotsky asserts that it is only as children grow older (after the age of three) that they will be able to select objects based on particular features that correspond with the meaning of the object they are intending to represent. Thus children discover that 'objects can indicate the things they denote as well as substitute for them' (Vygotsky 1978: 109). This is second-order symbolism in the sense that the object itself is used as a sign to signify the meaning of something else independently of gesture. The object is acting as a metaphor. However, in these examples, although the children made their selections based on the physical characteristics of their chosen objects/tools, the *meaning* of 'grass' or 'snow' was manifest when these objects were used in combination with gesture.

Other tools were chosen because of the children's prior knowledge of the textural qualities they could create using them. For example, one child initiated using the drinking straws to suck up and blow paint, saying, 'You can make the oozy mud go splat splat like this' (Figure 5.5). In doing this, he seemed to be making a connection between the textural qualities of mud and paint and drawing on a previously known method for generating splattered paint. He may also have been making the connection between the sound made by splattering paint in this way with the onomatopoeic words used in the story to allude to the sound of wading through the mud, 'squelch, squerch'. Also in the visualisation of the mud, children selected sponges saturated with paint to create similar textural effect, pressing them down onto the paper as they said the words, 'squelch, squerch' in a rhythmical correspondence with their actions.

Many of the children used their hands as representational tools for painting, creating a variety of effects through employing varied techniques, again appropriated for each environment. Finger tips were employed, as fine tools in order to generate defined patterns reminiscent, for example, of ripples on a water's surface. For other visualisations, children chose to use the palms of their hands for mark-making, often in combination with movement, creating less defined marks and covering larger areas of the paper. I surmise that these actions were more concerned with exploring the textural qualities of the paint (particularly in the case of the mud visualisation) and with creating a large 'wet' surface in the case of the river visualisation.

In the same way that the children deployed tools for a range of representational purposes and reasons, their selection of materials displayed a variety of cognitive processes. There appear to have been two main ways in which the materials were used throughout the visualisation sessions: for representational means and as simulacrum of the natural environmental substances. In many instances, I sense that the children moved back and forth between these different approaches, as though in dialogue with

Figure 5.5 Splattered paint. (Photographer: Gemma Cozens)

the media and the unfolding visualisation. As Bruce (1991) explains, 'children make decisions about visual structure from moment to moment in free-flowing play with the drawing medium' (cited in Matthews 2003: 131).

As discussed previously (Figure 5.1) it can be seen in the children's visualisation of the long tall grass that, in addition to representing embodied actions, children also used materials and tools for purposes of visual realism: to represent the appearance of grass.

In 'a deep dark forest tree' (Figure 5.6) one child mixed grains of couscous with brown paint 'to look like the soil'. After gluing some of this 'soil' to the area of the paper she had been working on, another child suggested that they 'need[ed] some soil on the ground', referring to the bottom of the page as he viewed it. He and one other had been working alongside each other, both using forks to paint the arcs of green paint representing grass. A denser mass of green paint at the bottom of the page thinned out towards the top where more individual marks or stalks of grass could be seen. He indicated that the soil should be glued below the area of dense green paint, suggesting that he was trying to represent the grassy environment from a singular viewpoint: a side elevation or cross-section.

In other instances, particularly in the case of the mud visualisation, children approached using the media less as representational tools with a fixed goal in mind (what the visualisation would 'look like') and more with a concern for their textural

Figure 5.6 'A deep dark forest tree'. (Photographer: Gemma Cozens)

possibilities. Through exploration of the 'feel' of wet paint on their hands, it became for the children a simulacrum for mud itself, rather than a medium for representing mud. In this sense, the children seemed to be using the paint as a representational plaything in its own right, rather than as a medium for representational mark-making. Considering children's use of objects in play for representational purposes, Vygotsky asserts that the 'sign' function of the object is dependent on the gestures performed on it. He suggests that an object used in play 'performs a substitution function' (Vygotsky 1978: 109) in the sense that it is used to stand for or signify something else. He stresses, however, that it is not physical, visual similarity between the object being employed and the object being represented that is significant, but rather that the 'child's self-motion, his own gestures, are what assign the function of sign to the object and give it meaning. All symbolic representational activity is full of such indicatory gestures' (p. 108). This is first-order symbolism arising from gesture. In discussing the stage in children's development when they begin to become increasingly concerned with the meaning of things, Vygotsky asserts that 'play provides a transitional stage in this direction whenever an object (for example, a stick) becomes a pivot for severing the meaning of horse from a real horse … the child makes one

Figure 5.7 'Look, we're all messy and muddy!' (Photographer: Gemma Cozens)

object influence another semantically' (1978: 97–98). To use Vygotsky's term, the paint, in the case of the mud visualisation, became a 'pivot' for severing the meaning of mud from real mud.

Through this kind of explorative play with materials, the children transgressed the functional categories of tools and media aimed at representation. Additionally, through this 'messy' play, they were experimenting (initially tentatively in some cases) with a newly found freedom to transgress beyond the boundaries of accepted practice, a way of playing that might in other circumstances be deemed 'misbehaving'. One child initiated this sensory play with the paint as mud saying, 'I'm going to make my hands all muddy' as she smeared her hands around in the paint tray. Cautiously, initially, two others followed the first's lead, glancing at me for reassurance that it was 'allowed'. With a smile of encouragement from me, they were soon all shrieking with laughter, clasping and squeezing their 'muddy' hands together, transferring the 'mud' to the paper, and pausing to look at their hands, exclaiming, 'Look, we're all messy and muddy!' (Figure 5.7).

I sense the children's transgression beyond the boundaries of accepted practice may have been due, for them, to the relationship between group work and play. Ordinarily, the children are required to participate individually in adult directed activities. This situation was novel for the children in the sense that they worked/ played in self-selected groups and were given a comparatively high degree of agency.

It may be that, associating collective activity with play, the children were able to approach their visualisations in a more playful manner than they usually approach adult directed activities that they work on individually. Vygotsky refutes the notion of transferable skills based on his experimental findings, which suggest that skills are, in fact, non-transferable (1978: 82). This theory could, I feel, be applied to the above example. Potentially, the children's inability to transfer their understanding of collaboration from 'play' to 'work' enabled them to view the visualisations as 'play' rather than 'work' and therefore approach them with more of the freedom that their play possesses than they would have been able to achieve if working individually.

Additionally, I feel the above example relates to Vygotsky's notion of the fourth connection between imagination and reality: *embodied imagination*. Vygotsky claims that this fourth aspect reveals the cyclical nature of the relationship. Embodied imagination refers to the point in the cycle when imagination becomes reality. I sense that in this example, this is what has happened. The children's real experiences of mud, coupled with their internalised understanding of the story have informed their combinatorial imaginations. In turn, the paint has taken on the meaning of mud through their play such that it has an externally embodied reality.

Matthews, in alignment with Vygotsky's educational recommendations, advocates the importance of allowing children the opportunity to explore, investigate and play with materials and tools as *processes* of interest and value in their own right, without the need for 'a fixed end in mind' (Matthews 2003: 28). Akin to the children who had explored the textural qualities of paint on their hands, one child experimented with the textural qualities of paint in a tray, releasing it from its functional category as a medium for making marks on paper. Moving from using the white paint to make swirling marks on paper to represent the dynamism of a turbulent snowstorm, he began to use his chosen tool (a cotton bud) to carve travelling loops into the viscous paint in the tray, exploring this property of the paint and noticing that negative marks or tracks remained intact as he dragged his tool through it (Figure 5.8). Commenting, 'It's like walking through the snow', it seems that he himself made the association between the tracks he was making in the paint with the tracks made when walking through deep snow (which he would have experienced for the first time the previous winter).

In doing this, the child was demonstrating the dependence of his combinatorial imagination on his own prior experience: Vygotsky's first theorised relationship between imagination and reality.

> By releasing objects and actions from their usual functions and meanings, the child is able to detect characteristics not otherwise revealed when these objects, and the actions performed on them are tied to adaptation to object-mastery.
>
> (Matthews 2003: 27–28)

Approaching the visualisation of the river, children again began to use the paint as a simulacrum for water, utilising its fluid property to simulate the 'wetness' of water: 'let's make it really wet'. Having applied liberal quantities of the wet paint to the

Figure 5.8 Tracks in the snow. (Photographer: Gemma Cozens)

Figure 5.9 Making ripples. (Photographer: Gemma Cozens)

Figure 5.10 'Splash splosh'. (Photographer: Gemma Cozens)

paper, the children then became concerned that their visualisation did not in fact 'look like' water and they responded by moving towards using media for representational purposes. Matthews argues that 'progress in drawing is unlikely to arise from the child being exhorted to somehow 'look more closely' at nature, but out of the child's looking at what emerges on the drawing surface itself' (Matthews 2003: 163). Responding to the emerging visualisation on the paper, children began to employ alternative materials, tools and representational techniques to resolve ambiguities as they saw them. One child began tearing up blue plastic bags and cutting foil and cling film into strips. She glued the strips onto the painted surface 'to make the ripples' on the river's surface (Figure 5.9). Using a different tool for the same effect, another child used a glue spreader to carve negative wave marks into the wet paint. I propose that the layering effect and negative marks indicate an understanding, not only of the form of ripples and waves, but also of the transparency of water. Additionally, it seems to me that the choice of foil as a material for representing water indicates a knowledge and understanding of the reflective property of water. Another child, considering the available materials, suggested that they could use a white plastic bag (which she tore into small pieces and scattered over the paper) 'for the splashes' (Figure 5.10). By making this suggestion, it appears that she is accessing internalised imagery of the white appearance of light-reflecting water droplets.

Conclusion

My intention has been 'to explore the value of multimodal creative processes involving explorative play and performance aspects for representational purposes and, specifically, to investigate the relationship between, and potential influence of, embodied action on subsequent visualisation'.

I have discussed how the visualisations formed part of a process in which I attempted to engage the children in a story. In alignment with Vygotsky's acknowledgement of the 'kinship' of gesture and drawing (1978: 108) and Matthews' notion of 'action representation' (1999, 2003), I have discussed my belief in the value of embodied action and its influence on the subsequent dynamism of the children's painting episodes. These painting sessions were dynamic in two ways: first, in the way in which the children mapped their embodied movements on to the two-dimensional surface, and second in the way in which the sessions were evolving multimodal processes in their own right. The children seized the opportunity for explorative play with materials and tools which paved the way for a dynamic, unfolding, dialogical process: a temporal 'conversation with materials and media' (Matthews 2003: 26). Moving fluidly between the modes of dramatisation and painting, the children's representational processes seemed to possess an explorative, ontological dimension (concerned with ways of being) as opposed to an epistemological dimension (concerned with ways of knowing).

I have contested the Vygotskian staged theory of sign development, regarding the perceived hegemony of one sign system over another, in favour of a perspective that values children's multimodal representational processes. I have argued that the children who I observed were employing the semiotic systems of symbols and indexical signs throughout their representational processes. Having analysed the children's selection and deployment of materials and tools for representational purposes, three categories of motivation for selection emerged. In alignment with Vygotsky's theories it is clear that, first, some tools were chosen on the basis of the sign function of specific features: second-order symbolism. Second, some were chosen based on children's prior knowledge of the marks they could create using them. Third, some materials were used as simulacrum for the thing being represented. Often this was achieved in combination with gesture.

I sense that, having *internalised* (integrated into their own consciousness) and physically embodied the story prior to the visualisation stage of the process, children were equipped and empowered to translate their acquired actional vocabulary into marks on a two-dimensional surface. By developing their use of dynamic actions to transform materials, children were able to explore the relationship between their actions and emergent marks on the paper surface. In effect, the paintings, in many instances, were records of movement, a process through which the children were developing a set of semiotic resources in the form of symbols and indexical signs (Vygotsky 1978; Matthews 2003). Through this process of semiosis they were learning that a mark can be used to stand for or represent something else: a movement, an experience, an object, an emotion.

References

Atkinson, D. (2008) 'Pedagogy Against the State', *International Journal of Art and Design Education*, 27 (3): 226–240.

Bruce, T. (1991) *Time to Play in Early Childhood Education,* London: Hodder Arnold.

Kress, G. and van Leeuwen, T. (2006) *Reading Images: The Grammar of Visual Design*, 2nd edn, London: Routledge.

Matthews, J. (1999) *The Art of Childhood and Adolescence: The Construction of Meaning*, London: Falmer Press.

Matthews, J. (2003) *Drawing and Painting: Children and Visual Representation. 0–8 years*, 2nd edn, London: Paul Chapman.

Rosen, M. and Oxenbury, H. (1989) *We're Going on a Bear Hunt*, London: Walker Books.

Vygotsky, L.S. (1978) *Mind in Society: The Development of Higher Psychological Processes*, M. Cole, V. John-Steiner, S. Scribner and E. Souberman (eds), Cambridge, MA: MIT Press.

Vygotsky, L.S. (2004) 'Imagination and Creativity in Childhood', *Journal of Russian and European Psychology*, 42 (1): 7–97. Trans. M.E. Sharpe Inc.

A response to 'Symbolic representational processes: a case for embodied practice'

Yiannis Hayiannis

I have been invited to respond to Cozens's case for embodied practice to make more explicit the implications for learning in art and design of an example taken from early years teaching. My argument is directed to notions of play, embodiment and representation. Before turning directly to these concerns, however, I wish to signal praise for Cozens's account. I believe that she persuasively combines reference to aspects of educational theory with her own project, in focusing on the ways in which children develop 'semiotic systems of symbols and signs to communicate meaning' across 'representational modes'. While I am sympathetic to this case, I propose here an alternative and complementary account of the educational value of play and embodied practice with particular reference to the practice of painting in secondary schools.

I wish to consider the relevance of play for older children engaged in learning in art and design with respect to the formation of rules. I will address Vygotsky's identification of rule-making as a characteristic of young children's play (1978) in order to consider ways in which the material affordances of painting practice can be made available for secondary school pupils.

With respect to representation, I wish to discuss the perceptual assumptions that are arguably apparent in Vygotsky's essay of 1930, 'Imagination and Creativity in Childhood' (2004), to which Cozens refers, and to attend to the debate regarding the question of the 'representational imperative' which she claims as a characteristic of the present skills-based National Curriculum. In presenting a brief account of embodied practice as it pertains to practices of painting, I wish both to discriminate between the understandings of embodiment that Cozens presents and to suggest that the significance of painting as an embodied practice deserves greater attention in the context of secondary art education.

Play

In addressing play with respect to learning and creative activity, I wish to attend briefly to questions of exploratory play and rule-making. In his account of young children's painting and drawing activity, Matthews (2003) shows how play is 'implicated in the child's understandings and use of symbols, signs and representations' (p. 27). Children, Matthews states, 'need opportunities to temporally uncouple means from ends in tasks, allowing them the opportunity to investigate processes as entities of interest in themselves and worthy of repetition' (ibid.). These opportunities, he continues, permit children to free 'actions and objects from their usual functions' and thereby come to use semiotic systems (p. 28). This process is apparent in Cozens's description of the children's 'explorative play with materials', play which gave them licence to transgress 'the functional categories of tools and media aimed at representation'.

In 'The Role of Play in Development', Vygotsky (1978) asserts that rules always apply to the imaginary situations in which children participate in play – 'not rules that are formulated in advance and change during the course of the game but ones that stem from an imaginary situation' (p. 95). Subordination to such rules in play, he observes, requires great self-control of the child (p. 99). Play, he continues, creates 'a zone of proximal development of the child' (p. 102) in that in play the child 'always behaves beyond his [sic] average age, above his daily behavior' (ibid.).

How might exploratory play and rule-making inform art and design educational practice at secondary level? I would suggest setting up a learning environment where young people are able to invent their own rules and procedures for the exploration of the properties and affordances of particular materials and tools (I refer here to those associated with painting). In the sense that older children are able to reflect productively on what they make and do (to consider the ways in which the affective or representational potential of certain materials may be recruited in their work, to think through the possibilities of rep-licating or refining certain processes or effects), such an approach could afford pupils at this level wider scope and greater responsibility for their meaning-making activity.

Rules could be set in place by pupils for restricting their choice of colours, for using specific densities of paint or thicknesses of brush. Particular procedures, indeed, could be formulated for starting, interrupting or ending a painting. Again, rules may only emerge for pupils in the course of practice and further develop in parallel with desired outcomes. Equally, they may be transgressed. The application of rules in practices of painting can of course be essayed both technically (with reference, perhaps, to Whistler's highly pre-scribed palette or the putatively scientific regularity of Seurat's colour combinations and brushwork) and conceptually (in terms of the chance procedures employed in the con-struction of paintings by Marcel Duchamp, John Cage or Tom Phillips).

I would qualify this approach, however, with reference to the different level of expectations that young people bring to art and design practice and to their own work. Cozens, drawing on Vygotsky (2004), observes that for young children, 'the value of creative activity lies in the imaginative process rather than in the end product'. My experience as an art and design teacher at secondary level suggests to me that the significance of creative activity for older children can often have as much to do with pride in finished pieces of work (work that is carefully carried home and displayed) as it does with the process of making itself. A balance needs to be achieved in pedagogic practice in fostering both the exploration of particular materials and ways in which such exploration may be harnessed for representational or symbolic purposes.

Representation and embodiment

In teaching art and design in a secondary school I was constantly reminded of the preference of most of the pupils for what may best be described as forms of photo-graphic realism; for painting and drawing that approximated as closely as possible the look of photographic source material. This was the case both with respect to their own work and to that of the artists to whom I introduced them and those that they themselves chose to reference. I would argue that the assumptions concerning photography and painting that underpin this normative predilection for 'accurate' visual realism need to be questioned by teachers in sustaining exploratory and embodied painting practice with pupils in secondary art education. How is it that particular materials permit particular painted surfaces to come into being? How might an emphasis on the materiality of paint inform possibilities for practice that exceed expectations based on the popular association of painting with verisimilitude?

Atkinson has analysed the imperative for accuracy in representation both in his discussion of standards in initial teacher education (2003) and in his critique of the assessment discourse of art practice in the National Curriculum, which 'assumes a clear uncomplicated relation between vision and representation' (2006: 141). The question of the correspondence between particular educational discourses and pressures and the unsubstantiated assessment of popular taste in painting I have presented above merits much greater attention than can be afforded in the present discussion.

I wish here, however, to turn attention to the distinction Cozens makes between the representational potential of embodied practice and 'the curricular objective for representation as mirroring' (the latter she describes as the visualisation of mental constructs 'without embodied explorations or dialogue with materials and tools'). As I will show, I believe that this distinction is of critical importance in re-evaluating the significance of painting at secondary level.

The notion of visual realism often prized by teachers to which Cozens refers, is arguably that which also informs Vygotsky's assessment of children's drawings in 'Imagination and Creativity in Childhood'. Here, Vygotsky refers to a notion of 'true representation and resemblance to reality' (2004: 78) in describing the developmental stages of children's drawings. These successive stages of development, evidenced by an ever-increasing correspondence between the perception of the child and her or his visual productions – the 'perceptualist' account of representation that Bryson (1983) emphatically critiques – can be seen in terms of a teleology of visual realism. In Vygotsky's 'The Prehistory of Written Language', this teleology is itself subordinated to that of the 'history of sign development in the child' (1978: 106), the end-point of which is written language. I agree with Cozens that Vygotsky's staged theory of sign development underestimates the potential of drawing as a mode of signification.

For Vygotsky, drawing from life is a reproductive practice rather than a strictly creative one. Vygotsky identifies drawing from life, 'the reproduction of previously experienced impressions or actions', against creative or 'combinatorial' activities which permit the 'creation of new images or actions' (2004: 9).

The perceptualist account of representation functions only if one accepts perception as an unchanging, universal given for human beings. Merleau-Ponty (2002) demonstrates that perception is not a given in this sense, that perceptual life is 'situated' – is 'subtended by an "intentional arc" which projects round about us our past, our future, our human setting, our physical, ideological and moral situation' (p. 157). In his characterisation of Merleau-Ponty's theory of perception, Crowther (1993a) asserts that 'perception is creative', that 'the body does not find meaning pre-existent in the world, but calls such meaning into existence, through its own activity' (p. 42). If perception can be considered an embodied, creative process, then so too can its interpretation through transformative engagement with materials, here through the practice of painting.

While I shall refer further to Merleau-Ponty in discussing painting as an embodied practice, I now wish to turn to the variety of understandings of embodiment and embodied practice to which Cozens refers in discussing the imaginative and creative practices of children.

In her chapter Cozens not only invokes Vygotsky's characterisation of 'embodied imagination' (Vygotsky 2004) in discussing imaginative play (the way in which, as she puts it, 'the products of our imaginations become embodied realities'), but also uses the term 'embodied movement' to describe the activity of the nursery children in the visualisations they performed of the picture book. Significantly for the view that I propose, Cozens also refers to embodiment in connection with painting.

In the description Cozens offers of her project with young children, she refers to the way in which one particular child moved 'between embodiment and representation', mapping 'his movements from the three-dimensional space on to the two-dimensional surface'. In addressing Cozen's account of the development of young children's meaning-making activity across representational modes, I wish to dwell here on the special meaning-making affordances of painting in particular; to suggest that the significance of painting hinges upon the way in which it can operate simultaneously as an index of different kinds of movements and as a means of 'standing for'. The mark afforded by the resistance of a particular surface to a paint-laden brush, sponge, finger or hand is not only a trace of the physical orientation of the body of the painter to her or his tools and materials and the decisions that these permit, but potentially a term in a narrative (that of a shooting star or a train), which can be understood with reference to what Matthews (2003) defines as 'action representation' (p. 24). In Matthews's analysis of the painting activity of young children, the latter refers to mark-making that describes the movements of objects in time and space. Again, it is worth observing that a mark may simply register the child's delight in manipulating paint, a joyful, perhaps exploratory gesture inaccessible in meaning to all but the child. Painting, as Atkinson (2011) eloquently demonstrates in his description of a child painting, is 'the ground of practice where there is no separation between acting, thinking, reflecting, desiring or feeling' (p. 7).

Matthews's identification of the cognitive and representational character of children's embodied activity in painting is worth quoting here at length:

> [W]hen young children use paint, their movements are far from merely mechanical in the muscles and joints; they look at what they do, and can vary what they do intentionally. They show and use knowledge; knowledge about the body and its potential in terms of action within specific contexts. Early childhood painting is a stunning example of a process of fluid adaptation to unique circumstances which co-ordinates and combines object mastery with the exploitation of body actions for expressive or representational messages.

> (Matthews 2003: 22)

If a case may be made for painting as an embodied practice in its scope for play, representation and learning in early years and primary education, how might such an understanding of painting inform art and design educational practice at secondary level?

In that much has been written on the subject of painting and embodiment by phenomenologists and philosophers, Cozens's statement that 'the influence of embodiment on painting and drawing' is a 'relatively unexplored concept' requires revision. The interrogation of painting traced by Merleau-Ponty in his celebrated essay 'Eye and Mind' (Merleau-Ponty in Johnson 1993), originally published in 1961, is a highly significant text for proponents of painting as an embodied practice in its emphasis on the embodied nature of perception. Merleau-Ponty's phenomenological approach to perception and painting has been the subject of much comment by art historians and theoreticians (Crowther 1993a, b; Follin 2004; Meskimmon 2002; Wentworth 2004).

In 'Eye and Mind' Merleau-Ponty proposes vision as 'a thinking that unequivocally decodes signs given within the body' (Merleau-Ponty in Johnson 1993: 132) – vision, he states, is '"incited" to think by the body' (p. 136). In 'The Visible and the Invisible', written contemporaneously with 'Eye and Mind', Merleau-Ponty urges us to conceive of every visible as 'cut out in the tangible', to accept 'that there is encroachment, infringement' between 'the tangible and the visible' (1973: 134).

I would assert that it is in the context of secondary education that the significance of embodiment with respect to painting deserves further exploration. A robust case for painting at secondary level can be made in emphasising its potential for embodied and transformative engagement with materials and tools in the context of representational aims (not, it is worth adding, with a view to dispensing with notions of representation altogether, but to temper the pre-eminence of a narrowly conceived approach to representation with the acknowledgment that painting involves the body).

Approaching painting in this way necessitates a pedagogical context in which pupils are permitted to engage with paint in an exploratory fashion – to test for those equivalences between visibility and tactility that working with paint affords, to exploit unconsidered technical possibilities and, indeed, to take ownership of such discoveries in their painting activity.

Conclusion

In concluding I want to suggest that the drive towards 'realistic' representation in the context of secondary art and design education is unhelpful in supporting and engaging young people in painting activity. The 'uncomplicated relation between vision and representation' that Atkinson claims informs the assessment discourse of art practice in the National Curriculum (2006: 141), needs to be productively challenged in secondary school art and design practice.

I would further suggest that the notion of skill needs to be wrested from the transmission model of education, where the educator transmits valued traditions of skilled practice to the pupil, and set free from unadventurous conceptions of representation. Skill in the context of painting in secondary schools might profitably be conceived as a set of resources which pupils can themselves determine through rule-making and experimentation, and develop in the light of their particular representational, symbolic or expressive interests. It is worth paying close attention to Cozens's account of young children's embodied meaning-making activities, including painting, in thinking through the ways in which painting might operate as a valuable form of embodied and interpretative practical engagement for older children.

References

Atkinson, D. (2003) 'Forming Teaching Identities in Initial Teacher Education', in: N. Addison and L. Burgess (eds) *Issues in Art and Design Teaching*, London: Routledge Falmer.

Atkinson, D. (2006) 'A Critical Reading of the National Curriculum for Art in the Light of Contemporary Theories of Subjectivity', in: T. Hardy (ed.) *Art Education in a Postmodern World: Collected Essays*, Bristol: Intellect Books.

Atkinson, D. (2011) *Art, Equality and Learning: Pedagogies against the State*, Rotterdam: Sense Publishers.

Bryson, N. (1983) *Vision and Painting: The Logic of the Gaze*, London: Macmillan.

Crowther, P. (1993a) *Critical Aesthetics and Postmodernism*, New York: Oxford University Press.

Crowther, P. (1993b) *Art and Embodiment*, New York: Oxford University Press.

Follin, F. (2004) *Embodied Visions: Bridget Riley, Op Art and the Sixties*, London: Thames & Hudson.

Johnson, G. (ed.) (1993) *The Merleau-Ponty Aesthetics Reader: Philosophy and Painting*, Evanston, IL: Northwestern University Press.

Matthews, J. (2003) *Drawing and Painting: Children and Visual Representation. 0–8 years*, 2nd edn, London: Paul Chapman.

Merleau-Ponty, M. (1973) *The Visible and the Invisible*, Evanston, IL: Northwestern University Press.

Merleau-Ponty, M. (2002) *Phenomenology of Perception*, London: Routledge.

Meskimmon, M. (2002) *Women Making Art: History, Subjectivity, Aesthetics*, London: Routledge.

Vygotsky, L.S. (1978) *Mind in Society: The Development of Higher Psychological Processes*, M. Cole, V. John-Steiner, S. Scribner and E. Souberman (eds), Cambridge, MA: MIT Press.

Vygotsky, L.S. (2004) 'Imagination and Creativity in Childhood', *Journal of Russian and European Psychology*, 42 (1): 7–97. Trans. M.E. Sharpe Inc.

Wentworth, R. (2004) *The Phenomenology of Painting*, Cambridge: Cambridge University Press.

Chapter 6

'Strangely delivered by Pyrates'
Illustration and the National Curriculum

Pam Meecham

I want to argue that we need history (albeit a rehabilitated and chastened, less mono-lithic and confident, history following its encounter with the postmodern turn) in order to understand better the ways that we establish hierarchies. Constructing bound-aries is not a neutral exercise in extracting facts but can be an exercise in power, open to revision. This chapter starts from the premise that seeing *history* in context is vital if we are to understand our current multifaceted conditions. I contend it is important to understand how our perceptions of others have changed across the centuries so as to inform our understanding of our own attitudes in the present as contingent and constructed. History requires an acknowledgement of time and space and, for young people in particular, images are an important non-verbal reference in visualising and imagining 'others'. Reflecting on images teaches us that they are not a mirror of essential, immutable truths but subject to interpretation and reappraisal.

In this chapter I want to argue for teaching and learning from pictorial illustrations, contemporary and historic, as a core element of the art and design curriculum. Rather than taking an ahistoric approach I make a case for teaching visual literacy rooted in reading illustrations critically and historically eschewing a philosophical approach indifferent to history. While ahistoric approaches may appear to offer 'secure' frame-works, they often fail to take account of distinctive national characteristics and diverse, conflicting histories. I argue that by acknowledging people outside of the law (transgressive: economically, morally and sexually) we can come to understand some-thing of the political, economic and social conditions that produce the 'outsider' and 'anti-hero' in specific historic moments. I would contend that the legacy of these conditions still resonates today. In particular, this exploration of pirates enables me to look at histories of sexuality.

Powerful visual images have structured, and continue to structure, our visualisation of the pirate: indeed illustrations have done much to fix pirate folklore in the popular imagination. Tracing changes in the visualisation of the pirate across media (book – *Treasure Island* [see N.C. Wyeth's 1891 illustration: www.wikipaintings.org/en/n-c-wyeth/billy-bones]; opera – *Pirates of Penzance*; exhibition – *The Captain Kidd Story*, Museum of London; and film – *Pirates of the Caribbean*) can also teach us much about the history of illustration, the technical aspects of skill-based work, and crucially the need to be able to read and re-read visual images as they are transformed according to historic and contemporary values.

It is a commonplace observation, at least in the West, that definitions of individual-ism, sexuality and even humanity are historically unstable: the process of disrupting the fiction of a progressive unified history underpins this chapter. Rather than see destabilising definitions as problematic in a classroom context, I want to argue that historical instability can be a strength in revealing notions of a constant, essential self as a fiction. Classroom discussion, particularly when accompanied by images, may offer solace and information to those unclear about their own identities and those entrenched in seemingly preordained roles. Removed from the moral imperatives of PSHEE (Personal, Social, Health and Economic Education) or Religious Education, the role of Citizenship or the forensic attachment to truth promoted in the Science curriculum, the Art and Design studio offers a space for the free-play of the imagina-tion because it can cross-over popular culture, fact and fiction. And yet unlike most subject disciplines the debates can also be allied to the practice of a craft-based skill, here in the form of illustration. Joanna Bourke in a recent historical study of the imposed, inconsistent, constructed boundaries of the 'unknowability of all beings', reminds us that the 'autonomous, self-willed "human" at the heart of humanist think-ing is a fantasy, a chimera' (Bourke 2011: 378).

In uncovering such a fiction, what has been termed 'the inattentive observer' (Althusser 1965) can be encouraged towards a greater alertness to reading visual images and creating alternatives to the regimes of truths often masqueraded as quality reassurance, improvement, best practice, etc. The 'curriculum' outlined below crosses boundaries and is a counter-discourse precisely because a moving target may evade the strictures that can turn the curriculum into a joyless exercise governed by a fugi-tive search for definitive standards and a bogus consensus. All too often the latter leads to the deadening hand of conformity even within an art curriculum.

Starting from this position, this chapter trawls through representations of pirates (including book illustrations, films on YouTube, images from contemporary popular culture, displays in museums and online archives) to re-read and re-visualise the ways that identities are constructed and crucially re-presented. In tandem with a framework around gender, sexuality and masculinity and a return to the unrealised project of the f-word: feminism, such groupings have much to offer the art curriculum especially where an attachment to making embraces a bricolage approach, to which I will return. Keying into young people's popular culture and returning to a skills base in graphic illustration, cross-disciplinary projects such as the one outlined below can be modi-fied to suit specific classrooms and made age-appropriate: the obvious divide between issues of sexuality, cross-dressing or tattoos come to mind. A visually critical approach to illustration can also enhance the skills element of the curriculum. I am not alone in wondering why there is no critical history of illustration. Rick Poynor (2010) calls for a critical history of image making that is interdisciplinary, crossing design criticism and history, art and its history combined with critical reflection on consumerism and the marketplace. The translation of images of pirates from historic print to commercial film calls for such an approach.

The art and design room is an exceptional learning space because it can trade in fictions, create untruths and through *visual imagery* imagine other realities: crucial for young people struggling to cope with rapidly changing political and economic realities. Moreover the notion of fixed identities, while comfortable for many, can be a burden for others less certain. The historic construction of the pirate is complex, but working across disciplines (*perhaps* with PSHEE or the History and English curriculums) much can be gained.

Terms of reference

As well as looking at imagery definitions (print, drawing, illustration, graphic design, documentary and so on) discussions need to include differentiation between pirate, privateer and buccaneer. All are commonly used but with slightly different connotations. In terms of periods and geographic locations the golden age of pirates is generally considered to be the seventeenth and eighteenth centuries when much activity was located in the Caribbean. However, to allow more nuanced debates around gender and geography, I look at visual representations under the red as well the black flag, acknowledging the pirates of South East Asia. In part, pirates are important in understanding that there were 'periods of history where sexual orientation, in the identity-forging sense, was a less significant interpretive force' than in contemporary society (Mills 2010: 85). Leaving aside the issue of social-constructionism in the history of sexuality verses one that maintains a 'core' of queer desire that is transcultural and transhistorical in essence (ibid.), it should be possible to 'disrupt' a constant narrative. It should also be noted that in pirate studies, whenever homosexuality is referenced it is usual to use the term 'sodomy'.

The 'Ship Ahoy' title of a *Dr Who* episode (Series 6 episode 3, May 2011) is evidence that at the time of writing pirates, both fictional and futuristic, are having their moment in the sun. The clichés ran thick and fast throughout, complete with walking the plank and piratical fashion, outsider behaviour, etc. Bookstores are cashing in on the popularity of the *Pirates of the Caribbean* series with the ubiquitous Johnny Depp as Captain Jack Sparrow. Sticker Dressing Pirate books abound and The Halliard 'Death of Captain Kidd' is available as a ringtone. Museums the world over are attracting large numbers to pirate events. Add to your diary along with LGBT (lesbian, gay, bisexual and transgender) history month, ITLAPD (International Talk Like a Pirate Day) every 19th September. It is the collapse of distinction between high and low art that occupies me here, and the commodification of museums with their unashamed embrace of populism and *faction* as history. For instance, the film *Pirates of the Caribbean IV* features Blackbeard's *Queen Anne's Revenge*, a former French slave ship. The raising of the ship's anchor, sunk off the North Carolina coast, was timed to coincide with the film's premiere. Linda Carlisle (the state cultural resources secretary) pronounced 'Blackbeard and piracy are important threads in eastern North Carolina's maritime heritage fabric .... The historic and economic value of this project is enormous' (Carlisle 2011). The *Queen Anne's Revenge* has already yielded 250,000 artefacts. The ship is also available in Lego. But Blackbeard's contribution to humanity may not be merely an economic one.

Honour and democracy amongst pirates

Jason Acosta's thesis (2006) argues that Blackbeard (Bristol-born Edward Teach, c.1680–1718) and Benjamin Franklin deserve equal billing for founding democracy in the United States and the New World. He argues that pirates practised the same egalitarian principles as America's Founding Fathers, displaying a pioneering spirit in exploring new territory and meeting native peoples and fighting on the side of the American Revolution. Other evidence cited includes: pirates had ship's charters signed by all and an assembly; voted for their Captain with a Quartermaster who acted as judge (1721); votes for all; compensation for those who lost a limb or eye. Acosta, descended from pirates, in comparing pirate charters with the Declaration of Independence and the US Constitution, may have overstated the case for democracy given pirates' often anti-social behaviour, but the rise of the Pirate Party across contemporary Europe might give some pause for reflection. Mostly known in the popular imagination through their eighteenth-century exploits, pirates nonetheless have a contemporary resonance in the Somalian pirates' almost industrial scale activity. In more 'legitimate' culture, as members of the Pirate Party in Europe, (apparently a response to disillusionment with the political elite; Virag Kaufer, *The Guardian* 2011) they are gaining ground. In Germany fifteen members of the Pirate Party won seats at the expense of the Free Democrats. With an average age of twenty-nine and a spin-off of the Swedish Pirate Bay Hacker movement with alternative views on sexual relationships, the economy and transport, they operate within the historic pirate tradition. They are democratic but not normative: even their dress codes owe much to the eighteenth-century pirate tradition. In cross-curricular work in schools they are a historic and contemporary gift for promoting discussions about dress codes, gender and sexuality, the right to privacy and famously in Sweden (with two Pirate MEPs) a campaign to reform and limit the patent and copyright law: unsurprisingly members of the Pirate Party are optimistic about the emancipatory potential of the internet. The Pirate Party's associated youth organisation, Young Pirate (Ung Pirat) was for part of 2009–2010 the numerically largest political youth organisation in Sweden.

The pirate ideal of a 'Brethren of the Sea' grew out of frustration with the maltreatment meted out by British Naval and merchant ships. Acosta claims 'It's no wonder that many sailors seized the opportunity to jump ship and search for a better way of life, namely piracy, which offered better food, shorter work shifts and the power of the crew in decision-making' (2006). The historian Christopher Hill takes the view that pirates dissented from the status quo of nationalism and class difference in the seventeenth century which had left them alienated and in poverty (Turley 1999: 80 and Hill 1986: 161–187). Beyond class-dissention and the rise of democratic idealism, notions of gender and sexuality left hanging earlier need to be revisited. A commonplace question in pirate studies asks: 'How did the pirate – a real threat to mercantilism and trade in early modern Britain – become the hypermasculine, anti-hero familiar to us through a variety of pop culture outlets?' (Turley 1999: dust jacket). While Turley's project (and amongst others, Barry Burg's) is rooted in changing historical images of the male pirate that have implications for shifting notions of self, masculinity and sexuality in contemporary Western culture, a more nuanced approach to the history of piracy incorporating images of female pirates from the Caribbean and the Far East, has much to say about the ways that men and women outsiders are 'illustrated' and perceived historically. Cordingly (1997) is a reliable source here offering a range of images, statistics and histories leading to informed debate. Reading a history of piracy outside its received history (brutal economic adventurers that become through Romanticism the anti-hero) is to encounter complexity. The homo-social spaces of prisons, boarding schools and so on have long been the subject of research about male behaviour, asking about spaces devoid of women. Growing recent research suggests that the spaces of the pirate ship were transgressive not just economically and socially but also for many men sexually. While accepting that the development of homosexually directed behaviour is psychodynamic and situational as well as cultural in nature, a study of pirates reveals schisms in contemporary scholarship. Burg (1983) for instance maintains that in the England of Charles II, the relative tolerance to sodomy in the vagabond societies,

> and a range of other factors allowed many Englishmen to establish homosexuality as a virtually normal pattern of behaviour and … many of these same men … [transported] their sexual practices to a Caribbean shipboard milieu where they became so well integrated into the total social equation that heterosexual contact became a genuinely exotic manner of sexual expression.
>
> (Burg 1983: 41)

Burg sees the origins of gay piracy in the seventeenth-century apprentice class and vagabond societies (a subculture of the destitute and depraved depending on perspective) as a consequence of poverty. Many from the apprentice class were press-ganged and found their way to sea.

It is also historically the case that where women were allowed on to ships (in the Far East in the eighteenth and early nineteenth century), they became hugely 'successful' pirate captains commanding fleets. The ships were unhindered by the misogyny that promoted superstitious notions of women as trouble on board ships. Mrs Cheng (Ching Shih; Cheng I Sao; Ching Yih Saou), the nineteenth-century Chinese pirate makes a good case study (see Figure 6.1). Whether Mrs Cheng justifies the claim that she was 'the greatest pirate, male or female, in all history is questionable, but for three years she controlled and masterminded the activities of one of the largest pirate communities there has ever been' (Cordingly 1997: 78). Numbers vary but one estimate has Cheng's fleet at 1800 and crew at about 80,000. Crucially in China families lived on board ship: one observer noting the vessels were filled with their families, men, women and children. It was not unusual for women to command the junks and sail them into battle. Cordingly (1997) observed: 'The sheer numbers involved in these pirate attacks make the activities of the pirates in the West Indies pale into insignificance. Sometimes Mrs Cheng's forces went into action with several hundred vessels and up to two thousand pirates' (p. 77).

Figure 6.1 Mrs Cheng (Ching Shih; Cheng I Sao; Ching Yih Saou), died 1844.

Allowing a different space for teaching gender and sexuality

Pirates, when viewed historically in terms of gender and sexuality, offer a way of discussing sexuality beyond the heroic tales of resistance and personal outing that have become orthodoxy. It is often the case that revealing hidden, repressed gay histories is accompanied by a narrative of personal coming out, the repeal of repressive legislation and so on. Mills states:

> It is difficult for LGBT public cultures to resist coming-out narratives ... to avoid the temptation of ... Foucault's ... 'repressive hypothesis' – [to] avoid the notion that Western cultures are characterized by a stiflingly Victorian attitude to sex that has been progressively unraveling since the 1960s.
>
> (Mills 2010: 82)

A historic approach eschewing personal narrative, no matter how compelling, leaves space for more general discussions of the ways that society has constructed and visualised gender and sexuality. As museums seek wider interpretive strategies, note the power of the pink pound and seek new audiences, sexuality often stalks the once hallowed, objective, heteronormative halls. For instance the Historic Royal Palaces are currently (2011–2012) looking at cross-dressing in the seventeenth and eighteenth century through fashion and costume. In particular, cross-dressing as an element of male and female fashions in the seventeenth century will be one focus of 'The Wild the Beautiful and the Damned' at Hampton Court Palace. Centred on the painting *Mary of Modena when Duchess of York* (*c*.1675) by Simon Verelst 'The Wild the Beautiful and the Damned' hardly sets a precedent for discussions of atypical women. But if, as the flyer states, such paintings are about lust, infidelity and death… with the gendered behaviours of the day as a focus, it should be possible to imagine a world 'other' where normative behaviours do not chime with our own. Arguably such an approach would help young people towards a greater awareness of the historical specificity of their own boundaries. Bourke (2011) suggests, 'Each person is born into a world forged by others. We resist, create and recreate – but always from a starting point that is never of our own choosing' (p. 378). Even the most conservative of museums and palaces are moving towards reading artworks within a range of social even contradictory and irreconcilable contexts, accepting difference, ambiguity and social dissonance rather than presenting a definitive reading of the past. *Zeitgeist* is not something art curriculums are good at embracing but in this instance it might be worth a try.

The contextual approach to history is important but needs some qualification here. Museums through LGBT History Month and since the repeal of Clause 28 in 2003 have made considerable strides towards more inclusive historical perspectives. In an analysis of the Museum of London's *Queer is Here* (2006) exhibition, Mills (2010) wondered if there was not room for a different approach to such subjects. In museums he wondered about translating into exhibitions queer histories that contest objectivity and self-evident scientific 'fact': he argues for a history in the museum that abandons linear narrative and is closer in style of presentation to stories 'that take as their point of departure sexual intensities, tastes and roles, gender dissonances, dispositions and styles, queer feelings, emotions and desires' (Mills 2010: 86). For our purposes here it is the presentation and visualisation of such histories that also needs reformation to include strategies modelled on 'scrapbooks and collage; in place of the representative "object", they [exhibitions] will appropriate fragments, snippets of gossip, speculations, irreverent half-truths. Museum-goers will … interact with exhibitions that self-consciously resist grand narratives and categorical assertions'. Mills continues that a 'mode of display, collecting, and curating [should be] driven not by a desire for a petrified "history as it really was" but by the recognition that interpretations change and that our encounters with archives are saturated with desire' (Mills 2010: 86–87). Even the most authoritative history of pirates is a blend of historical fact and fiction (during the Enlightenment period, history was categorised as literature). In particular, Captain Johnson (possibly a pseudonym for Daniel Defoe) wrote a definitive history (1724) which was in part the documenting of individual lives but also of mythical constructs; composite characters. Importantly Johnson (and his readers) did not distinguish between fictional or factual pirate histories.

It has been argued that books such as Turley's *Rum, Sodomy and the Lash: Piracy, Sexuality, and Masculine Identity*, enable us to rethink both the history of piracy and the history of sexuality by rethinking sodomy and piracy as part of the eighteenth-century cultural imagination. Gender is often overlooked (or at least marginalised) in most of the histories of piracy but there is now a growing body of scholarship on women pirates: see in particular, Klausman *et al.* (1997). But the inclusion of piracy in the Far East can also encourage students to see other possibilities for gender and sexuality and the role of cross-dressing. There are few images of Mrs Cheng, the Chinese pirate, and of these many are composite images, some incorporating elements of Mary Read and Anne Bonny. The latter two women are particularly important in establishing that women were also compelled to go to sea to escape domestic servitude. Grenada, the Bahamas and Jamaica have postage stamps dedicated to Read and Bonny using the earliest known images. Mills has argued that 'gay liberation movements have fore-grounded sexual orientation over gender ... [and that] this produces a set of boundaries and omissions' (Mills 2010: 83). Gender dissidence Levin (2010) maintains was one of the casualties of such an approach. Reintroducing gender dissidence through pirates can tell us a great deal about gender construction.

Entertaining pirates in the art room allows the breaking of codes, working with the margins (illustration) and offers a challenge to the conformity of the centre. It also offers the chance to bring to the art room images that in our age of mechanical and electronic reproduction have been marginalised by a grand narrative of the autonomous artist bent on creative self-expression. Pirates allow back into the classroom the extraordinary achievements of illustrators, from the sixteenth-century's John White (c.1540–c.1593) and Theodor de Bry (1528–1598), to Alexandre Exquemelin, (1678) with his *Buccaneers of America* (see Figure 6.2) and the anonymous printmakers of numerous pirate histories. Moreover it allows discussion of the Brandywine School of Illustration and Howard Pyle's (1853–1911) *Book of Pirates* and the work of his legendary pupil Newell Convers Wyeth, whose seminal image of *Treasure Island*'s Long John Silver echoes, along with his other characters, across the centuries, for example in John Ryan's *Captain Pugwash* or when Kermit the Frog becomes the honourable Captain Smollett.

Important too in the lexicon of written and visual imagery of the eighteenth-century's quest for a transgressive place safe from the conformity of domestic heteronormativity and capitalism is Daniel Defoe's *Robinson Crusoe* (1791). Crusoe was finally, you might remember, 'strangely delivered by Pyrates' (frontispiece). The definitive illustrations were done by N.C. Wyeth again, but the frontispiece to the original downloadable Defoe publication is also worth comparing with Wyeth and subsequent film adaptations such as the French television version of *Robinson Crusoe* shown by the BBC in 1964 (available on YouTube). Alexandre Exquemelin's *Buccaneers of America* and the many subsequent translations and amended editions are easily sourced on the web. The reproductions from Captain Charles Johnson's *A General History of the Robberies and Murders of the Most Notorious Pyrates* (1724) are also easily available and do not lose any 'aura' from being downloaded and printed out. As a primary source for the way that pirates dressed and with descriptions and bibliographic details pirates are a relatively easy subject for research. The primary sources for pirates although few are available online. Institutions such as the Museum of London, (in 2011 hosting an exhibition on *The Captain Kidd Story*, the privateer turned pirate, hung at Tilbury in 1701) are investing resources into the history of pirates. The opening up of archives by the Museums, Libraries and Archives Council (established 2000, abolished 2011) has meant there has been considerable willingness to make sources available. The record of Captain Kidd's trail for instance is kept at Kew National Archives with eyewitness accounts, illustrated

Figure 6.2 Johnson, Buccaneers of America 1678 (illustration from *The Buccaneers of America* (Dover Maritime) by Alexander O. Exquemelin, Harmondsworth: Penguin Books).

with Kidd hanging in a gibbet. It would be timely for students to ask their own questions about the representation of pirates in histories, media and political parties.

Investigating pirates through visiting exhibitions (and their websites) enables looking, research and talking, giving an insight into the debates around the often male space of ships. But perhaps most significantly, bringing a contested pirate history into the classroom is to deal in 'transgressive data'.

Contingent histories

A return to history is overdue in our art classrooms, not because we need a Gradgrindesque attachment to 'facts' but because the past offers a way of seeing the world conceptualised and constructed differently. A close look at history reveals the construction of our own naturalised assumptions: enabling us to think otherwise. It is a commonplace observation that contemporary fine art, often of a conceptual nature that poured scorn on traditional skill-based art, has dominated the art curriculum since the introduction of the National Curriculum for Art in 1991. In part a response to years of moribund skills teaching that offered just technical skill devoid of critical thinking, the imperative to work in galleries with contemporary artists was a welcome release from slavish tasks. Reform was argued for using the language of emancipatory teaching and learning: empowerment, student voice, constructionism, etc. What is perhaps surprising given this rhetoric is that the gap between what pupils wanted (often reflected in their home-art, inflected with popular culture) remained at odds with school art. One of the casualties of both what might be termed a modernist curriculum and a broadly postmodern curriculum is graphic illustration. All the more surprising as children often come to visual art through the storybook or animated cartoon. Adept at an early age at reading even the most esoteric of illustrators, illustration is rarely used in the art classroom: a casualty of modernism's hostility to art that was 'merely' illustrative. Slavish adherence to the rhetoric of originality and fine art militated against the use of picture books, photography and film, leaving picture books in particular a curiously overlooked resource. It is still the case that illustration struggles against its overbearing cousin, fine art. For instance, a survey exhibition on *Alice in Wonderland* at Tate Liverpool (2011) that includes graphic illustration can still elicit the remark that situating the exhibition in the art gallery rather than in a library might seem 'surprising' (Warner 2011). But of course it is John Tenniel's visualisation of the two Alice books (1865 and 1871) that has fixed her in the public's imagination.

The unravelling of myths, fictions and a bit of history is an under-utilised possibility in the National Curriculum for Art and Design. In discussing the ways that sexuality and gender have been defined and represented historically and within contemporary culture it is hoped young people will come to a more informed understanding of the ways that illustrations signify and can both confirm and refute stereotypes and prejudice. Moreover, even a cursory glance at pirate flags (Lane 1998: 173) will demonstrate that design is contingent and dependent on more than aesthetic considerations. Discussed within an art, fiction and crucially historic context, contemporary assumptions and common-sense wisdom around identity politics can be better articulated. The benefit to the art curriculum, could be a concentration on popular culture, illustration, fashion and a move away from an exclusive concentration on 'self' that many contemporary art works extol. The importance of fictions, historic and illustrative, can be used to develop an understanding of the contingent and fleeting construction of gender and sexuality.

Our conception of the way a pirate *looks* owes a debt to N.C. Wyeth's definitive 1911 illustrations for Robert Louis Stephenson's *Treasure Island* (1883). Stephenson is responsible for maps with a telling X marking the spot, talking parrots, hidden treasure, walking the plank and other clichés indispensible to any self-respecting pirate script. *Treasure Island or the Mutiny of the Hispaniola* was first published in 1881–1882 under a pseudonym, Captain George North, in *Young Folks*, a UK children's literary magazine (*Young Folk – 1871–1897*). Given such child-focused publications it is perhaps surprising that camp pirates seem to dominate contemporary imagery.

Camp pirates before Captain Sparrow

Burg (1983) maintains that there was an almost pathological rejection of effeminacy amongst seventeenth-century Caribbean pirates. Calling male pirates by female names, what Christopher Isherwood termed 'low camp', was according to Burg almost unheard of. He cites the very few pirates with effeminate nicknames as evidence of a rejection of effeminacy that is mirrored in Ancient Greek culture where being a warrior and same sex activity were not mutually exclusive.

Camp sailors, however, abound in the illustrations and literature. Although there was no intention to attribute 'gay' behaviour to pirates aboard the *Black Pig* in John Ryan's *Captain Pugwash*, urban myths abound. However, in De Rijke and Hollands' (2007) 'The Thing That Is Not There? A Psychoanalytic Reading of Mervyn Peake's Captain Slaughterboard Drops Anchor', the illustration of Timothy Twitch, 'the most elegant [pirate] in battle, his left hand especially' (p. 3), is an unsubtly camp stereotype. De Rijke and Hollands take a Judith Butler perspective on the performativity of the pirate body, suggesting 'a queer reading of *Slaughterboard*, where "queer" in this sense is less an identity than a critique of (fixed) identity, so that subjectivity is always a role of development, a site of permanent "becoming"' (De Rijke and Hollands 2007). Holding in abeyance Butler's psychoanalytical readings of the body, it might be useful to return to a neostructuralist approach and uncover historical readings (accepting that all readings are in part fictions and subject to re-telling).

More compelling than Butler's thesis is Turley's in *Rum, Sodomy and the Lash: Piracy, Sexuality and Masculine Identity* (1999) that pirates' sexual behaviour was considered normal, rather than a challenge to heteronormativity. However, rather than concentrate on pirates' sexual practices Turley is more concerned about the wider relationship with society arguing that in eighteenth-century literature, sexuality became a component of identity. According to Turley sodomites were defined by their sexuality and criminalised. However, he maintains that extremely masculine pirates could also have been sodomites. This view that only heterosexuals (and often hyper-masculine heterosexuals) can be masculine is questioned and overturned by Ancient Greek culture. Transgression, a trope in contemporary theory, takes on a different normative aura here making our definitions of sexuality, eroticism and even camp historically contingent (see Meecham 2008).

The *Sacred Band of Thebes*, a huge if 'unrealistic' lion monument in Greece, marks the site of a famous battle that took place in the fourth century BC. Built in 300 BC and rebuilt in the twentieth century, the Lion Monument is significant for my purposes in that the notion of homosexuality as an effete practice, marked by camp and effeminacy, is countered by the warriors who died here. The men belonged to the Sacred Band of Thebes, an elite group of 150 male couples who fought together (one [slightly] older man and one youth in the Greek tradition). Plutarch's records maintain that the rationale for such a fighting force was based on Plato's *Symposium*: a stated assumption that male lovers would be less prone to dishonour and fight harder to protect their lover. The Sacred Band of Thebes had a formidable reputation winning battles against great odds, finally dying together at the Battle of Chaeronea in 338 BC (see in particular 'Out in the World: A Global Gay History' BBC Radio 3, October 2011). This diversion into ancient Greece is to argue that sodomy between men is not viewed consistently across time and cultures.

The Tomb of the Unknown Craftsman, by Grayson Perry at the British Museum (2011) includes a homage to the Chevalier d'Eon (the guiding light behind the Beaumont Society, founded for transgendered and cross-dressing people in 1966). The cross-dressing spy, diplomat and soldier eventually lived as a woman. Noteworthy here is the contention that d'Eon too was 'also pretty macho'. He can be found in numerous illustrations of the late eighteenth century (d. 1810). In particular see Charles Jean Robinson's satire of a fencing dual between Monsieur de Saint-George and Mademoiselle La Chevalíere d'Éon de Beaumont at Carlton House in 1787 (*Chevalier: Le Chevalier D'Eon* is the title of a well-known manga animation based loosely on the eighteenth century D'Eon. The animation could be critiqued against historic illustrations of D'Eon but as some manga is violent it comes with an age appropriate warning).

Burg (1983) similarly argues that there was no contradiction between sodomy and uber-masculinity. Such debates require a reflexive approach and while recovery of the past is another fugitive enterprise, pillaging the past for images consistent with contemporary beliefs is also problematic. For instance the cover of Burg's *Sodomy and the Pirate Tradition* shows that Blackbeard could be read as camp (as perhaps intended by Burg) in the sense that we use the term today. But the historic evidence is against such a reading.

However, what is clear is illustrations are often forced to play handmaiden to ideological positions: their meanings are simply changed. Another example may illuminate.

Changing signification of tattooed bodies

The tattoo, familiar as part of a pirate's armoury and shown in detail on many images of pirates (historical and fictional), can be re-read. Fuelled by changing ideas about the ways physical and psychic attributes are connected, the tattoo has changing significations. Rather than being seen as transgressive, the tattoo was initially evidence of status and power, as seen in the sixteenth-century John White drawings of the Algonquinians. However, early anthropologists and later Charles Darwin rewrote the tattoo as a sign of primitivism; evident in the ability to bear pain for the purposes of decoration and paganism. Often a feature of freak shows in Europe and North America, tattooed bodies were one of the wonders of eighteenth-century world exploration. By the mid-1800s the tattoo had also become a sign of sexual permissiveness and criminality, particularly evident in the work of Cesare Lombroso (1890s), the founder of positivistic criminology. Albert Loos in *Ornament and Crime* (1908) considered the tattooed Papuan had not evolved to a moral and civilised state, was degenerate or a criminal. From Captain Pugwash to Charlie Choke 'covered all over with dreadful drawings in blue ink' (Peake, Captain Slaughterboard) to today's fashion statements, tattooed bodies have had a chequered history.

By the nineteenth century, however, tattooed people from the Far East, the South Sea Islands and South America in particular were identified as 'primitive'. In the earliest images of Native Americans, the Inuit, the North Carolina Algonquians and the Timucuan Indians of Florida recorded by Jacques Le Moyne de Morgues (c.1564), widespread use of body painting and tattoos was recorded. Pictured by John White in the1580s, the paintings show body adornment was related to class and power in much the same way that it was in Europe. If the appropriation of tattoos by Europeans was seen as an outsider, even transgressive, practice, their use in some non-Western tribes was restricted to the chief and his wife. Moreover, according to Kim Sloan (2007), images of first peoples were subject to revision, neither Le Moyne or White 'averse to adapting European conventions they were familiar with to fit missing details in their recollected views of the New World' (Sloan 2007: 134). In *The wyfe of an Herowan of Secotan*, Wingina was 'pownced', that is tattooed in blue on her face, arms and legs. It is important for our purposes for young people to note that even a so-called 'naturalistic' image is not a neutral, value-free depiction of an a priori, external world. While the images painted by White are naturalistic in style they owe much to classicism and to an imperative to create a particular image to read 'back home'. Chaplin argues that White's images of non-threatening, smiling Indians placed in a theatrical setting were a counterfeit staged to encourage colonisation: a 'propaganda campaign intended to promote the tiny English outpost' (Chaplin 2007: 51).

Nonetheless, first impressions were of 'very handsome, and goodly people, and in their behaviour as mannerly, and civil, as any of Europe' (Morison 1971: 624). Moreover, far from the savage, tattooed and bloodthirsty Indians of later legend, Barlowe wrote of an Edenic paradise:

> Wee found the people most gentle, loving and faithful, void of all guile and treason, and such as lived after the manner of the golden age. The earth bringeth foorth all things in aboundance, as in the first creation, without toile or labour.
>
> (Morison 1971: 624)

We can see further adjustments to images if they are traced from original to later editions. John White's *The Wife of a Timucuan Chief of Florida after Le Moyne* was developed after the Huguenot artist, Jacques Le Moyne de Mortgues (1533–1588): the later images of White and Le Moyne's work through de Bry's widely available engravings. The latter (1590s) Theodor de Bry work is instructive: the reworked illustrations being altered not just by adding objects to create context but through reworking the physical characteristics of Native Americans to be more European, stylised in attitudes even more in debt than White's to classical poses and modelling.

What is important here is that the *native* body complete with painted or tattooed adornment could be overwritten. The tattooed Indian also appears in Benjamin West's revolutionary depiction of a modern heroic 'history' painting *The Death of General*

Wolfe (1770). In the foreground appears a powerfully built, tattooed Indian, a model of enigmatic restraint reflecting in *Thinker*-like pose on the unfolding of a seminal moment during the British army's defeat of the French at Quebec. Subsequently, the Native American painted body in nineteenth-century frontier disputes was reconfigured to contribute to the image of the savage (Meecham and Sheldon 2008).

Changing significations of male sexuality

Sodomy too has a changing and contingent history particularly during times of political and social unrest. Burg (1983) argues charges of sodomy were used politically, citing the anti-Catholic Popish Plot during the Stuart restoration between 1678 and 1681. However, differentiating between sodomy and homosexuality, he maintains that accusations of sodomy disappeared in English politics once the hysteria of the Popish Plot was over. It re-emerged briefly in about 1699 in relation to homosexuality, when it was popularly believed that there was 'a large network of homosexuals' (Burg 1983: 29). What is noteworthy is that 'sodomy was often mentioned in relation to other crimes such as sedition, murder, conspiracy, perjury, rape, bribery, subordination, and treason … sodomy was the least serious crime … often associated with general duplicity' (ibid.). Moreover historically there has been little consistency in the public perception of sodomy, in its punishment and so its censure. This is an important point even in modern history, Burg argues that 'there was not even following the Popish plot and the Rigby case … a wave of revulsion or hostility toward sodomy' (Burg 1983: 30).

> Despite the draconian proscriptions against sodomy in seventeenth century England, the legal reality was very different. Fines, abbreviated stays in the pillory, and often exoneration were the fates of those accused. … Accusations of sexual irregularity were occasionally employed against political foes for ridicule, to punish other crimes, or perhaps to obtain property.
>
> (Burg 1983: 40)

Changing significations of women pirates

From a vengeful Jane de Belleville (1345) to a national icon, the Irish Grace O'Malley (*c*.1530–*c*.1603) (well-known through the engraving of her meeting with Queen Elizabeth I), there are many images of women pirates that key into popular folk heroes, as pirates and outlaws share similar philosophies and appeal (Seal 2001). To return again to Anne Bonny, and Mary Read: the original sources for these women are few, but the ways in which the images change to comply with changing sensibilities are telling. Grace O'Malley undergoes considerable 'enhancement' to be compliant with the current sexualised demands of Hollywood, etc. Bonny and Read's images also change across the centuries, but even close to their time, the collapsing of sexual licentiousness, criminality and outsider status is easy to read. Arguably a reaction to repressive heterosexual norms and balefully narrowly defined Victorian family values of 'the angel in the house', the romance of the seas must have seemed a viable option to modernity, industrialisation and increasing urbanisation. The fast pace of techno-logical change can also be seen as a reason to retreat to another perhaps less audited world: topics that can be explored with young people. Not all the issues raised above would be suitable for the Key Stage 3 classroom but most are.

Looking at historic and contemporary images, across domains, drawing, painting, film and photography with critical reflection on conflicting historical information has been successfully used in museums. *Outlawed! Rebels, Revolutionaries and Bushrangers* at the National Museum of Australia (NMA) comes to mind. Working across gender, time and cultures with a global perspective and citing Eric Hobsbawm's *Social Bandits* (1959) as a touchstone for the debate about outsiderness, the exhibition was dependent on wide-ranging historical images. It sought to uncover the motivations for the 'inter-generational chain of heroisation' that outsider cultures can impel (NMA 2004: 7). Pirates too have their advocates and detractors. Putting the debates into the classroom means asking why images change over time: to ask how culture is transmitted. It is curious that such questioning is often the preserve of the history department. With visual images at the crux of the issue, the art department is well positioned to encourage the interrogation of the illustrated image and its development for a contemporary age.

References

Acosta, J. (2006) University of Florida PhD Thesis. Online. Available at: http://news.ufl.edu/2006/06/28/pirates/ (accessed 29 January 2012).

Bourke, J. (2011) *What it Means to be Human: Reflections from 1791 to the Present*, London: Virago.

Burg, B.R. (1983) *Sodomy and the Pirate Tradition: English Sea Rovers in the Seventeenth-Century Caribbean*, New York: New York University Press.

Butler, J. (1999) *Gender Trouble*, New York: Routledge.

Chaplin, J.E. (2007) 'Roanoke Counterfeited According to the Truth', in: K. Sloan (ed.) *A New World: England's First View of America*, London: British Museum Press.

Cordingly, D. (1997) *Under the Black Flag: The Romance and the Reality of Life among the Pirates*, New York: Random House Harvest edition.

De Rijke, V. and Hollands, H. (2007) 'The Thing that is Not There? A Psychoanalytic Reading of Mervyn Peake's *Captain Slaughterboard Drops Anchor*', in: J. Plastow (ed.) *Children's Literature Annual, No 2: The Story and the Self Children's Literature: Some Psychoanalytic Perspectives*, papers and presentations from the 2007 conference, Hertfordshire: University of Hertfordshire Press.

Exquemelin, A.O. (2010 [1678]) *The Buccaneers of America (Dover Maritime)*, Digireads.com Publishing.

Gilbert, W.S. and Sullivan, A. (1880) *The Pirates of Penzance: The Slave of Duty*, 1983 film version starring Kevin Kline.

Hill, C. (1986) in: *The Collected Essays of Christopher Hill, Volume 3: People and Ideas in Seventeenth-Century England*, Amherst, MA: University of Massachusetts Press.

Hobsbawm, E. (1959) *Social Bandits and Primitive Rebels*, republished (1965) under the title: *Primitive Rebels: Studies in Archaic Forms of Social Movement in the 19th Century and 20th Century*, New York: W.W. Norton.

Johnson, Captain Charles (1998 [1724]) *A General History of the Robberies and Murders of the Most Notorious Pirates*, with an introduction and commentary by David Cordingly, London: Conway Maritime Press.

Kaufer, V. (2011) Cited in: H. Pidd 'Pirate Party Leads New Breed out to Change European Politics', *The Guardian*, 28 October.

Klausman, U., Meinzerin, M. and Kuhn, G. (1997) *Women Pirates and the Politics of the Jolly Roger*, Montreal: Black Rose Books.

Lane, K.E. (1998) *Pillaging the Empire: Piracy in the Americas 1500–1750 (Latin American Realities)*, New York: M.E. Sharpe.

Levin, A.K. (ed.) (2010) *Gender, Sexuality, and Museums: A Routledge Reader*, London: Routledge.

Meecham, P. (2008) 'Reconfiguring the Shipping News: Maritime's Hidden Histories and the Politics of Gender Display', *Sex Education*, 8 (3): 371–380.

Meecham, P. and Sheldon, J. (2008) *Making American Art*, London: Routledge.

Mills, R. (2010) 'Queer Is Here? Lesbian, Gay, Bisexual and Transgender Histories and Public Culture', in: A. K. Levin (ed.) *Gender, Sexuality, and Museums*, London: Routledge.

Morison, S.E. (1971) *The European Discovery of America: The Northern Voyages A.D. 500–1600*, New York: Oxford University Press.

NMA (National Museum of Australia) (2004) *Outlawed! Rebels, Revolutionaries and Bushrangers*, Canberra: NMA.

Poynor, R. (2010) 'The Missing Critical History of Illustration', *Print*, June. Online. Available at: http://www.printmag.com/Article/The-Forgotten-History-of-Illustration (accessed 29 January 2012).

Seal, G. (2001) *Encyclopedia of Folk Heroes*, Santa Barbara, CA: ABC-Clio.

Sloan, K. (2007) *A New World: England's First View of America*, London: British Museum Press.

Stephenson, R.L. (1911 [1883]) *Treasure Island*, illustrations by N.C. Wyeth, London: Cassell.

Turley, H. (1999) *Rum, Sodomy and the Lash: Piracy, Sexuality and Masculine Identity*, Albany, NY: New York University Press.

Warner, M. (2011) '"The Dream Child" Review of *Alice in Wonderland*, Tate Liverpool, 4 November 2011 to 29 January 2011', *The Guardian Review*, 29 October, pp. 16–17.

Part III

Debates beyond the classroom

Chapter 7

Cultural diversity, creativity and modernism

Rasheed Araeen

Introduction

An enormous confusion reigns about cultural diversity, which has obscured both the question of its necessity to society and also its relationship to creativity. If human society comprises a multiplicity of diverse cultures, then something must bring them together into a communion of exchange for their mutual enrichment. The history of the last six thousand or so years shows us how humanity has advanced, carrying with it all the ideas produced by the interaction between different cultures within particular civilisations, as well as across those boundaries. It is therefore imperative that we approach the question of cultural diversity historically, in order to understand its significance to the post-war, post-colonial and multiracial society of Britain today but also globally.

Our concern here is not merely with cultural diversity per se but with its relationship to human creativity, particularly that which produces art. Diversity of cultures and diversity within art must therefore be recognised as two different things, and diversity in art should not be considered necessarily a mirror image of cultural diversity. The passage of diversity from culture to art involves a complex intellectual process which occurs when the individual imagination is relatively free both from the demands of society and the culture of which art is a specific formation and expression. It is therefore requisite to separate the process of creativity from what already exists within society, either as cultural heritage or a multiplicity of cultural traditions. These traditions, of course, define the nature of society and provide it with an overall cultural framework that can be dynamic and inspire individual creativity. But what emerges from this individual creativity *as art* does not always replicate or display particular cultural forms.

The separation of art from the overall cultural milieu of society does not, however, diminish the importance of the diversity of cultures. They play a fundamental role in defining society and its identity. But if this identity becomes frozen in conformity, society will succumb to cultural fragmentation, intellectual stagnation and eventually decay and decline. Only when people have freedom to think, to reflect and contemplate, can they confront the norms that have become fixed dogmas, and so reactivate society's creative energy. In other words, new ideas produced by individual creativity, underpinned by freedom of thought, create a society able to change and transform itself into a dynamic force in history.

A brief journey through history

Since early history, when human groups began to communicate with each other, diversity has been fundamental to cultures. When two or more cultures met and interacted, inevitably, an interface was created from which emerged a diversity of new cultural forms that enriched the cultures collectively and enhanced individual creative imagination. Out of such imagination, when it was free to think and act, emerged what we now call art.

The increase in travel and speed of communication, facilitated by the rise of modern science and technologies since the Renaissance, has created a constant flow of ideas between peoples, nations and cultures across the world. As ideas often tend to gravitate towards a dominant centre or centres, and since Europe emerged as a major political power following its 'discovery' of the 'New World', knowledge began to accumulate in the major European cities. This accumulation at the beginning of the twentieth century, particularly in Paris, 'capital of the world', is of particular significance. Historically, it laid the foundation for what in my view became essential to the cultural diversity of modernism. Examples abound, Cubism and Surrealism for instance, besides the many individuals whose work was influenced by their admiration of art from Asia, Africa and native cultures of the Americas, proof that the issue of cultural diversity in art cannot be understood without looking at it historically.

Cultural diversity has been very much part of the emergence of new ideas in recent history. Only when this is understood, both in terms of the role of diversity in producing new ideas and of the failure of Eurocentric discourse to recognise the centrality of this role in the art of the twentieth century, will it be possible to reclaim the critical position of cultural diversity within art history beyond the practice of marginalisation on the basis of exotic otherness. We have to make clear the difference between appropriation of other cultures as exotic within Eurocentric art history and their true role in twentieth-century art. While exoticism ignores or undermines this critical role, by banishing it to the margins of history, a proper understanding challenges this marginalisation by invoking and recognising the historically central role of cultural diversity in the formation of modernism at the beginning of the twentieth century.

The very basis of modernism, particularly that which emerged with Pablo Picasso's *Les Demoiselles d'Avignon* in 1907, was an emergence of critical 'dialogue' with cultural difference. Although this dialogue was determined within a colonial frame, the resulting discourse managed to come to terms with what was inevitable at the beginning of the last century: a move away not only from one's own cultural specificity but also from the specificity and the homogeneity of Western traditions in art in order to construct a new order which could claim to be universal.

Cultural diversity and modernism

The interrelationship of many world cultures in European modernism is extremely complex and problematic. What follows here is intended only to show that it was the presence of cultural forms from other parts of the world entering Europe, particularly in the latter part of the nineteenth century, that, by becoming part of European consciousness, both changed the course of European art and influenced art all over the world. This presence coincided with the discovery of photography, which challenged the very foundation of European art. When it became clear that photography could achieve similar and indeed better results than European 'realist' painting had produced, and that there were radical alternatives offered by other cultures, the iconic pictorialism of European traditions in art began to collapse. This created a crisis in what was historically perceived, via the idealist philosophy of G.W.F. Hegel, to be the progressive mainstream that began its journey thousands of years before when humans first left their marks on the walls of caves. But with this also arose an awareness that the resolution of this crisis lay in the alternatives offered by other cultures.

If perspectival depth combined with the chiaroscuro technique of a European tradition in art created an illusion of reality, Japanese painting, as it became available to view in nineteenth-century Europe, was free of this illusion. This opened up entirely new vistas for European art. Artists now began to realise that art was not only about representing reality through illusionism. There were other different ways of looking at and representing the world.

Until then, the role of line and colour in post-Renaissance, European art had been to follow faithfully the contours and features of what one observed, so that the result was a representation of what one experienced in nature. If there was an occasional deviation from this norm, it was either to emphasise some important aspects of observed reality or to deal with social disturbances, caused by war or other disasters. Francisco Goya's Black Paintings (1819–1823), made after the upheavals of the Napoleonic War, represent the first example of this deviation in the recent history of Europe, permitting the artist to abandon faithful representation of what one observed. Goya's work, rare in the trajectory of European painting, predates the awareness of the alternatives offered by other cultures some fifty years later, yet foreshadows what became dramatically obvious only when art encountered these alternatives. Line and colour were no longer subservient to the realistic depiction of things but followed whatever the artist could perceive intellectually. This would not have happened without the presence of Asian and African cultural forms in Europe. This shift towards a freedom to perceive and conceive, without recourse to normative realism, was the beginning of modernism in art.

One can cite in particular the late nineteenth-century examples of Paul Gauguin, Vincent van Gogh and Paul Cézanne, whose work was transformed when it came into contact with the ideas as well as art forms of non-European cultures, and which then opened the way forward. The role of other cultures in the modern transformation of European art becomes much more determined when we enter the twentieth century. It was the time of great change, with new ideas in science (Albert Einstein), music (Claude Debussy followed by Arnold Schoenberg and Igor Stravinsky), philosophy (Henri Bergson), literature (James Joyce, Ezra Pound and T.S. Eliot), and so on. But my concern here is with visual art, as it was the form most influenced by the presence of many cultures and their art in Europe at the turn of the century.

One might actually describe the beginning of the century as the beginning of cultural diversity, as European culture mingled with many other world cultures. And, although one can begin the century with the art of Henri Matisse, one of the first artists to encounter and become fascinated by African sculpture and whose later work was directly influenced by his visits to North Africa, it was in Pablo Picasso's work that the meeting of Europe and Africa first took place.

At the time, *c.* 1907, Picasso faced difficulty in continuing his work, as the consciousness of the history in which he found himself located was not only insufficient but had itself become the problem. This is of course oversimplified, but European artists of the time undeniably faced a complex socio-historical situation which they could not resolve within the iconographic realm of Western tradition and still produce something new. It was also a moment significantly reflective of the changes taking place in Western society. It was this situation which led Picasso, among others, to the different world of African and Oceanic art.

When Picasso saw the African and Oceanic artefacts – as they were then called – in the museum at the Trocadéro, he was amazed not only by the freedom of imagination that had created them, but by his own realisation of a potential alternative way of representing the world. Although a radical shift had already taken place in Western art, in the work of the post-Impressionists and Fauves, Picasso's *Les Demoiselles d'Avignon* has been seen as the first real work of twentieth-century modernism. It laid the foundation for Cubism and triggered a historical process based on dialogue between different cultures. When we look at this great painting, *Les Demoiselles d'Avignon*, what do we see? The heritage of Western culture – El Greco, Cézanne, and others – and forms from African and Oceanic cultures, intermingled and interlocked with each other, creating an interface that was to become fundamental to the relationship of different cultures within modernism for the rest of the twentieth century, and also beyond as part of late-twentieth-century globalisation.

One can also take the work of Matisse and Paul Klee to illustrate the main point, that of a dialogue between the West's iconographic traditions and the Islamic tradition of North Africa. This 'dialogue' is full of problematic, if not unresolved, contradictions – to which I shall return. However, while picture-making dominates their canvases, it is the tension between the iconography of their work and what had been historically in defiance of and a challenge to European pictorialism that makes this work historically significant. This challenge has existed ever since the emergence of an Arab Islamic civilisation and art in the seventh century. But it was dismissed from Europe's historical trajectory as philosophically conceived by Hegel and others. Now, in the early twentieth century, Islamic culture entered into the dynamic force of modernity and began to show a way forward in history (Araeen 2009: 3–14) In other words, it was on the basis of modernism's ability to incorporate the problematics of cultural difference within its mainstream that modernism was able to claim its universality, spreading its wings over the whole world and providing the contexts for other cultures to enter into a discourse that claimed progress and advancement.

Colonialism and modernism

I have put the word 'dialogue' in quotes in order to highlight the problem that has remained the basis of a divided world today. Globalisation might seem to reduce division by offering all cultures of the world a common space in which to manifest themselves.

This 'equalisation' of cultures is an illusion created by the triumph of the neoliberal/ capitalist system whose chief concern is not with the history of ideas and those who have been its agents, but the marketing of commodities. This history has been brought to an end with the mistaken notion that what was meant to be achieved historically has been achieved, and that there is nothing further we can learn from it for the future.

What is this history which has 'ended'? Why can it not now be re-examined and revised? Why are art historians reluctant to recognise its missing parts, particularly those which would reveal its cultural diversity? The answers to these questions will reveal the hidden agenda of bourgeois humanism that has been used to justify colonialism, and why globalisation is now being deployed to undermine and 'end' what began as an anti-colonial struggle.

A collusion between modernity and colonialism is well recognised in what is generally called the radical discourse of philosophy and social sciences. Enough philosophical ideas have by now emerged in the West that question the division of humanity on the basis of the Self and the Other – the former being European subjectivity and latter its colonised others. What lies beneath this division is the agency of history attributed exclusively to European (by implication, white) subjectivity, while the colonial other is reduced to the mere victim of history, incapable of self-definition, of determining their destination and entering history. What is remarkable here is not primarily the inferiorisation of the colonised, but that a colonial attitude towards the racially different on the part of the European encompasses an admiration for this difference, and a desire to help and guide them in the march of history.

Colonialism has been and is still a brutal force which dehumanises both the coloniser and the colonised. But it also has a liberal benevolent side which regards the colonised with sympathy and fascination. It has often sided with the colonised and helped them gain post-colonial independence as nation states. But this benevolence does not go far enough, and leaves untouched what is enshrined deep within the ideology of colonialism, failing to allow the colonised to define themselves as free subjects by confronting the so-called master–slave relationship that underpinned colonialism. The slave can demand freedom, and the benevolence of the master can allow the slave to go free; but without the master giving up his own ground.

My concern here is with this benevolent face of colonialism which effectively denies others their human subjectivity, and without which others cannot rid themselves of their Otherness and enter history. This is particularly important when we consider the struggle of art, not only in those areas of the non-European world both during and after the time when these were occupied by the colonial powers, but also in its continuous striving for modern subjectivity in the metropolis. An example from art history will show what I mean. From Matisse to Picasso, Klee and Brancusi to the Surrealists, each and all were fascinated by the artistic forms of other cultures, especially those of Africa and Asia, and they made these forms part of their work. Some of them even went further in their admiration and expressed their support for and solidarity with the struggles in the colonies. But that is where the solidarity ended, because when they actually encountered someone from the colonies who had come to the metropolis to pursue a course similar to their own as modernist avant-garde artists, there was either suspicion or disbelief that such a person could have ability equal to theirs. Suspicion still prevails, even now that there is overwhelming evidence that others entered the central core of modernism as talented subjects, defying and confronting that which persists in keeping them outside history, and thus demolishing the very basis for white supremacist exclusivity in modern art history. Something deeply entrenched within the European colonial psyche prevents it from recognising equally the intellectual ability of other human beings within modernity.

The dialogue between Europe and the rest of the world has remained problematic to this day. This is not due to the inability of other cultures to find their place subjectively in history or as equal partners in this dialogue. But the space within which 'dialogue' took place was constructed on the basis of a colonial view that divided the world into ruler and ruled, conforming to the Hegelian construct of master–slave relationship, and also apparently fixed this relationship eternally. Master and slave can indeed speak to each other, both have their voices, but only one has significance – that of the master. The master can speak even with the voice of the slave and sympathetically represent the predicament of the slave. But the slave must not claim any subjectivity or agency that might threaten or undermine the power of the master. The struggle of the colonial other is therefore against the supposed benevolence of the colonial master. For if the other were ever to find a place as an obvious agent of history *within* history, this assumption of the benevolent master would collapse, and so liberate the space within which both had been confined in the slave–master relationship.

Benevolent colonialism and struggle of art

It is important nevertheless to recognise the positive aspects of what I call benevolent colonialism, even when this paradox has collapsed along with the failure of its attempted modernising projects. Whatever it achieved, in its efforts to bring the colonised into the orbit of the progressive march of history, has remained contained within the self-interest of colonialism. What concerns me specifically is its educational programme, part of which was to persuade indigenous peoples to adopt Western ways of thinking and living. While missionaries were busy destroying Africa's ancient artistic heritage, often simply burning its artefacts, liberals of the colonial administration encouraged and promoted those who would adopt a Western way of making art. Art schools were set up, particularly in India, and stocked with teachers from the art schools of London. The idea was to lead the native artists on to the path that would eventually lead them to modernism along a track laid down by Europe and the West.

But things do not always go according to a predetermined plan. It is in the nature of humanity not to accept subservience or dominance, not permanently. There comes a time when the oppressed rise up, either to demand equality or to revolt against what is imposed. Many artists confounded the expectations of their patrons and supporters, even when they were genuinely helped in pursuit of their ambitions. There are many instances of artists being sent to the metropolises of London and Paris by their well-wishing colonial patrons. For example, Uzo Egonu from Nigeria went to London with the assistance of a colonial friend of his father (Oguibe 1995) Aubrey Williams from

British Guiana was persuaded by his colonial friends to leave the political turmoil of the country and go to London (Araeen 1988), and so on. Colonialism was not always a blunt instrument of oppression but frequently provided or created a space in which both the coloniser and the colonised could exist in a mutually sympathetic relationship, giving the colonised the means for the self-realisation of their own humanity, and allowing them to exceed the expectations of their empathetic masters. Behind this paradox lies a deeper unresolvable contradiction, for when the colonised do exceed expectation, sometimes surpassing the ability of the master, what can the master do? Recognise the achievement of the colonised? How can that be? Would it not demolish the very basis of colonial power?

My assertion here may seem crude, but how else can one penetrate the complexity of such an ambivalent relationship and reveal what lies behind it? It involves a sophisticated system that maintains the coloniser and the colonised in mutual dependence and admiration. By invoking the bonds of common humanity, they can even seem to love each other and share each others' pain. But when the colonised try to confront this relationship by asserting their humanity in their own way, this relationship breaks down, often producing the extreme violence that has been a hallmark of anti-colonial struggle.

This relationship had a specific significance in art, particularly during the 1920s and 1930s in Paris when there was great fascination with so-called 'Negro art', described by some historians as Negrophilia (Archer-Shaw 2000). It was during this time that an extraordinary event of historical importance also occurred in Paris, which turned the whole business upside down. Ernest Mancoba, a black South African, set an example of what an individual artistic imagination can do to defy the seductions of colonial predetermination, and offers us allegorically the way forward to the real liberation of humanity. He has shown that the colonised can enter the central core of modernism's genealogy and thereby assert the common humanity of both the coloniser and the colonised.

Ernest Mancoba and the liberation of the colonised imagination

Ernest Mancoba was born in 1904 near Johannesburg and educated at the Christian school of Pietersburg. He also learned to sculpt there, in a European style, producing a work in 1929 called *Bantu Madonna* (see http://www.artubuntu.org/projects_em_gallery.php) which caused a scandal, followed by a series of works that established him as an important sculptor. In 1936 he was offered a lucrative government job but declined it.

> The Commissioner for Native Affairs in Pretoria ... decided that I should take part in the upcoming British 'Empire Exhibition'. The idea was ... to develop the indigenous art trade by selling all sorts of pseudo-tribal figures for tourists. He offered me a good job with a fine salary, to gather young Africans to provide for this kind of traffic. I was shocked and, as politely as possible, refused the proposition.
>
> (Obrist 2010: 373)

He goes on to elaborate his position:

> Some of my political friends told me that the artistic activity was not the most urgent thing to concentrate upon, while our people were undergoing such a terrible plight, but I believed, on the contrary, that art was precisely also a means to favour a great consciousness in Man, which, for me, is part of the struggle for any human liberation, and without which any practical achievement would probably, sooner or later, deviate and miss its point. Therefore, making art, I thought, was as urgent as for working the political evolution, which, at the time, anyhow seemed still a faraway prospect. *So I decided to engage upon a debate with European artists by coming to Europe.*
>
> (p. 376; my emphasis)

Despite his poverty Mancoba came to Europe:

> As I had absolutely no means to travel, I had the good fortune to be helped by missionary institutions, and when I arrived in London, I lived with Bishop Smythe, whom I had known as the head of my student hostel at Fort Hare. ... Through Bishop Smythe's connection in Paris, I got into the Ecole des Arts Decoratifs.
>
> (ibid.)

When Mancoba arrived in Paris in 1938, the city was still in the grip of 'Negrophilia' and the ideas of Negritude (Epko 2010). But he turned his back on both of them, with a defiance that required tremendous courage, leading him to the discovery of the power of free imagination.

> [T]he true universality is a common goal on the cultural, political and spiritual horizon that will be reached only when all ethnic groups achieve, through an authentic dialogue, the many-faceted diamond shape and the full blossom of the deepest and widest human integrity.
>
> (Obrist op. cit.: 379)

His work of 1939 and 1940 was a precursor to one of the most important post-war avant-garde movements in Europe, CoBrA (Copenhagen, Brussels and Amsterdam). After the war, and his release from internment, he went to Copenhagen, where in 1948 he met Asger Jorn and Karel Appel and took part in the Host Exhibition. In the following year, 1949, he became involved in the founding of CoBrA. But no history of CoBrA mentions Mancoba (Smalligan 2010). A few years before his death in 2002, Mancoba reminisced about his association with CoBrA:

> The embarrassment that my presence caused – to the point of making me, in their eyes, some sort of 'Invisible Man' or merely the consort of a European woman artist [his wife, Sonja Ferlov] was understandable, as before me, there had never

been, to my knowledge, any black man taking part in the visual arts 'avant-garde' of the Western World. ... Some critics totally obliterate my participation in the movement, as modest as it admittedly has been, on the reason that my work was suspected of not being European enough, and in his words, 'betraying (my) African origins'.

(Obrist op. cit.: 383)

Mancoba's work is neither European nor African but in a dialogue with them both. He has created a space in which such a dialogue can and should take place, although this cannot be recognised by the colonial mindset trapped in the power it continues to entertain and enjoy. And thus we have humanity's separation on a racial basis:

but I'm not thinking about an artistic one. For me, what is still not realised is a common acceptance and understanding between whites and blacks (as the most contrasted opposition in terms of colour, but between other races as well). The dialogue has not started yet.

(Obrist op. cit.: 384)

Which brings me to the core of my argument, that the colonised, while struggling to liberate themselves, also liberate the colonisers. Ernest Mancoba's achievement has not only secured his place within the historical genealogy of modernism, but, perhaps more importantly, with this he liberated modernism from its Eurocentric framework *by infusing into its central core an African vision and placing Africa within it with its own authentic modern voice.* It is in such an achievement that there exists, historically, true cultural diversity in art. (Examples of Ernest Mancoba's work can be found at: http://www.artubuntu.org/about_mancoba_4.php).

African and Asian artists in post-war Britain

Ernest Mancoba's release from war-time internment in France, and his subsequent extraordinary achievement in art, unprecedented during the classical period of colonialism that produced its most barbaric form in South Africa's apartheid, offers us an appropriate metaphor for the beginning of the collapse of the West's colonial empire and the release of a creativity that enters the European body to liberate it from its self-imposed assumptions of intellectual superiority and supremacy. Surprisingly, even paradoxically, it was a *white* South African in London, Denis Bowen, who recognised this liberated creativity and called it 'a breath of fresh air'. Bowen constantly struggled, along with artists from Asia, Africa and the Caribbean who began to arrive in London soon after the war, against the division of humanity into racial or cultural differences (Santacatterina 2008).

However, my concern is primarily with those who faced the problem of being seen, due to their racial difference, as 'others', and who became 'black artists' in the white art world of Britain. Even when they were right at the centre of modern developments in art, they were seen as merely representing their own Asian, African or Caribbean culture. And with regard to the diversity and experimental nature of the avant-garde activities in 1960s London, Guy Brett has highlighted the problem:

> These qualities have never been recognised by British art history. In fact the entire mainstream historical writing and exhibition-making has been concerned with constructing a national image of British art ... ignoring or excluding the work of those foreigners which cannot be assimilated within the national canon. By the cruel logic of chauvinism, official aspirations to make London an international art centre have only resulted in obliterating London's cosmopolitan reality and the actual ferment of its cultural life.
>
> (Brett 1995: 50)

'London's cosmopolitan reality' comprised not just members of the European avant-garde but the active presence of artists of Asian and African origins ('black artists') that turned this reality into a culturally diverse art world. When both white and black artists showed in the same galleries, the basic premises of the modernist avant-garde were transformed into a culturally diverse discourse. Unlike the early part of the twentieth century, when the role of other cultures within modernism was enacted through their cultural objects penetrating into it and precipitating a transformation, now this penetration was that of a *subject* who challenged Eurocentric modernism and liberated it from its white ethnocentrism. When we link this achievement to the exemplary one of Ernest Mancoba, and those of many others in the modern world, we have a completely different history. It is no longer exclusively the history of the achievement of European or Western culture in art but a history that has engaged in defiant challenge to the colonial frame of modernism and has given to modernism what the West had always claimed for it, its universality, now truly meaning the liberated subjectivity of all humanity. In short, the true history of modernism and the avant-garde is the history of many diverse cultures of the world.

Diversity and art in Britain

With the change in its demographic map, resulting from the arrival of people from Asia, Africa and the Caribbean after World War II, British society could no longer be considered an exclusively white society but a multiracial and multicultural one. This has been constantly reflected in art during the last sixty or so years, producing what is and should be recognised as the historical accomplishment of Britain's cultural diversity. What is striking about this success story is that it is located at the centre of British mainstream and not as a separate cultural entity – or a specific 'sector', of the sort institutionally promoted in Britain, representing only what is described in the Arts Council's *Cultural Diversity Action Plan 1998–2003* as 'African, Caribbean, Asian and Chinese Arts'. The Arts Council's report, we should take note, describes cultural diversity as 'ethnic diversity resulting from post-war immigration'. This is not simply a 'misguided' perception due to ignorance or the legacy of benevolent colonialism still embedded within the art institutions (Araeen 2000: 125–144), but, more disturbingly, a denial of the reality of what has been historically achieved in the art of Britain and a perpetuation of the institutional suppression of the actual facts of cultural diversity in art. Which raises some very disquieting questions. If cultural diversity has been an integral part of the British mainstream, why is there institutional insistence on its separation and exclusion from that mainstream? And why are millions being spent in the official support and promotion of this version of 'cultural apartheid'?

The facts of cultural diversity within the mainstream are well known. The art establishment has been constantly reminded of the importance of these facts for a culturally integrated multiracial British society. And yet these facts are persistently ignored and this ignorance is institutionally advanced by publicly funding separatist art projects based on ethnic or racial categories. I do not wish to invoke the former apartheid policy of South Africa, but questions must be asked in the interest of a society that has consistently declared its opposition to all kinds of discrimination. I do not doubt that British society truly aspires to be an integrated multiracial society. So how can exclusion from British art history of those artists who have been historically responsible for the cultural diversity within the mainstream be explained or justified? Why instead are racially based separate categories of cultural diversity being officially supported?

I am aware of the complexity of the problem and know that these questions alone will not provide for sufficient answers. One must go beyond simplified polemics. There is a genuine desire for radical change, no doubt, but this desire is itself trapped in the very perception that also traps 'black artists' in their presumed displacement from their own cultures, which it is believed, prevents them from being creative. Hence it becomes policy to help them recover from this loss. Being helpful to others in this way blocks the recognition of the reality that such recipients in fact do not require this sort of help but are confronting the very basis of this benevolence.

Free imagination is fundamental to creativity. This imagination may carry with it personal experiences involving 'diversity of culture' but its creativity cannot be predetermined by these experiences. They may appear as part of what emerges from it as art, though not necessarily in a way that clearly or simply reveals its specific cultural roots. It is more likely, instead, that when creativity faces a culturally specific precondition or an institutionally imposed cultural framework, it will lose its vital force. I am not denying the role of one's culture in what one creates as art, but when this is seen ontologically as the predetermination of creativity, then its power becomes limited and contained; and consequently it is prevented from giving rise to what can claim to be profoundly and historically a significant idea performing a social function. The ambition of art throughout history, both in national pursuits and across all cultures of the world, has been either to reflect what society aspires to collectively or to suggest a way for it to move forward.

Art history and diversity

The role of history is fundamental to creativity, as history is the motor of art. Its history will also define the space in which this movement occurs. In other words, the movement of art in Britain defines the nature of British society. If this movement is recognised as only that of a certain racial group, then the space of movement is defined only by this group. If the history of art in Britain is the history only of white artists – as it is institutionally recognised and promoted – then Britain is a society defined by these artists. If this is what should be accepted wholeheartedly and without critical thought, then what is expected from Britain's non-white population? To remain at the margin of this society without any active and equal part either in its formation or definition? Has this not created the problem of a culturally divided Britain? It seems that society is aware of this division and suffers from its resulting conflicts, but is unable to deal with the underlying causes of this division. Awareness of this problem was publicly expressed in 1999 by none other than the then Secretary of State for Culture, Media and Sport, Chris Smith:

> If we have a national identity, as I'm sure we do, then that presupposes we have developed a common cultural heritage and history, and we are aware that we have developed it. In representing and reporting that heritage, we need to look closely at how it has been done in the past, at who has done it, and how we can do it better in the future.
>
> (Smith 1999)

He then goes further on to elaborate his point:

> Cultural professionals should be aware of how narrowly based their own inter-preters of history can be. … They need both to employ people with a wider vision and undertake projects that focus on missing history. As Secretary of State for culture, I want to see organisations working in this field – I would put this very strongly – providing a more complete version of the truth.
>
> (ibid.)

What is significant about Smith's view is not only his awareness of the role of history, of its 'complete version of the truth', but also his knowledge that something important is missing from dominant British history. He goes further, in the same speech, to emphasise the importance of 'a common cultural heritage' that includes all people, without which those who are excluded from it will look to their own cultures outside Britain:

> Without a recorded history, nothing else can follow: no celebration of achieve-ment, no development of a common cultural heritage. This results in immigrant populations looking outside these shores for their history and cultural points of reference.
>
> (ibid.)

Chris Smith was then head of a government department that decided the cultural policies of the country and funded the institutions to implement them, and which, a few years after his speech, funded the Arts Council England to the tune of twenty-nine million pounds in setting up *ethnically based separate organisations* and projects. How can one explain this backslide and contradiction? Was Smith unaware of what his department was doing to promote the fragmentation of British society into ethnic ghettos? What happened to his idea of 'a common cultural heritage and history' and the elements he suggested were missing from it? And what happened to his aspiration for 'a more complete version of the truth'? My experience has shown me that there has been little actual concern with 'missing history' or to pursue 'a more complete version of the truth'.

It is common knowledge that what is being taught as art history in Britain is racially constructed in favour of the white race and at the expense of those who are not. I say this not because I demand the inclusion of 'black artists' into this history, regardless of the nature or quality of their work, simply to make it a 'multiracial' art history, but with a knowledge of those who have been at the centre of important developments in post-war British art; those who have been at the forefront of post-Abstract Expressionism, Kineticism, Minimalism, Post-Minimalism and Conceptualism. Those who have been part of the new experiments by which the 1970s are identified (Araeen 1989). So why are they excluded from these developments as narrated in official British art history? I ask this not merely because of their race but because their innovative work placed them at the centre of modernism's mainstream, and in so doing they have redefined the central core of the British nation as multiracial and multicultural. British art institutions have not yet fully come to terms with the changed reality of post-war Britain.

The facts are plain. The 'missing history', invoked by Chris Smith, was in fact presented to the public in an exhibition at the Hayward Gallery in 1989 (Araeen 1989). But the question remains: What is still missing from the recognition of the specific nature of discrimination in art that a 'racial equality scheme' will not suffice to address? It cannot just be about 'cultural variations' in society which can be seen celebrated every day in British cities without hindrance. Even when the concern is about those described as 'Black and minority ethnic artists', it is not clear who these artists are. If this includes artists like Anish Kapoor, Yinka Shonibare, Chris Ofili and so on, then there should be no problem. Don't they represent the success of what the art establishment perceives as 'cultural diversity'? This paternalistic view separates those who are seen to be different from the indigenous white people of Britain and has led to the division of society into two different discourses: one for the dominant white majority whose creativity is believed self-generated without outside help; and the other for the non-white minority, defined racially or ethnically, who must be told how to be creative. Thus the former becomes part of the mainstream history, while the latter must linger at the margins to reinforce the white centrality of society. This paradigmatic division of British society has been determined not by the reality of what it actually is, and what it has achieved historically in art as part of its post-war post-colonial transformation, but by a deep-lodged perception unwilling to accept this achievement as precisely that of cultural diversity within the mainstream that unites the society (Araeen 1989).

The achievement of cultural diversity in art in Britain

What Guy Brett calls the extraordinary 'cosmopolitan reality' of post-war art in Britain looked forward to a racially integrated multicultural *one* society. A transformation took place because there was a space in which different cultures could meet and intermix and provide an interface from which emerged a notion of modernism that was previously absent in Britain. This modernism gave Britain its post-war national identity. And although this development was at first welcomed – in fact celebrated in the case of some artists – it became a problem for the writing of history. There was a clash of views within British society about what this history should represent and how it should be written. Some wanted it to represent the new multicultural reality of post-war Britain, while others, like Enoch Powell, saw such an inclusive history as a threat to British culture, whose values could only be defined and protected by its indigenous people. However, the struggle for a society in which all people, irrespective of their racial or cultural differences, would have equal rights and would be part of Britain's new identity and history did vigorously proceed. But as British society began to perceive post-war immigrants from the British Commonwealth as a social problem, the impetus for change lost its ground to the notion of immigrants as a separate entity in need of separate development. Thus emerged the idea of 'cultural diversity', based on the ethnicities of the diverse minorities, which masked the real struggle between equality and exclusivity. And with this, as 'black artists' became 'foreigners' (Brett 1995: 50), their place within British art history became untenable. But these 'foreigners' could not be sent home; nor could their demand for equality be ignored. The conundrum demanded a resolution for the good of all society, but that became increasingly difficult as the fear of other cultures grew. This fear had less to do with the presence of other cultures in Britain than with their critical potential to intervene in what was perceived to be indigenous British culture and change its basic character. This fear became acute when Margaret Thatcher, following in Enoch Powell's footsteps, declared in 1978:

> I think it means that people are really rather *afraid* that this country might be swamped by people of a different culture. ... The British character has done so much for democracy, for law, and done so much throughout the world that if there is any *fear* that it might be swamped, then people are going to be rather hostile to those coming in. ... We are a British nation with British characteristics. Every country can take some minorities, and in many ways they add to the richness and variety of this country. But the moment the minority *threatens* to become a big one, people get frightened.
>
> (Thatcher 1978: my emphases)

If we compare Thatcher's declaration with Chris Smith's vision for 'a common cultural heritage and history', then we can better grasp the nature of the rift I have underlined. Thatcher's triumph commandeered the future of British society and left the issue of 'British character' unchallenged.

What was this fear Thatcher was referring to, if not the very one regularly implanted in the gullible public by a reactionary element within British culture to maintain its power? This power has never come to terms with its past and continues nostalgically to celebrate the glories of colonialism, and stubbornly opposes any attempt to transform Britain into a racially equitable post-colonial society. But if, at the same time, the aspiration of British society is to become an equitable society, how can this be achieved without confronting the beliefs enshrined in Thatcher's notion of the 'British character', which clings to the colonial past? Did this not create an irresolvable contradiction within a power structure that still wished to maintain the status quo of this 'British character', and to thus subject a section of society to *minority* status, preventing it from claiming equal rights within the mainstream? Did this not then lead to riots in the major cities of the United Kingdom in 1981?

Following the riots in Brixton, Liverpool, Manchester, and other cities, Prime Minister Thatcher appointed Lord Scarman to investigate the matter, and he, in his report, suggested special funding for the promotion of the cultures of 'ethnic minority communities' as a solution to what was a socio-economic problem. At the time, unemployment in Brixton stood at 13 per cent and 26 per cent for ethnic minorities, while among the black youth it was estimated at 55 per cent.

It comes as no surprise that Thatcher provided funds for this programme in 1986 in support of what she called 'people of a different culture', and thereby reinforced the separate cultural status of those who might otherwise have changed the 'British character' of this nation.

History is our best guide to understanding the present and constructing the future. What we face today are the mistakes of the past and its results in the present; but they can be rectified if we are prepared to look at things historically. Historically, there have been two cultural models: one emerged from the freedom of imagination and is integrated within the mainstream; the other was imposed on a section of society on the basis of its assumed separateness. The former was hailed by Chris Smith who wanted it to be the basis of the unity of British society; while the aim of the latter was to suppress or mask a conflict that could not easily be resolved. The continuing non-recognition of the former and the institutional perpetuation of the latter comprise the problem of our divided society today.

The question remains: What do we really want? Should we adopt a model of cultural diversity that brings us all together in a cohesive whole, or accept the attitudes that promote the division of society into unrelated fragments? If society's true aspiration is the former, then we must listen to Chris Smith and pursue what he suggested; otherwise, we will leave society as it is, to undergo further conflicts and violence.

References

Araeen, R. (1988) 'Conversation with Aubrey Williams', *Third Text 2*, 1: 25–52.

Araeen, R. (1989) *The Other Story: Afro Asian Artists in Postwar Britain*, London: Hayward Gallery.

Araeen, R. (2000) 'The Art of Benevolent Racism', *Third Text 51*, 14: 57–64.

Araeen, R. (2009) 'Preliminary Notes for the Understanding of the Historical Significance of Geometry in Arab/Islamic Thought, and its Suppressed Role in the Genealogy of World History', *Third Text* 106, 24 (5): 3–14.

Archer-Shaw, P. (2000) *Negrophilia: Avant-Garde Paris and Black Culture in the 1920s*, London: Thames & Hudson.

Brett, G. (1995) *Exploding Galaxies: The Art of David Mandalla*, London: Kalla Press.

Epko, D. (guest ed.) (2010) 'Special Issue: Beyond Negritude: Senghor's Vision for Africa', *Third Text 103*, 24 (2).

Obrist, H. Ulrich (2010) 'An Interview with Ernest Mancoba', *Third Text 104*, 24 (3): 373–384.

Oguibe, O. (1995) *Uzo Egonu: An African Artist in the West*, London: Kala Press.

Santacatterina, S. (2008) 'Denis Bowen: The Universality of Abstraction', in: *'A Very Special British Issue', Third Text 91*, 22 (2): 157–162.

Smalligan, L. (2010) 'The Erasure of Ernest Manchoba; Africa and Europe at the Crossroads', *Third Text 103*, 24 (2): 263–276.

Smith, C. (1999) 'Whose Heritage?', paper given at *The Museums Association Conference*, Manchester, 1–3 November 1999.

Thatcher, M. (1978) quoted in the editorial of *Black Phoenix*, 2: 3.

Chapter 8

From trance-like solipsism to speculative audacity?

Young people's learning in galleries today

Emily Pringle

In Iris Murdoch's novel *The Bell* (2004 [1973]), Dora, the young female protagonist, visits the National Gallery in London during a period of great stress in her life. During this visit, which is described in some detail, Dora, who 'had been to the National Gallery a thousand times' (p. 194) is initially calmed by the familiarity of the paintings, as they are well known to her. Yet, as she progresses she sees the work afresh, prompting her to think about both the art and herself anew:

> Dora was always moved by the pictures. Today she was moved, but in a new way. She marvelled, with a kind of gratitude, that they were all still here. ... It occurred to her that here at last was something real and something perfect. Who had said that, about perfection and reality being in the same place? Here was something that her consciousness could not wretchedly devour, and by making it part of her fantasy make it worthless ... the pictures were something real outside herself, which spoke to her kindly and yet in sovereign tones, something superior and good whose presence destroyed the dreary trance-like solipsism of her earlier mood. When the world had seemed to be subjective it had seemed to be without interest or value. But now there was something else in it after all. These thoughts, not clearly articulated, flitted through Dora's mind. She had never thought about the pictures in this way before; nor did she draw now any very explicit moral. Yet she felt she had had a revelation.

> (Murdoch 2004 [1973]: 196)

Although published originally in 1973, there is much in this extract that I believe is relevant to learning in galleries today. In particular, Murdoch draws our attention to the potential for art to engender significant shifts in thinking and feeling; that art has a capacity to communicate, to console, to uplift and to challenge and that through encountering and engaging with works, even if they are familiar to us, we can reach new understandings about ourselves and art.

For gallery learning professionals, facilitating experiences such as Dora's represents a key ambition. Those working within learning departments aspire to provide the context and opportunities for the visitor or participant in an outreach project (particularly those not familiar or confident with art) to engage with art and with the other participants in profound ways and to learn. This aspiration is not just held by gallery and museum staff, for, around the world, interest from policy makers and educationalists in how learning about, with and through art in galleries and elsewhere can support young people's learning especially remains strong. In the United Kingdom, significant financial support was provided through policy initiatives under the previous Labour government (1997–2010), which enabled gallery education programmes to develop across the country, and much valuable and innovative work was undertaken. However, circumstances are changing, not least because of global financial constraints and shifts in UK governmental priorities in relation to formal education, and consequently the gallery education sector faces challenges in terms of maintaining staff, supporting programme development and attracting schools that may not have art as a priority in their curriculum. Furthermore, despite many years of good practice some persistent questions remain unresolved, not least how we understand, capture and account for the benefits to young people of engaging with art in rigorous and meaningful ways to those working in the sector, funders and policy makers. In recent years gallery education professionals, with other educationalists, have sought to articulate the nature and value of the practice through research-led initiatives, (for recent examples see 'enquire' [www.enquire.org.uk] and Documenta 12 [Mörsch 2009]) and surface new insights through constructing pedagogy in relation to a range of theoretical perspectives (see in particular Atkinson [2011]; Burnham and Kai Kee [2011] and Pringle [2011]). Taking account of these developments and current challenges it is timely to look at how young people's learning in galleries is constructed today.

Whilst it is understandable that attention has been paid to the outcomes of gallery education interventions, there is also value to be gained by looking at the contexts and processes of learning in order to comprehend what happens and, moreover, how and why it happens. We need to address not only the impact on individual learners but also to interrogate what occurs in the moment, in the particular environment of the gallery. From here we can consider what needs to be put in place to facilitate learning for everyone. The experience described in *The Bell* provides a starting point from which to examine different constructions, constraints and opportunities and contribute some observations on the implications of these for practice going forward. With this in mind, there are particular aspects of learning in the gallery that I see articulated in the extract above which I want to focus on; the concept of the learning event, the dialogic nature of the encounter and nature of the knowledge gained through the experience, the significance of the gallery context, and an explication of what has been learnt.

In the extract, Iris Murdoch describes one learning moment and articulates how a particular scenario can prove revelatory. In the simplest terms, a young woman looks at paintings in the context of a gallery and is moved to think and feel differently. Drawing on the ideas of the French theorist Alain Badiou, Dennis Atkinson has recently identified how a learning event of this kind can be understood in terms of a shift from one state to a new, previously unknown, one (Atkinson 2011). Key to this possibility is that the learner, in this case Dora, needs to experience a momentary state of uncertainty prompted by the realisation of something unexpected. Here it is Dora's confrontation with the alternative reality of the paintings; their existence beyond and outside her subjectivity. This 'event' brings about a temporary ontological space or vacuum that exposes, in this example, the existing limits of Dora's comprehension of herself and her agency (she had previously been caught up in her own all-encompassing subjectivity, which prevented her from imagining alternatives to the suffocating situation within which she found herself).

Grasping this unpredictable event and allowing herself to go with the new perspectives it has engendered bring Dora to a new state of being, one in which the limitations of her previous world view are exposed. She experiences a moment of 'real' learning, where the 'event of learning precipitates a new order of becoming that has the potential to invoke new states of existence' (Atkinson 2011: 9). In this context the 'real' refers to the shift in perspective from one standpoint to another; it can be understood as a disturbance to the learner's customary ways of understanding that is prompted by a specific event, which, in turn, enables that learner to think something new. In Dora's case this learning event brings about a changed mindset that allows her to make certain decisions about her future. She moves from a state of confusion to one of greater clarity and purpose. This is shown by the acknowledgement at the end of the chapter that 'She remembered that she had been wondering what to do; but now without her thinking it had become obvious' (Murdoch op. cit.: 197).

The framing of learning as an event is a useful starting point, as it suggests how and why the learner is transformed. It draws attention to the importance of risk and experimentation and the openness that is required to move into a space of not knowing in order to gain new insights.

A second and significant aspect of this particular learning process is the specific pedagogic relationship established between the viewer and the paintings. Dora's learning takes place through an engagement with art in the context of the gallery. She comes face to face with paintings, which disturb her customary ways of knowing. But despite the suggestion of confrontation it is important to recognise that this encounter is essentially a dialogic process. We are told that the paintings 'spoke' to Dora, suggesting to her alternative ways of thinking and being and that she in turn responds to them. Each painting has its own existence (for example, Murdoch describes 'the solemn world of Piero della Francesca' (op. cit.: 197) and Dora's new knowledge is precipitated by her engagement with this 'otherness'. She views the works, asks questions of herself and them, and takes in what the paintings communicate to her. Her ideas are shaped by that ongoing communication.

In this way learning with art is framed as a dialogue, wherein the art object actively contributes to the construction of meaning. Here the use of the term 'dialogic' is intended to draw attention to the dynamic and generative nature of the process of engagement with the artwork. Artworks cannot literally 'speak', but they communicate provisional and shifting meanings, which inform viewers' interpretations. The US gallery educators Elliot Kai Kee and Rika Burnham describe this learning process as 'like a fruitful conversation' (Burnham and Kai Kee 2011: 61), wherein the dialogue between artwork and viewer encourages ideas and speculations that open up possibilities, rather than limiting them. As with all good conversations, this process takes time to develop, requires focus and is easier if the participants have sufficient ability to communicate effectively. This suggests, in addition to the requirements for learning outlined above (namely openness, experimentation and risk-taking), that curiosity, appropriate communication skills and time are needed also.

Here we need to take a moment to consider the significance of what the learner brings to the conversation with art. Returning to Dora it is clear that the experience of the work is fundamental, as it is through looking at the work she is brought to a new state of awareness. But Dora enters the gallery with her own set of intellectual and emotional frames. She is troubled and confused and is unable, in her words, to 'tell the difference between right and wrong' (Murdoch op. cit.: 195). Dora visits the gallery to seek comfort, reassurance and guidance. Yet at the same time she is someone who is familiar with and knowledgeable about art. In an earlier passage in the novel we are told that Dora, who is a graduate of the Slade School of Art, 'did not need to peer. She could look, as one can at last when one knows a great thing very well' (ibid.). Dora, this implies, is empathetic and knowledgeable and because of this she is able to reach new understandings, simply by skilful observation. Thus we are presented with a learner who is clearly not an empty vessel to be filled, but a complex individual who connects with art on intellectual and emotional levels. It can be seen that her particular insight is determined to some extent by her emotional and epistemological frameworks. These enable her both to reach deeper understandings (she is equipped with the necessary intellectual and social tools for looking at works of art), but also to shape what that new knowledge might be. As many previous cultural educators and writers have done, we can deduce from this that in the context of the gallery, as elsewhere, knowledge is essentially constructed by learners, who actively generate meaning through discovery, discussion and making connections, rather than passively received from external sources. And because learning is not only an intellectual, but also a social and emotional process, these aspects need to be recognised as well.

So what is it that Dora has learnt? It would appear that in this instance Dora has not specifically acquired new knowledge about the paintings' formal qualities (she does not, for example, learn more about Piero della Francesca's use of colour). Neither does she seem to gain greater insights into art history, as there is no mention of either of these in the book. Furthermore there is no suggestion that her new state of awareness is predicated on her receiving specific art historical or contextual information about the paintings. What the passage above suggests is that Dora's learning concerns what art represents and how it exists in relation to her. It is important to stress that this is her particular insight, which derives from her experience. It is clearly not the only one available and there is no suggestion that it is the 'right' one (indeed some may be troubled by Murdoch's construction of artworks as objective, let alone 'superior and good'). Dora could, in fact, on a different visit, acquire entirely different insights and knowledge. But what is crucial is that in this specific situation, having this experience, she was prompted to think differently and to construct new meanings. This is the learning.

Before moving on I would like to return to the suggestion that Dora 'looks' and that her looking is made possible, because she 'knows a great thing very well'. In an earlier telling extract from the novel Dora comments scathingly on the 'poor visitors armed with guidebooks who were peering anxiously at the masterpieces' (Murdoch

2004 [1973]: 195). By using such language Murdoch appears to imply that viewing art is essentially an aesthetic experience capable of transforming spectators, but only those who are already knowledgeable and sympathetic. This has echoes of the view put forward in the early twentieth century by the British art critic Clive Bell and others who argued that viewers need neither specialist knowledge nor even familiarity with art in order to identify 'significant form' and be moved by it (Bell 1993 [1914]: 113). For Bell appreciation of art was projected as an innate gift, a 'sensibility', rather than an acquired ability. Just as Murdoch infers that those who do not have the expertise to 'look' are incapable of true understanding, for Bell (1993 [1914]) such cultural ignoramuses are 'deaf men at a concert. They know that they are in the presence of something great, but they lack the power of apprehending it' (ibid.). Both writers make a clear distinction between those who 'know' and those deficient in sensibility; who cannot know. Furthermore, by discrediting those visitors with guidebooks, arguably Murdoch implies that telling people what to look for is not the answer since, without knowing how to look, at best, these individuals will only ever 'peer'.

Yet there are differences between what Murdoch and Bell are suggesting. Whereas Bell argued that the appreciation of art is gifted to some who are inherently capable, without the need for specialist knowledge gained through particular education or experience, Murdoch makes clear that Dora has benefited from schooling in art and hence, 'knows' how to look at paintings. In some respects she is acknowledging what the French theorist Pierre Bourdieu has argued. In his study of French museums in the 1960s, Bourdieu identifies that comprehending works of art requires education and 'cultural capital', which is a form of class distinction more than an inherent gift (Bourdieu and Darbel 1997). Cultural capital represents an individual's accumulated knowledge of, and familiarity with, cultural practices and is acquired through the development of certain skills, attitudes and abilities and, above all, education. It is a person's degree of cultural capital that determines the extent to which they can make meaning from art. This is because, for all their physical accessibility, art objects remain out of reach of the unfamiliar viewer owing to the theoretical discourse that surrounds them.

In Dora's case she is possessed of significant cultural capital, hence is able to engage readily and deeply with the art. But as the novel shows, not everyone who enters the gallery is in a position to do this. It is here that many of the key questions confronting galleries are encapsulated. How can the institution provide for all its visitors, irrespective of their existing knowledge of art, with that same set of skills, knowledge and experience to afford them the opportunity for the revelatory learning experience that Dora has in the National Gallery? What happens when the museum seeks to work with those who do not feel confident in the learning context of the gallery, who do not come with the knowledge of art and who, indeed, consider that art has little or no relevance to their lives?

These questions raise yet more issues. In trying to support those for whom visiting the gallery and studying art is an unfamiliar experience, should the gallery revert to a more traditional approach, providing in the first instance information that will provide visitors with core knowledge from which they can start their explorations? And through seeking to include the visitor through the transmission of expertise, does it then provide a platform from which individuals begin to learn? Or does it start from a recognition of equality of 'intelligence' rather than 'knowledge' between learner and teacher. Here I am drawing on the understanding of these terms outlined by Jacques Rancière in 'The Ignorant Schoolmaster' (Rancière 2011 [1987]). Rancière introduces the term 'intelligence' to denote the equal aptitude and willingness to learn exhibited by students in relation to the teacher. In the specific pedagogic context Rancière describes, 'intelligence' is contrasted with the idea of 'knowledge' which is perceived to be held by the teacher and transferred to the student; this latter construction assuming an inequality between the more knowledgeable teacher and ignorant students. In contrast, Rancière's more egalitarian concept of 'intelligence' suggests that is it possible for teachers and learners to work towards a shared redistribution of knowledge and co-construction of meaning. Later in this text I will return to these questions, but prior to that let us consider the role played by the gallery context in learning.

The language used to describe the paintings and the gallery itself in *The Bell* brings to mind a contemplative, almost religious realm, where worshippers come to pay homage to great works of genius. Yet within this space Dora undergoes a significant and disruptive shift in her thinking. This suggests that the gallery can be a space where the familiar can become unfamiliar, where 'normal' views of experience are interrupted and transformed, because art objects have the capacity to destabilise conventional modes of thinking. Maxine Greene (1988) the veteran American philosopher and educator draws on Dewey's idea that experiences with artworks are distinct and separate. She recognises that art objects:

> When authentically attended to ... enable persons to hear and to see what they would not ordinarily hear and see, to offer visions of consonance and dissonance that are unfamiliar and indeed abnormal, to disclose the incomplete profiles of the world.

> (Greene 1988: 129)

Taking us back to the notion of 'real learning' as a process of moving from the familiar to the previously unfamiliar, one involving exploration and risk-taking and the generation of new knowledge, Greene's observation also implies that the gallery needs to provide a space where there is freedom for individuals to experience work in such a way as to make possible these leaps of understanding into the unknown. In such a gallery learners feel confident enough to become de-familiarised; they are able to feel comfortable not knowing. It is a space of potential that is open, non-judgemental, that permits new ontologies and does not introduce premature closures of meaning. She refers to this ideal pedagogic context as a place that permits 'speculative audacity', since here students can grasp the unpredictable event and follow its consequences through a series of inquiries, questions and decisions that bring about a new situation.

In contrast with this scenario is one where practices, discourses and rituals conspire to prohibit opportunities for such speculative audacity. In these circumstances rigid curricula and tightly managed assessment cultures, at times combined with entrenched behaviours, serve to deny learners the chance to experiment or often fail to support or validate students' new, but potentially destabilising, insights. Here the learner receives information that others have already identified as significant and success is judged according to the extent to which this knowledge is acquired, memorised and reproduced (Carnell and Lodge 2002). Potentially the modern and contemporary gallery, where meanings are not necessarily fixed and where the art itself is frequently concerned with speculation, should be the ideal space for unconstrained enquiry. Yet such museums are also the holders of valuable knowledge and expertise and for the majority of the twentieth century (and arguably into the twenty-first) galleries have understood their role to be primarily concerned with the accumulation, conservation and dispensation of this knowledge. It is only relatively recently that art institutions have acknowledged the need and value of engaging in more open, dialogic relations with visitors and co-constructing knowledge. It is within this still contested terrain, where institutional expertise confronts or comes together with visitors' knowledge and experiences that gallery learning programmes operate.

Looking at examples of programming involving young people, we can begin to understand how these tensions are addressed in practice. Alongside its provision for adults and schools and teachers, Tate Gallery has been a pioneer in developing programmes with and for young people aged between thirteen and twenty-five. With the intention of making art relevant and enjoyable for young people, Tate's Young People's Programme includes consultation, peer-led programming and peer-to-peer learning. Such programmes function outside of formal education (with the associated qualifications agenda) and aim to attract those who would not necessarily visit the gallery in order to enable them to 'create and acquire knowledge, related to culture and transferable skills' (Miller 2011: 1). Central to these programmes is the negotiation between the expertise and interests of the young people and the institutional discourse, since there is a recognition that, particularly with this demographic, there is a need to develop 'ways of working that relate directly to the lives of the young people, so they don't view art from the within prescribed paradigms of skill and practice, thus largely excluding themselves' (Atkinson 2011: 64). Consequently, projects make connections with exhibitions and displays and embrace multiple cultural practices beyond fine art (music, fashion, street art, digital technologies) in part to facilitate young people's engagement with works in the Collection and encourage the formation of their opinions and ideas in relevant and meaningful ways. The empowerment of the learner is uppermost; hence a key indicator of 'success' is the extent to which young people feel comfortable in the gallery and able to construct new knowledge for themselves.

As identified in the questions raised above, when working with those unfamiliar with art the relative positions of those functioning as teacher and those identified as learner can be redefined if learner 'intelligence', rather than 'knowledge', is foregrounded and the issue of institutional and participant equality is brought into sharp focus in these projects. Programmes which work toward empowering the learner attempt to move away from the model of the expert imparting information to the novice and aim instead to construct pedagogic environments whereby learner and teacher develop understanding through questioning, disruption and experimentation. The 'Youth Art Interchange' project (which involved young people at Tate Britain) sought to bring about a successful working method with a practising artist, in order to create methods or interventions which allowed for participation and creative development. The project was led by an artist, Raimi Gbadamosi, whose role was to enable young participants to develop a reflective process founded on critical thinking, whilst gaining knowledge and understanding on the theme of democracy. As he acknowledged, his relationship with the young people was grounded in a recognition of their skills: 'It was clear to me right from the start that all the young people were capable artists in their own right, and as a consequence my interest was in finding ways to pull all the evident skills together' (Gbadamosi quoted in Miller 2011: 12).

The project was constructed as a collaboration; therefore, rather than assuming an authoritarian role, Gbadamosi set about creating a permissive space for ideas and questions to materialise and dialogue to develop. The resulting installations and event in Tate Britain drew on works in the Gallery to examine hierarchies of power, social and cultural change and democratic representation, (visit http://young.tate.org.uk/events/late-tate-borders-and-territories).

What is not perhaps evident in this short description is quite how skilled this pedagogic process needs to be. For, as important as it is to recognise the 'intelligence' of the young people and to value their experience and expertise authentically, it is *as* crucial that the knowledge of the art institution and the educator is not denied. In his reflections on Youth Art Interchange, Gbadamosi acknowledges the value of the Tate Collection as a 'storehouse' of ideas that can challenge and inspire. He also recognises the responsibility he has as an artist to use his own knowledge to effect change with and for others. This suggests that he sees the danger of withholding expertise in order to avoid being perceived as patronising or overly didactic. Indeed, with youth-oriented projects there is a risk that in the drive to ensure participants are not alienated, the particularity of the art and the discourses surrounding it, as well as the knowledge and skills of the educator, are dissipated, if not rendered invisible. Or, as Frances Borzello (1995) has identified:

> So keen are we to show we are on the visitors' side that we play down that we have knowledge to impart. We want to launch the young visitors on a voyage of discovery, yet we are uncomfortable with the idea that to do this we have to pass on information from a position of authority.

> (Borzello 1995: 6)

So how then do those working in galleries negotiate between authority and authoritarianism? An answer lies in the scenarios outlined above; namely the specific learning context that allows for experimentation, risk-taking and speculation and the centrality of dialogue within the learning process. In effective learning programmes with young people, practitioners scaffold and sustain conversations, model thinking out loud, engage with higher-order questioning and give time for thinking and reflecting. At the same time, rather than ignoring the content of the works, the existing language of art and the institutional discourse, the challenge implicit in working with young people in the gallery is to make these explicit so as to foster learning from a position of equality. Gbadamosi and other artists working on such projects, attempt to celebrate, pull together, dismantle and redistribute knowledge, within a supportive environment, in order to develop participants' cultural capital. In other words, artist educators in the context of the gallery seek to equip each individual with the necessary intellectual and social tools for looking at works of art through deconstructing and co-constructing knowledge. Young people are not told what to think, but are supported to take intellectual and emotional risks, much as Dora is able to do.

Final thoughts – making the learning visible

Early in this chapter I drew attention to the continuing and arguably unresolved need to understand, capture and account for the benefits to young people of engaging with art. For despite the publication of numerous research projects and evaluation reports addressing learning in cultural institutions (for example, in addition to those texts referenced above, a significant amount of research has been conducted under the auspices of the 'Creative Partnerships' initiative (www.creative-partnerships.com) that addresses creative learning in schools and with galleries), our comprehension of the experience remains incomplete. Indeed, part of the attraction of examining the extract from *The Bell* is that it provides a rare example where the learning process and outcomes are clearly articulated. We see here how Dora is transformed by engaging with art and why this is helpful to her.

Yet Murdoch's novel also illuminates why these challenges exist, since the phrase 'without her thinking it had become obvious' and the earlier comment 'these thoughts, not clearly articulated' suggest that much of the learning for Dora is tacit. We the reader benefit, not from Dora articulating what her learning has been, but from the brilliance of Murdoch who describes it for her. Murdoch has the novelist's privilege of reading Dora's mind and the language to make visible what the experience has meant. The former scenario cannot exist for researchers and educators who are tasked with making visible what so often remains hidden. And herein lies the challenge, for although assumptions have been made in the past, increasingly there is a need for those involved with learning in galleries and elsewhere to move beyond inferences based on superficial evaluative statements to gain a richer understanding of the quality of the learning for young people. Or, to put this another way, in order to understand better the ways in which learning occurs and why young people gain in positive ways we need more than a comment by a young participant such as 'I really enjoyed my day' from which to deduce that the learning experience has transformed the individual. And although valuable insights can be gained from observations and third-party narratives, what is needed is for learners to have the language to describe their learning.

This focus on making the learning experience explicit suggests that galleries should enable, not only the skills to be able to engage with the art, but the language with which to articulate what that engagement has engendered. Projects need therefore to consider how to allow participants to focus, reflect on and describe their learning processes as well as content, both during and after the event. Through articulating what they have learnt, but also how and why, learners not only have a voice with which to represent their experience (rather than having it represented for them), but more importantly gain a richer conception of learning and a greater range of learning strategies which they can then apply in the future. Reflecting on the learning process (or 'meta-learning') enables participants to 'make sense' of the experience and to own it; they can review learning activities to assess what was effective for them and gain greater understanding of how and why they learn. In this way becoming familiar with the language of learning supports the young person's learning process, as well as aiding those who are seeking to capture and understand better what new insights are emerging.

Working in dialogic, collaborative and open ways, where learners are encouraged to share ideas and reflect critically through conversation, supports meta-learning. It is a relatively small additional step from encouraging young people to engage actively in constructing meaning and take responsibility for their learning to ensuring that they monitor and articulate the progress of their learning, either through dialogue with others or through writing it down. By doing this, gallery learning professionals can increase self-awareness amongst learners, which translates into greater confidence in negotiating the gallery and the displays. As noted by Bourdieu (Bourdieu and Darbel 1997), unfamiliarity with interpreting art can act as a barrier to cultural engagement, since artworks appear intimidating and impenetrable. But by becoming more conscious of learning strategies employed effectively, young people can become confident, active and strategic in the gallery, and gallery professionals can know more about the learning they hope to facilitate. Whilst not all young people might want to describe their experiences as Iris Murdoch portrays Dora's, through making learning explicit they can move from trance-like solipsism to greater speculative audacity.

References

Atkinson, D. (2011) *Art, Equality and Learning: Pedagogies against the State*, Rotterdam: Sense Publishers.

Bell, C. (1993 [1914]) 'The Aesthetic Hypothesis', in: C. Harrison and P. Wood (eds) *Art in Theory 1900–1990: An Anthology of Changing Ideas*, Oxford: Blackwell.

Borzello, F. (1995) 'Art Gallery Education: Have we Progressed?', *Journal of Education in Museums*, 16: 6–7.

Bourdieu, P. and Darbel, A. (1997) *The Love of Art: European Museums and their Public Culture*, Cambridge: Polity Press.

Burnham, R. and Kai Kee, E. (2011) *Teaching in the Art Museum: Interpretation as Experience*, Los Angeles, CA: The J. Paul Getty Museum.

Carnell, E. and Lodge, C. (2002) *Supporting Effective Learning*, London: Paul Chapman.

Greene, M. (1988) *The Dialectic of Freedom*, New York: Teachers College Press.

Miller, M. (2011) Unpublished evaluation of the Youth Art Interchange Project.

Mörsch, C. (ed.) (2009) *Documenta 12 Education II: Between Critical Practice and Visitor Services. Results of a Research Project*, Zurich: Diaphanes Press.

Murdoch, I. (2004 [1973]) *The Bell*, London: Vintage Books.

Pringle, E. (2011) 'The Artist, the Gallery, the Art and Learning: Negotiating Theory to Understand Practice', *engage*, 27 (June): 151–156.

Rancière, J. (2011 [1987]) 'The Ignorant Schoolmaster', in: F. Allen (ed.) *Education*, London: Whitechapel Gallery and MIT Press.

Chapter 9

Critical about design

Helen Charman

Design occupies a unique space amongst human activities. Located where culture and commerce intersect, design is the activity that connects what we need (the problem, gap or opportunity that inspires the designer), with what we make (the product or service the designer plans for), with how we experience and appreciate the world (the way the product looks, or the service works, and what its appearance means), with how we now live (the purchase and consumption of the product), with our impact on the world (the resources the product consumes).

Consequently, thinking about design can be a complicated process, one in which commercial, aesthetic, symbolic and environmental aspects all jostle for attention. Those who teach, study and practice design need to know what good design looks like, feels like, and does; they need to know how design has developed, and where it is heading. But there is more to understanding design than being able to hone a dove-tailed joint beautifully: they must also be able to stand back from the process, practice and product, to say: this is what 'design' *means*.

This ability to take a step back from design – intellectually and emotionally – and consider its wider context and question its role is at the heart of critical approaches to design. And in a world, which Design Museum director Deyan Sudjic describes as 'drowning in objects' (Sudjic 2009: 5), a critical approach to design should be an essential component of all design education. Such an approach enables students to develop a discourse or language around the category 'design' that will foster greater understanding of the subject. This chapter considers how people have written about these questions in the past, and at the new directions that writers and designers are taking in their approach to these questions in the last decade.

When thinking about design, we need to acknowledge that it is an inchoate field. As an attribute of almost everything in the material world, it eludes easy definition. Descriptions are many and varied, ranging from discrete forms of practice, processes and activities to characterisations and outcomes. For teachers of design in schools, the diversity of the field is reflected in the formal curricula that include design within both Art and design, and Design and technology. The separation of design across two different curriculum areas is not a clean divide. Textile design and graphic design feature in both subjects. Similarly, aspects of engineering, such as the design of levers and exploration of resistant materials, can be found in both the Science and Design and technology curricula. The point of this snapshot of design across the National

Curriculum is to illustrate its diffusive and ubiquitous character. At university level design practice further proliferates into (currently) fourteen different areas, increasing again if we include architecture and design history (see HESA codings for Design Studies at: http://www.hesa.ac.uk/dox/jacs/JACS_complete.pdf).

There are pragmatic reasons why art and design teachers, as much as design and technology teachers, need to be familiar with the multifarious and complex world of design. Numerous design industries which your students might wish to pursue in higher education and professionally, such as fashion and textiles, graphic design, web design, product design, exhibition design, interior design, jewellery, furniture design, architecture, glass and ceramics, film, photography and TV – and even automotive design – are located in the art and design sector, as illustrated in the recent response of the National Society for Education in Art and Design (NSEAD) to the 2011 Curriculum Review (www.nsead.org). Additionally, there is shared territory with the creativity which sits at the heart of design, even if and when it is used for more obviously utilitarian ends than might be found in art practice, as expressed in the 'Cox Review of Creativity in Business' (2005): '"Design" is what links creativity and innovation. It shapes ideas to become practical and attractive propositions for users or customers. Design may be described as creativity deployed to a specific end.'

Contemporary designer Martí Guixé makes an interesting provocation in the description of design as, usually … a problem-solving discipline and Art a trouble-making one. In both you are confronted with a situation where you react, solving or sabotaging. But you can solve sabotaging, and sabotage solving' (Guixé 2003: 14). What he means by this is that design, like art, has the capacity to problematise itself, and to come up with new questions and new ways to look at things. It can be propositional and conceptual, as well as a practical and experiential.

Yet despite the extent to which our lives are infused with and shaped by design, it is not a subject accorded much critical attention, certainly not when compared to fine art criticism. How many contemporary art critics can you call to mind (for example, people who write regularly for broadsheets, blogs or are featured on the radio)? Now try to think of the same number of design critics. Suffice to say, critical discourse and reflexivity about design is, at best, in its nascent stages, and certainly little more than a footnote to a design student's educational experience. The reasons for this are explored in Section II of this chapter. But first we need to formulate an understanding of what people who care about design say that design is; how they describe the activity of design, and how they draw a line around it to distinguish it from other activities, particularly fine art. This is the task of Section I. Having established some parameters for design as a category, Section II then introduces, in summary form, arguments for developing a more critical approach towards design than can currently be found, in product reviews, press releases, magazines and on blogs. The intention here is to map the contours of the debate and offer some provocations about the value of design criticism. Section III 'Critical practice' looks at examples of design that are self-aware, meaning that they ask questions about the role and meaning of design, and also at examples of design that 'rolls up its sleeves' and directly engages with the social, political and economic contexts of twenty-first century life and in doing so offers a critical perspective on design in today's complex world. In conclusion the role of the designer is briefly examined, and some suggestions are put forward for introducing critical approaches to design into classroom practice.

Section I: Disciplinary context – understanding design

Distinguishing design from related academic disciplines and professions, especially fine art, is not without its complexities and controversies. Most pertinently, with regard to the curricula context, design has a deeply ambiguous relationship to fine art. Boundaries are blurred and there is little consensus and much contestation about the distinctiveness of each discipline in relation to the other. However, design and art are not alone in this contestation. Mieke Bal's critical notes in 'The Discourse of the Museum' consider the arbitrariness of disciplinary boundaries, and the subsequent responsibility of the museum to exercise criticality towards its operations as a site of knowledge, one that discursively produces and defines such boundaries (Bal in Greenberg *et al.* 1996: 201). Nowhere is this more explicitly apparent than in the commercial world of the art market where a hybrid known as 'design art' has been growing as a principal force in the twenty-first century (although whether this is about design acquiring a newfound cultural currency or solely to do with commercial gain is a matter for debate beyond the focus of this chapter). While art and design have jostled one another over the centuries, the emergence of hybrid design practices into the physical and conceptual space of visual art, both through exhibitions and critical discourse, merits attention. This is particularly pertinent given the pairing of art and design within the national curriculum. On the one hand 'Design Art', exemplified in Marc Newson's *Lockheed Lounge* 1986, a work that was the first of this category to sell in excess of one million dollars, is steadily gaining commercial recognition in the art gallery context. On the other hand, 'Critical Design', such as the work of Dunne and Raby discussed in Section II, or that of political–social design activists kennard-phillipps, is defining itself as a form of design practice using languages of reflexivity and self-awareness more traditionally associated with modern and contemporary visual art. Seemingly, the relationship between art and design in the exhibition context is both contested and continuous.

While by no means the only way to address the breadth of writing about design, in this summary I locate design within three broad taxonomies. These taxonomies single out design history, design culture and design studies as ways to understand how design has emerged historically as a subject in its own right, ripe for critique.

Design history

Broadly speaking, design history focuses on single objects and the impact of creative individuals (McDermott 2007; Naylor 1990 [1971]; Pevsner 2005 [1936]; Sparke 2004 [1986]; Walker 1989). Design culture considers the impact of design as part of wider social interactions (Highmore 2009; Julier 2007) and design studies seeks to understand what it is that positions design as an activity apart from all other pursuits (Buchanan and Margolin 1995; Cross 1995; Shiner 2001). Each of these perspectives offers valuable disciplinary coordinates for understanding design.

The development of design history as an academic subject in its own right marks a key moment in the recognition of design as a distinct discipline. McDermott (2007) describes the formalisation of design history through a series of significant contributions both by individuals committed to the subject – in particular Sigfried Gideon (1888–1964), Nikolaus Pevsner (1902–1983) and Herbert Read (1893–1968) – and as a result of momentous changes in British art and design education in the 1960s and 70s. The inception of the Design History Society in Britain in 1977 and the launch in 1975 of the Open University's course 'The History of Modern Architecture and Design from 1890–1939' are noteworthy for setting design history apart from the history of decorative or applied arts, two subjects within which design history had been previously subsumed. However, the way they present design history through the work of a small number of significant individuals has its critics. For example, Judy Attfield (2007) critiques the provenance of design history through modernism as one within which women's contribution is absent, rendered silent, hidden and unformulated. Although design history could be studied as part of both art and architecture degrees, it was not until the Coldstream Report (1960) that the diploma for design was upgraded to a degree, (one-fifth of which comprised historical or contextual studies) and design history found its feet as a discrete field of study and entered the academy.

The relationship between design history and design practice at degree level has its own tensions (Russell 2002; Wood 2000). These continue to be debated today and are of direct import to the display of design in the gallery context, both in relation to framing design both as idea/process (creative, generative, iterative and commutative) and as object (aesthetic, formal, autonomous). The question of the credibility and status of studio practice in relation to academic research lies at the heart of the debate, concerning the extent to which the practice of design is required to demonstrate sound intellectual foundations, through design history, a subject for which pedagogical methods have set it apart from those of the design studio. While pedagogical methods for both design practice and design history continue to develop apace, the literature suggests that their differences are yet to be fully reconciled to the satisfaction of practitioners and academics.

Today, the intellectual base of design history is increasingly multidisciplinary, drawing on analytical methods from sociology, anthropology, geography and political economy and conversant with new histories of design such as women's studies and material culture. Alongside expanded readings of design history examining the role of design in society, the growing interest in design as an interdisciplinary field has given rise to a nascent new area of study, design culture (Forty 2005 [1992]).

Design culture

Design culture readily acknowledges its roots within design history and material culture. Just as readily, it critiques these subjects for what are regarded as significant shortfalls. Design culture critiques design history for overlooking the experience of everyday design and focusing on objects designed by key individuals. A further charge is levelled at how style and formal qualities are prioritised over process or social impact (Highmore 2009; Julier 2007). Although 'material culture' studies is recognised as redressing the balance by focusing on how consumers read and understand products, it too is criticised for focusing too exclusively on objects in the domestic context where the individuated consumer is privileged. Design culture negotiates between design history and material culture, exploring the range of human experiences (social, cultural, political, or economic) produced through networks of designers, designed objects, their intermediaries and consumers (Molotch 2003). This network is central to design culture and is perhaps its most ambitious characteristic:

> It extends design studies beyond the realm of goods (the products of industrial designers, fashion designers, architects and so on) and into the whole panoply of interconnections between the material and the immaterial, between humans and things, between the organic and the inorganic.
>
> (Highmore 2009: xiv)

The relevance of design culture to teaching design is in the explicit recognition of the rich interconnections between humans and the designed environment ('things'), for this is where meanings are formed and knowledge is generated. Put simply, design culture recognises that design is everywhere in the world, and affects everyone.

Design studies

Design culture is not alone in its attention to design-as-process. It complements developments in design studies (also known as design thinking and used interchangeably here). Design studies proposes design as a systematic discipline with principles and methods distinct from other related fields of knowledge (Archer 1979; Buchanan and Margolin 1995; Cross 1995). Most notably for critical approaches to design, which move the focus of discussion away from design's formal qualities to its broader contexts, Buchanan argues that the formal qualities of design are not simply about making things look good stylistically – although design historian Adrian Forty wryly observes that anyone reading design literature in the mid to late twentieth century would be forgiven for thinking so (2005 [1992]) – but where the creative and iterative design thinking process is revealed, 'expression does not clothe design thinking: it *is* design thinking in its most immediate manifestation' (Buchanan and Margolin 1995: 46). Therefore students need to develop their skills of looking at, reading and deconstructing design with the same visual attention they would an art work.

A second notable feature of design studies concerns the influence of social, institutional and intellectual changes on the formation of the discipline of design. Design thinking flourished in the twentieth century through a small but hugely significant number of institutions dedicated to design education, commencing with the establishment of the German Werkbund in 1907 and continuing in the Bauhaus School of Design in Weimer, Germany (1919–1933), under the direction of Walter Gropius, and thence to the New Bauhaus and to Ulm (Buchanan and Margolin 1995: 35–38, McDermott 2007). The extent to which design thinking can be regarded as a discreet discipline is an ongoing concern to scholars and practitioners of design today (Norman 2010). While pluralistic in nature, a common thread in Design Thinking revolves around the specific characteristic of design being distinguished by 'abductive' thought, that is, the concern not with how things are but with how they *might* be – what we might summarise as the essence of design's questioning approach.

The significance of reviewing the disciplinary contexts of design resides in an understanding of design as a distinctive discipline, which can be deconstructed through a critical language – a language as yet in its nascent form. In Section II we consider key arguments put forward for the value of developing a language of design criticism, and then in Section III introduce the field of design practice known as critical design.

Section II: Design criticism

What is design criticism? In its loosest sense design critics write about the works of designers, in the same way that art critics write about the works of artists. But current thinking about the state of design criticism today, as manifest in the majority of writing about design in blogs, magazines and exhibition reviews, is that it is too journalistic and promotional in flavour – that is, too related to design's commercial context and goals – to be genuinely critical. There is a chasm between academic writing about design and design's market context.

In 'Where are the Design Critics?' design critic Rick Poynor takes such journalistic criticism to task. He puts forward an alternative cultural criticism: an intellectual, historical, self-reflexive activity in which thinking and writing has a deep ideological purpose, is socially transformative, oppositional and often identified with the left (Poynor in Jeppsson 2010). Pulling focus to *design* criticism, Poynor goes on to offer a menu of key ingredients as follows:

- Design Criticism should take a critical view of design's instrumental uses, its wider social role, or lack of it.
- Design Criticism should engage with the political, economic and social contexts in which design is both produced and consumed.
- Design Criticism should be timely and relevant, because 'no one will care what critics say if their concerns don't capture something in the air'.
- Design Criticism should promote in-depth examination of particular design artefacts, images and experiences.
- Design Criticism should reveal the critic's personal position on design, manifest through the recurrence of key themes and concerns.

(Poynor in Jeppsson 2010: 54)

The key point here is that design criticism is not a neutral, objective endeavour but is writing about design that speaks from an engaged and personal position; there is an ethics to design criticism. In this regard, Poynor differentiates design journalism, which may indeed be critical or sceptical about design, from design criticism, which is defined by ideological intent. In such a differentiation, design journalism is so closely tied to the professional context of design that it more readily aligns itself with promotional rather than critical goals. As such, design journalism's default position is one embedded in its commercial environment and commensurate culture of consumption, one of capitalism's most obvious expressions (Poynor in Jeppsson 2010: 49).

Arguably, the paucity of writing about design as a serious subject for mainstream cultural analysis can be attributed to the dominance of commercial and utilitarian contexts for design. These override and crowd out the space for a more nuanced, complex and emotional understanding of design. This is not to say that such approaches are entirely absent, but rather that they occupy marginal territory in writing and thinking about design. Examples of such writing include: Roland Barthes *Mythologies* (1957) in which meanings attributed to everyday cultural phenomena including consumables such as soap powders and detergents are deconstructed; Jean Baudrillard's *The System of Objects* (1968), which focuses on consumerism and the construction of consumerist 'needs' as opposed to their innate existence; Csikszentmihalyi and Rochberg-Halton's *The Meaning of Things: Domestic Symbols and the Self* (1981), which explores the role of objects in people's self-understanding, concluding that people select objects in order to give meaning to their lives (Csikszentmihalyi and Rochberg-Halton 1981); Adrian Forty's *Objects of Desire* (2005 [1992]), which critiques design since 1750 as a socially value laden activity; and Deyan Sudjic's more recent publication *The Language of Things* (2009), which explores how design defines us – and why we seem to be 'inescapably in its grasp'. Sudjic notes that whereas the shelves are crowded and creaking under the weight of art criticism, there is space aplenty for similarly insightful writing about design. In this regard, Gareth Williams, Senior Tutor in Design Products at the Royal College of Arts, proffers the optimistic view when he claims: 'design thinking is beginning to be more and more critical of itself, in just the same way as art practice in the late nineteenth and twentieth centuries became pre-occupied with its own discourse' (Williams in Jeppsson 2010: 27).

What all of these texts share is the recognition that the meaning of a product extends far beyond its direct function, and this is where thinking critically and analytically about design finds its foothold. Max Bruinsma's 1995 lecture 'We Do Not Need New Forms, We Need a New Mentality' (Bruinsma in Jeppsson 2010) argues that behind function per se lie ethical questions with which the designer has to grapple, in addition to those of utility and aesthetics. For Bruinsma, these questions relate to the contexts in which the design artefact, service or experience will function. What are they, and within these contexts, what is the socially and morally desirable 'right use' for the design? In a world groaning under the weight of material culture, with yet more objects being designed, produced, consumed and discarded at a terrifying pace, Poynor's call for time-sensitive design criticism that is at once cognisant of, and situated within, the complexities of modern day life is directly and urgently relevant to teaching and understanding design today. One of those complexities that can be exploited to the advantage of a developing language of and readership for design criticism is web 2.0. Complementary to writing and publishing in print form, the interactive, democratic and collaborative space of web 2.0 offers emerging and established design critics a limitless platform for design writing and readership. Currently most design website and blogs are predominantly industry facing, but critically engaged sites such as www.designobserver.org offer spaces for design writers to explore, engage, experiment and evolve critical thinking about design.

Yet the difficulty for design criticism is that in critiquing the political, social and environmental contexts for design – which usually means challenging consumer lifestyles – it stands to bite the hand that feeds. One way of responding to this challenge has been for design practice itself to get critical, on the one hand through design which is *explicitly* described as Critical Design and on the other, through the growth of alternative design which is *implicitly* critical in its stance towards mainstream design for which it seeks to provide other possibilities. Section III presents two short case studies of each of these categories of design.

Section III: Critical design practice

Case study 1: The Placebo Project 2001, Dunne and Raby

'Critical design practice is rapidly reshaping design's conception of itself … it is removed from concerns of mass production and utility but exists to comment on the process of design production and consumption' (Williams in Jeppsson 2010: 27). Williams' definition of critical design suggests an area of design practice deeply at odds with itself – if, that is, we take a limited perspective on design as predicated on mass production and utility, with some stylistic charm to boot. Hopefully the preceding discussion on design criticism will have persuaded the reader that there is more to design than simply a judgement on whether it looks good/works well or vice versa – or an unhappy combination thereof. Sudjic (2012) argues that critical design has a history as long as industrialisation, commencing in the unlikely figure of William Morris. Acknowledging the difficulty of positioning Morris as a design revolutionary given the rare, high-end market for his hand-crafted wallpaper and furniture that only the wealthy could afford, and his preparedness to employ children whose small fingers could achieve the requisite level of fine detail in his weaving workshop, Sudjic suggests that by eschewing the industrial process of mass production and the moral void it created for the worker, Morris succeeded in problematising and politicising design's role in industrial production.

Contemporary designers Dunne and Raby continue in this problematising vein by using design as a medium to stimulate discussion and debate amongst designers, industry and the public about the social, cultural and ethical implications of existing and emerging technologies. Their projects include: 'Hertzian Tales' (2005), a combination of essays and design proposals exploring aesthetic and critical possibilities for electronic products that challenge design to engage with the social, cultural, and ethical implications of the technologies it makes so desirable; 'Placebo' (2004/2005), a collection of electronic objects exploring well-being in relation to domestic electromagnetic fields; 'Designs for Fragile Personalities in Anxious Times'; and 'Technological Dreams

Series: no.1, Robots' (2007). They define critical design practice as that which 'rejects how things are now as being the only possibility: it provides a critique of the prevailing situation through designs that embody alternative social, cultural, technical or economical values' (Dunne and Raby 2001: 58). This calls to mind Poynor's argument for design criticism as a form of oppositional practice that works against orthodox understandings of, and approaches towards, design. Such orthodoxies are termed 'affirmative design' by Dunne and Raby, a practice which 'reinforces how things are now' (ibid.). That Dunne and Raby's work is as likely to be found in the museum or gallery context as it is in the commercial design environment signals the potential of the museum to afford design a conceptual space for criticality, where questions of cultural value, meaning and interpretation can come to the fore. Teachers wishing to inculcate critical approaches to design would do well to embed visits to design exhibitions within their core curricula, not least because design curating is an emergent area of professional curatorial practice which, like design criticism, is currently evolving its own distinct languages and practices and can be as much a focus for critique as the design content of the exhibitions themselves.

The Placebo Project is a particularly interesting case study of critical design by virtue of its trans-disciplinary inflections, which interweave languages and strategies of conceptual art, formalism and artist intervention with design languages of prototyping, market research and end-user. Dunne and Raby describe the project as 'an experiment in taking conceptual design beyond the gallery into everyday life' (Dunne and Raby 2001: 75). They devised and made eight prototype objects with the aim of exploring peoples' attitudes to, and experiences of, electromagnetic fields in the home, describing how, once electronic objects enter people's homes, they develop,

> private lives, or at least ones that are hidden from human vision. Occasionally we catch a glimpse of this life when objects interfere with each other, or malfunction. Many people believe that mobile phones heat up their ears, or feel their skin tingle when they sit near a TV, and almost everyone has heard stories of people picking up radio broadcasts in their fillings. We are not interested in whether these stories are true or scientific, we are interested in the narratives people develop to explain and relate to electronic technologies, especially the invisible electromagnetic waves their electronic objects emit.
>
> (http://www.dunneandraby.co.uk/content/projects/70/0)

After a period of research, consultation and development with visitors as part of a residency at the Victoria and Albert Museum, these prototypes were then 'adopted' by volunteers who lived with them at home for a month, recording their experiences of living with the objects, before they were returned to the museum and exhibited as series of interventions in the twentieth-century galleries. Dunne and Raby describe the works as designed to elicit stories about the secret life of electronic objects – both factual and imagined. The works were purposely diagrammatic, based on furniture archetypes such as tables, chairs, ladders and lights, so as to be vaguely familiar in formal qualities, but with curious and surprising functions, so as to be 'open-ended

Figure 9.1 The GPS table, 2001, Dunne and Raby. (Photographer: Jason Evans)

enough to prompt stories, but not so open as to bewilder'. Examples of Placebo objects included 'the GPS table', at first glance an unremarkable domestic table but on closer investigation one with a small display set in the table-top, which revealed either the word 'lost', or its coordinates, depending on its location (Figure 9.1).

This display comprised a global positioning sensor that could only locate and indicate its position when able to receive a clear satellite reception, free from other forms of electromagnetic interference. The prevalence of other electronic objects in the domestic environment confounds the function of the GPS table, leading the designers to muse that 'people might feel a little cruel keeping it indoors' (Dunne and Raby 2001: 79), evoking the emotional relationship between people and objects referred to earlier in the work of Csikszentmihalyi and Rochberg-Halton, and the way that design decisions have the potential to shape behavioural and emotional responses.

When relocated to the twentieth-century gallery context at the Victoria and Albert Museum, the objects in the Placebo Project initiated formal and conceptual visual dialogues between the temporary and permanent objects, the contemporary and experimental, and the historical and traditional. For example, 'loft', a lead-clad box atop a ladder, which needed to be scaled in order to use it (Figure 9.2), shared formal qualities with the art deco furniture in the surrounding display, but its function as a safe place to store precious magnetic mementos such as answer phone messages, audio cassettes or floppy discs from potentially harmful electromagnetic fields set it apart, with the act of climbing the ladder described as part of a ritual to safeguard objects with personal value (Due 2003).

Figure 9.2 'Loft', 2001, Dunne and Raby. (Photographer: Jason Evans)

Other works in the piece included:

- Electro-draught excluder: Strategic positioning of this device helps deflect stray electromagnetic fields.
- Electricity drain: By sitting naked on a stool, accumulated electricity drains from the body into the chair then out of the house through the earth pin of a special plug.
- Nipple chair: Nodules embedded in the back of the chair vibrate when radiation passes through the sitter's upper body reminding them that electronic products extend beyond their visible limits.
- Parasite light: A light that feeds off the leaky radiation of household electronic products; it only works when placed in electromagnetic fields.

Figure 9.3 'Huggable Atomic Mushroom', 2004–2005, Dunne and Raby.
(Photographer: Francis Ware)

- Phone table: The mobile phone is given manners; the phone's ring is silenced when it is placed inside the drawer and instead, the table top gently glows green when the phone is called.

'Designs for Fragile Personalities in Anxious Times' (Dunne and Raby 2004/2005) included a soft, coral coloured cushion entitled 'Huggable Atomic Mushroom' (Figure 9.3). Impassively described on the website as 'for people afraid of nuclear annihilation … . Like treatments for phobias they allow for gradual exposure through different sizes', this piece is not, of course, designed to mitigate such anxiety. Rather, it makes a political point about design, evoking the more deadly uses design can be put to through conflating the comfortable world of domestic soft furnishings and children's oversized toys, with the menacing one of potential violence and the catastrophe of technological warfare.

Dunne and Raby's practice can be located within a critical design trajectory initiated by the design avant-garde that emerged amidst the politically unstable environment of Italy in the late 1960s in the work of design studios and collectives such as Archizoom Associati and Superstudio. In producing manifestos, articles and conceptual products, the Italian design avant-garde sought to critique the limitations of conventional design objects and to challenge, with wit and verve, the predominant mode of capitalist production, such that,

> design could become pure research, freed of the demands of production, or price or brand. Designers could stop listening to anything as tiresome as a brief, or a budget, or a marketing strategy, but instead get on with the altogether more congenial task of speculation and criticism.
>
> (Sudjic 2012)

An alternative to the predominantly conceptual approach of critical design, also termed 'anti design' or 'radical design' can be found in the field of design practice originally known as 'alternative design', but today more commonly identified as 'sustainable design'. Sustainable design not only shares critical design's aim of critiquing our relationship with design as it is engendered through the economic and commercial context of production and consumption, but also goes beyond that aim to effect changed and new design understanding and behaviours in the real world of design production and consumption.

Case study 2: Sustainable Futures at the Design Museum

Austrian-born design critic Victor Papanek opened his seminal text *Design for the Real World: Human Ecology and Social Change* (1972) by roundly and soundly criticising the designer's role in the production of consumer goods.

> There are professions more harmful than industrial design, but only a few of them ... by creating whole species of permanent garbage to clutter up the landscape, and by choosing materials and processes that pollute the air we breathe, designers have become a dangerous breed.
>
> (Papanek 1972: 3)

He went on to challenge designers to focus on social needs rather than consumer demand, for example by providing design solutions to the problems of education, people with disabilities and the developing world. Sustainable design, to use the more recent term to describe this field of practice, is an interesting case study for teachers wishing to introduce critical approaches to design in the classroom, because it is so obviously and directly rooted in the political, economic and social contexts that give rise to its production. As such it cannot help but provoke discussion.

In 2010 *Sustainable Futures* was presented at the Design Museum, London. This was a multidisciplinary exhibition that explored a range of products, concepts and projects addressing issues of sustainability in their design, including prototypes, samples, products, installations and film. Presented around five themes – Cities, Energy and Economics, Food, Materiality and Creative Citizens – the exhibition also cast light upon the changing role of the designer. Charles Eames is famously quoted to have said that the designer should be the perfect dinner party host, 'all of whose energy goes into trying to anticipate the needs of his guests' (online at: http://www.bustler. net/index.php/event/eames_designs_the_guest-host_relationship/). Sustainable design extends this notion by bringing a more participatory flavour to the table: the guests all bring a dish with them, preferably of the organic, locally sourced variety. This notion sees co-dependency as the most important factor. In the professional world of the designer, co-dependency plays out across a variety of contexts, including consumer psychology, environmental sustainability and networked communities of practice. Summarily put, sustainable design asks that the consumer change their behaviour, and consumers of sustainable design willingly participate in this change.

The *Sustainable Futures* exhibition, curated by Nina Due, Head of Exhibitions at the Design Museum, in consultation with MA students following Kingston University's Sustainable Development course and a panel of design sustainability experts, included exhibits that ranged from a model for the world's first carbon neutral city to PUMA's 'Clever Little Bag', designed by Fuseproject under the creative direction of designer Yves Behar. 'Clever Little Bag' does not conform to the status quo of shoebox packaging. Rather, it is designed to reshape itself within its commercial context. Fuseproject describes it as an innovative new approach to shoeboxes designed to radically reduce PUMA's carbon footprint, recalling the term 'radical design' discussed above. Sustainable design focuses on reducing the impact of design on the real world. The production and discarding of shoeboxes, even when secondary usages are taken into account, results in millions of tons of waste annually. 'Staggering' was how the exhibition text described the amount of resource that goes into packaging a single pair of trainers. Thinking both literally and metaphorically outside the box, Fuseproject discarded the idea of the shoebox entirely and instead designed a bag. This bag uses 65 per cent less cardboard than the standard shoe box, has no laminated printing, no tissue paper, takes up less space and weighs less in shipping, and replaces the plastic retail bag. The stated figures propose that the 'Clever Little Bag' will reduce water, energy and diesel consumption on the manufacturing level alone by more than 60 per cent a year: approximately 8,500 tons less paper consumed, 20 million megajoules of electricity saved, 1 million litres less fuel oil used and 1 million litres of water conserved. During transport 500,000 litres of diesel will be saved and by replacing traditional shopping bags the difference in weight will save almost 275 tons of plastic (http://www.fuseproject.com/products-47). Such arguments also translate into a canny marketing strategy, recalling the opening definition of design as at the intersection of culture and commerce.

Behar is a passionate advocate for sustainable design and can be heard speaking on the subject in a podcast at http://designmuseum.org/exhibitions/2010/sustainable-futures. He also designed 'One Laptop Per Child' (OLPC), an ambitious project imagined by Nicolas Negroponte with the aim to provide 150 million of the world's poorest, undereducated children with a laptop costing no more than $100 each, purchasable by governments, charities and world organisations. The OLPC project is about making social advances in bringing technology and education to children in areas of severe poverty, rather than advances in computing or technology. By designing a laptop for a completely new market — one where there is no feasible profit – OLPC also radically rethinks the purpose, role and impact of design. See www.designmuseum.org/discoverdesign.

Conclusion

In 2007 the Design Council's annual conference, entitled *Intersections*, brought together leading thinkers in design to explore how design is evolving and how this evolution affects its relationship with other fields of creative and business practice. The conference also highlighted the changing role and identity of the designer as part of today's rapidly moving and complex world. Four prospective identities emerged through the conference papers and debates. The first, 'Designer as Strategist', sees the designer emerge from the micro level of addressing a particular design problem in business to being increasingly involved in the bigger picture of design innovation in its social and environmental context, a touchstone for 'the what and why of innovation, and not just the how' (Myerson 2007: 6). The designer as strategist introduces a way of practising design which proactively and urgently engages with social and environmental concerns. The second identity, 'Designer as Co-creator' is part of a shift from the design silo (where designers work on a single specialist area of design) to the network, expressed in multidisciplinary and collaborative professional practice. The third identity, 'Designer as Rationalist' challenges the idea of the designer as strategist by arguing that designers are refocusing their attention on real technological solutions irrespective of their wider real-world contexts (this was the most controversial of the propositions). Finally, the 'Designer as Storyteller' proposes a role for designers in the urban realm in which the opportunities for convergence between communication media and architecture (be it buildings, public spaces or exhibitions) are realised.

In thinking critically about design, and providing opportunities for students to do likewise, the notion of the designer as storyteller is apt. What stories do the practice and consumption of design tell us about ourselves, about our society, about our values and priorities? Where do teachers and students place themselves in those stories? How do they locate themselves in the expansive field of design which is constantly redefining itself? The intention of this chapter has been to map out some recent thinking and debates on critical approaches to design and to introduce the practice of critical design. In conclusion some ideas for introducing and nurturing a critical approach to design in the classroom are offered below:

- foster opportunities for students to talk and write regularly about design, for example by reviewing an exhibition or using a particular design work to initiate discussion; this is essential in order that students develop their own critical voice and start to work out their design preferences and values;
- encourage students to read the design press, for example, magazines such as Blueprint, exhibition reviews, and blogs such as Design Observer (www. designobserver.com);

- develop students' research skills as a formative aspect of their design practice, for example, by keeping research logs for their own design practice, including contextual material informing their work;
- create a design library in your classroom, or see if you can organise borrowing rights from local university library.

Being critical about design means being self-aware, and reflecting on individual attitudes and responsibilities as inhabitants of a designed world. Objects do not have implicit meanings but acquire them through use and impact. Not every student will progress to pursue a career in the design profession, but all are inhabitants in, and consumers of, the designed world. As such, the need to develop a critical sensibility towards design is inarguable. The time to be Critical about Design is now.

References

Archer, B. (1979) 'Design as a Discipline', *Design Studies*, 1 (1): 17–20.

Attfield, J. (2007) *Bringing Modernity Home: Writings on Popular Design and Material Culture Studies in Design*, Manchester: Manchester University Press.

Bal, M. (1996) 'The Discourse of the Museum', in: R. Greenberg, B.W. Ferguson and S. Nairne (eds) *Thinking about Exhibitions*, London: Routledge.

Barthes, R. (1957) *Mythologies*, Trans. A. Lavers and C. Smith (edn 1990), London: Jonathan Cape and New York: Hill & Wang.

Baudrillard, J. (2005 [1968]) *The System of Objects*, London: Verso.

Buchanan, R. and Margolin, V. (1995) *Discovering Design*, Chicago, IL: Chicago University Press.

Coldstream, W. (1960) *First Report of the National Advisory Council on Art Education*, London: HMSO.

'Cox Review of Creativity in Business' (2005) London: Her Majesty's Treasury.

Cross, N. (1995) 'Discovering Design Ability', in: R. Buchanan and V. Margolin (eds) *Discovering Design*, Chicago, IL: Chicago University Press.

Csikszentmihalyi, M. and Rochberg-Halton, E. (1981) *The Meaning of Things: Domestic Symbols and the Self*, Cambridge: Cambridge University Press.

Due, N. (2003) 'Critical Attitudes in Design', unpublished MA dissertation, Kingston University.

Dunne, A. and Raby, F. (2001) *Design Noir: The Secret Life of Electronic Objects*, Berlin: Birkhauser.

Forty, A. (2005 [1992]) *Objects of Desire: Design and Society since 1750*, London: Thames & Hudson.

Guixe, M. (2003) 'What is design? Questions and Answers', in: E. Annike and I. Schwartz (eds) *Bright Minds, Beautiful Ideas*, Amsterdam: BIS Publishers.

Highmore, B. (2009) *The Design Culture Reader*, London: Routledge.

Jeppsson, F. (ed.) (2010) *In Case of Design – Inject Critical Thinking,* Stockholm: Jeppsson.

Julier, G. (2007) *The Culture of Design*, 2nd edn, London: Sage.

McDermott, C. (2007) *Design: The Key Concepts*, London: Routledge.

Molotch, H. (2003) *Where Stuff Comes From*, London: Routledge.

Myerson, J. (2007) 'Are Design Schools the New Business Schools?', Design Council Intersections Conference 2007. Online. Available at: http://www.designcouncil.org.uk/resources-and-events/Designers/Intersections-071/Intersections07/Design-schools/ (accessed 30 January 2012).

Naylor, G. (ed.) (1990 [1971]) *William Morris by Himself: Designs and Writings*, Boston, MA: Little, Brown & Company.

Norman, E. (2010) 'The Silent "D"', *Design and Technology Education*, 15 (2): 3–5.

NSEAD (National Society for Education in Art and Design) (2011) 'Art and Design Teacher Survey #2'. Online. Available at: http://www.nsead.org/Downloads/EBac_Survey2.pdf (accessed 15 July 2011).

Papanek, V. (1972) *Design for the Real World: Human Ecology and Social Change*, New York: Pantheon.

Pevsner, N. (2005 [1936]) *Pioneers of Modern Design: From William Morris to Walter Gropius*, London: Yale University Press.

Russell, K. (2002) 'Why the Culture of Academic Rigour Matters to Design Research: Or, Putting your Foot into the Same Mouth Twice', *Working Papers in Art and Design* (2).

Shiner, L. (2001) *The Invention of Art: A Cultural History*, London: University of Chicago Press.

Sparke, P. (2004 [1986]) *An Introduction to Design and Culture*, 2nd edn, London: Routledge.

Sudjic, D. (2009) *The Language of Things: Design, Luxury, Fashion, Art: How We Are Seduced by the Objects Around Us*, London: Penguin Books.

Sudjic, D. (2012 forthcoming) *A to Z of Design*, publisher yet to be confirmed.

Walker, J. (1989) *Design History and the History of Design*, London: Pluto Press.

Wood, J. (2000) 'The Culture of Academic Rigour: Does Design Research Really Need it?', *Design Journal*, 3 (1): 44–57.

Part IV

Debates in-between

Chapter 10

Art practice as a form of research in art education

Towards a teaching artist practice

Panagiotis Dafiotis

Introduction

All too often art teachers in schools find that their art practice falls away as the demands of teaching take over from their own creative practice. But is this separation inevitable? In this chapter I examine the ways in which, what I call, the 'teaching artist' might prevent this disjunction by crossing the borders between art and art education. What I propose here is a hybrid field in which the hierarchical distinctions, for example between teacher and learner, word and image, are questioned and the voices of students legitimised.

I present here the educational research I developed for my doctorate which was premised on a symbiosis of art practice and theoretical investigation. This practice comprised a series of installations encompassing a relational dimension (Bourriaud 2002; Kester 2004), a relationality that I wish to ally with education. In 2009, I co-authored an installation, ('Tunnel Vision'), with a small group of sixth-form students which became a hub, a relational space where the participants could intervene physically, interact, discuss, and hold sessions. I envisaged it as a stimulating environment aimed at producing relations. In this sense, its artistic as well as its educational essence was located in the interactions and discussions it provoked rather than its visual impact. From this I developed a further installation, 'The Benevolent Trap' (2010) which I offer up as an instance of practice. I do so not as a blueprint but as a possible source of inspiration and encouragement for fellow practitioners. The approaches that emerged during its construction may prove pertinent for teaching as well as helpful for educational investigations.

At this point, I invite the reader to visit the website: www.practiceledresearch.com where a visual account parallel to this chapter can be found. This will not merely give access to illustrative material; it will help the reader to gain insights into how the arguments for this chapter are embodied within, as well as advanced, through art practice. In addition, it is an ongoing, participatory site, which aims to promote practice-led methodologies.

From art teachers to teaching artists

Encouraging educational exchanges through arts methods in secondary schools is a quest conditioned by the ambiguity of the 'teaching artist' persona. I use the term 'teaching artists' to differentiate between art teachers, and artist teachers who come from an arts background. Teaching artists predominantly rely on heuristic, that is, discovery-based paradigms of creating, as well as communicating, knowledge. While their artistic background calls for open-ended approaches, which draw upon the affective potential of art, the reality of a secondary school gravitates towards conformity with institutional expectations and habituated practices (Bourdieu 1977). Therefore, teaching artists often perform their newly gained pedagogised identities against the grain, thereby pathologising themselves in the process (Atkinson 2003: 189).

In my experience, as for many art teachers who initially trained as artists, art education in secondary schools was an unwelcoming place. Art education, as practised, presented a set of historically sedimented skill-based procedures hinged upon a somewhat vague curriculum that continuously frustrated the novice. On the one hand, the new teacher was expected to navigate the curriculum's uneven borders and, on the other, to conform to a prescriptive school culture imbued with perfunctory exchanges. On top of that, the unfavourable status of art education within the hierarchy of secondary-school subjects increased the pressure on the teaching artist who had to defend and assert his/her position.

Within contemporary culture, the relationship between art and learning is often related to art's capacity to unsettle and provoke critical and reflexive thinking (Van Alphen 1992; Crowther 1993). The lack of a workable framework to encourage reflexive thinking (through making) in secondary art education becomes more detrimental within an uncritical, target-orientated and increasingly instrumentalist school culture (Usher and Edwards1994; Abbs 2003). Artists often embark on secondary education oblivious to the realities and complex demands of their task, clinging to their artistry and tending to downplay, or even deny, the educational dimension of their professional identity. This imbalance between the two elements makes it even more difficult to construct a new, hybrid 'teacher-artist' identity (Addison and Burgess 2005).

The fact that art teachers in Europe commonly hold a degree in fine arts from a university has, nevertheless, its implications: the hard-won skills over a period of four or five years of intensive study cannot be sidestepped without consequences. The knowledge about the manipulation of materials, the critical skills gained, and all the more, the *way* these competencies have been acquired, are not dispensable. An educational framework, hinging on the ways artists learn through reflexive practice facilitating in turn others to learn, is by no means nation-specific. My experience of the Greek context can easily be extrapolated to much of the 'so-called' Western world and perhaps beyond. I propose that by engaging in practice-led research, art teachers can move towards becoming teaching artists, a process that will enable them to sustain their art practice while simultaneously developing pedagogic knowledge.

Art practice as educational research

The discussion about practice-led research projects in the visual arts (see Macleod and Holdridge 2006; Holly and Smith 2008) is mirrored in the field of art education, in which new possibilities for doing research are tentatively explored (Eisner 1974; 1998; Sullivan 2005; 2008; Cole and Knowles 2008). Arts-led methods seem increasingly to appeal as a form of art education research by offering an alternative to standard social research methodologies:

A common call heard across email listserves, in conference corridors, within seminar sessions and among an increasing number of graduate students, is to question how it is that studio art has become so estranged from art education research.

(Baxter *et al.* 2008: 4)

The main characteristic of practice-led research is that it does not argue about something, rather it realises it. The strength of such a method is that it 'brings to life'; it presents a new possibility within secondary art education. I do not imply by this that social research methodologies, which are dominant in educational research, are inferior to practice-led ones. However, within the field of art education, there is scope in affording forms of practice-led research, especially when it is based on emergent methodologies, improvisation and reflexive approaches. For many artists, and increasingly educators, it is the work of Gilles Deleuze that has offered up ways to reconceptualise, or possibly reconfigure practice, so as to recognise the way art works. I want to look briefly at aspects of his thinking to suggest how art teachers might fruitfully adopt his approaches.

Art education as a hybrid space

For Deleuze (2003 [1981]) philosophy proper is about the invention of concepts, but according to him, one may think without using concepts; for example artists can think using visual configurations. He argues that philosophical thinking not only necessitates the employment of concepts, but should ideally engender them. However, he credits twentieth-century artists with being more advanced in comparison to their theorist 'counterparts' in 'creating concepts' by investigating the premises on which representation is based (Deleuze 2003 [1981]). This indicates the ability of 'sensation' and affect to provide insights into how representation and meaning making work. Artists seem to be better positioned in comparison to theorists, as they tap into what Bourdieu (1990) calls 'embodied knowledge' in his *Logic of Practice* or what Polanyi (1964) names 'tacit knowledge'. Deleuze (2003 [1981]) suggests that '... philosophers still have much to learn from painters'. In his introduction to the book on Bacon by Deleuze (Deleuze 2003 [1981]) Smith quotes Bacon himself claiming that 'painting is its own language and is not translatable into words'. Teaching artists are expected to talk or teach art through language, but is it not possible to teach art through art and 'its own language'? Although this very question might appear a futile exercise in word gaming, it is premised on the idea that art and language form a 'rhizome' or a 'fold' in Deleuze's terms (Deleuze 1993).

'Rhizome' and 'fold' are not interchangeable terms. However, they both underline the interconnectedness of things/domains, which, according to Deleuze, are artificially segregated and in reality form an inseparable continuum, a 'rhizome'. 'Fold' as a term, conveys that the differentiation between inner and outer is equally arbitrary; what is outside of something 'folds' into it, (e.g. what education, or art for the same matter, address, embody, perpetuate/rupture, is not in reality outside them).

I therefore make a case for art education as a triadic fold (Deleuze 1993), collapsing together different modes, different voices in dialogue, and finally different fields: namely, art practice and educational theory. The first 'fold' is to use the modalities of the self-contained artwork with those of artistic installation (e.g. drawings, written texts, constructions, animations, sound), a compound of modalities where none is privileged. The second fold pertains to dialogic and participatory strategies. It is premised on the impossibility of working in isolation when researching dialogue and negotiated meaning making, processes that invariably underpin education. The two above-mentioned folds are inextricably linked, as any form of dialogue as well as communication is essentially multimodal (Kress and Van Leeuwen 2001). The third fold regards theory and art as symbiotic, conceptual categories that gain meaning only in relation to each 'other'. Art and theory draw upon each other in order to develop. Theory about art and the theoretical discussion that art embodies form a continuum; art is not formed in a vacuum. Art can be the visualisation of a specific intellectual–conceptual context, one that it can embody and even reshape. In the same vein, arts-led methods in art education necessarily draw on relevant theory.

In practice-led research, the relationship between the written text and the visual element is a contested point: does the text accompany, interpret, describe, enrich, or complement the artworks produced? My favoured approach is a symbiotic relation between text and image or, for the same matter, theory and art. Theoria as discussed by Nicholas Davey (in Macleod and Holdridge 2006) provides a pertinent vehicle: 'Theoria opposes the theoretical overdetermination of art practice and resists any theoretical under-determination of art' (p. 25). Davey enunciates that 'If the roots of modern theory are traced back to the ancient Greek conception of theoria (contemplation) and theoros (participant), a path to rearticulating theory as a mode of participation in practice is opened' (p. 23). The notion of the engaged participant becomes central to this conception. Unlike Davey I will not suggest a specific scheme, a possible fusion between practice and theory by means of argumentation, but by creating dialogic and participatory installation artworks.

Instances of practice-led research

'Tunnel Vision'

In 2009 I ventured to use one of my installations as a learning resource, or in other words as a 'context provider' for educational exchanges inviting four sixth-form London-based students to work with me in one of the University art studios. Initially I created an installation (see Figures 10.1 and 10.2), albeit an incomplete one, in order to trigger responses to it and create an environment that was intended to be informal, ambiguous and stimulating at the same time. Students were 'briefed' to avoid thinking of their artworks as objects to be shown in an 'exhibition' but rather constitutive of the space-as-installation. The way students understood the loosely broached topic ('ways of seeing and the impact of technology'), and the way they put to use their skills and semiotic resources, resulted in an assemblage, turning the 'classroom' itself into an installation artwork.

Figure 10.1 'Tunnel Vision', 2009 (detail). (Photographer: Peter Thomas)

In one characteristic instance, a participant's use of video installations was a departure from his usual practice which had been exclusively two-dimensional. The 'call' to the third dimension, to engage with different methods seems to have opened up not only a modal possibility but, all the more, an opportunity to convey thoughts for which the skills that he had at his disposal (i.e. basic drawing skills) were not adequate or relevant.

Within the four designated days contributions were hybridised, reconfigured, negotiated. During the last stages, I took more liberties by making and altering (having gained the participants' permission to do so), not in an effort to embellish or make the installation comply to certain aesthetic criteria, but as a further elaboration on the educational exchanges that took place in that space. My intervention was an effort to use their configurations as a canvas on which I inscribed my understanding of the whole event along with the issues it raised, becoming part of it and hopefully amplifying it.

In one of the student contributions, the crudeness of the construction, along with its garish colours, suggested 'another example' of school art, but also of poor craftsmanship. This otherwise playful (but arduously made) construction could be seen as a direct comment on schooling, as it eschewed the neatness of 'well made' school art. In my response to it, nevertheless, I 'sought recourse' to the rather crass act of diluting its visual impact. This instance of intrusive 'curating' was undeniably a demonstration of power relations. A lesson was learned by me here, and I tried to avoid such impingements during the next collaborative installation.

The limitations of dialogical 'critical' educational practice have been analysed by Burbules (in Trifonas 2000) and invariably involve the paradox of dialogue as a power-related encounter with invested 'modes of address' (Ellsworth 1997). That is to say, dialogue depends on the ways it is being framed, while even 'radical' or critical pedagogies are not immune to becoming prescriptive if not coercive, all the rhetoric notwithstanding.

Figure 10.2 'Tunnel Vision', 2009 (detail). (Photographer: Peter Thomas)

'The Benevolent Trap'

> The question is not: is it true? But: does it work? What new thoughts does it make possible to think? What new emotions does it make it possible to feel? What new sensations and perceptions does it open to the body?
>
> (Massumi 1992: 8)

The installation, 'The Benevolent Trap' (May 2010) marked a turn towards relational aesthetics (Figure 10.3). It became a hub where postgraduate students from several departments converged and held discussions, exchanged opinions or simply spent time. Initially this space had been envisaged as a hybrid between a relational artwork and a collaborative installation, viewers being encouraged to intervene, reconfigure the space and give new directions to the project. As the installation progressed over a period of four weeks, it became a relational space. The accumulation of visual texts instigated numerous conversations within an environment which functioned as a 'discussion machine'. It was an undecidable space inviting participants to revisit methods, roles, and thereby, think on their subjectivities. In this perplexing but also convivial space, participants made their own connections. They often left a mark, either by means of making or by conversing.

Several discussions took place within this ambivalent space, which simply would not have happened elsewhere. There was a widespread sense amongst the users of the space that 'The Benevolent Trap' provided and embodied physically, conceptually and institutionally a place where things happened differently. As an unclassifiable, yet thought-provoking and emotionally 'charged' space, it left open the question of

Figure 10.3 'The Benevolent Trap', 2010. (Photographer: Peter Thomas)

whether it was a happening, a prototype, an installation/relational artwork – or all of these at the same time.

'The Benevolent Trap' was conceived as a hybrid and ambiguous space where art and education meet halfway. It occupies a middle ground, the 'volatile space' to paraphrase Ellsworth (1997) between the modalities employed by artists and those used by educators. In this project, an environment was created which took the form of a 'crossbreed' between an art classroom, a snug living room and an art installation. The space was designed to function as a place for learning about art, while it was also envisaged as a space for informal, relational encounters and dialogue, and last, but not least, it was intended to retain its function as artwork, that is enabling and inciting thoughts and interactions vis-à-vis the encounter with a stimulating and multimodal art installation.

From the outset it is obvious that these different aspects do overlap, interpenetrate, and fold into each other. Such a space functions as an inviting, unconventional spatiotemporal context to facilitate relational exchanges, thus falling under 'the purview' of relational aesthetics (Bourriaud 2002). In her discussion of Deleuze's thinking about architecture, Grosz conceptualises buildings as texts, which 'do things, perform connections, bring about new alignments' (cited in Davies and Gannon 2009: 133). 'Classrooms are thus places which ideally should be open to their outside, where outside is not understood only as an outer space but also, and more importantly, as what is different, unassimilable, and as yet unthought' (ibid.).

The space of 'The Benevolent Trap' is reminiscent of a 'model classroom' or an experimental setting. To a certain extent it was set up as an experiment, not in the sense of designing a controlled environment in order to observe how it works, but in the sense that it was an improvisation which – through making – leads to new sensations, new alignments and connections between participants. As it was a

Figure 10.4 The wall of 'The Benevolent Trap', 2010. (Photographer: Nicholas Addison)

co-authored (and not interactive) space, my role was that of setting the stage for what would follow without knowing what that would be exactly. After the initial launch of the installation it took on a life of its own, people responding to each other's interventions usually in a non-synchronous way. Therefore, my role became that of one amongst regulators, curators, authors of an ever-evolving space. The input of participants took unpredictable turns, eliciting responses that would not have been conceivable without it, moving the entire installation towards new directions. For example, one participant wove a thread through the cardboard walls. The use of thread running throughout or stitching elements together was developed and appropriated by others, mutating into other uses for the material, serving different, albeit interconnected ideas.

The installation's multifaceted nature ensured that most participants/visitors found some resonance with their own areas of interest:

> A learning space that follows Reggio Emilia principles is multisensory 'not so much in the sense of being simply rich in stimuli but having different sensory values so that each individual can tune into his or her own personal reception characteristics' (Ceppi and Zini 1998: n.p.) An unstimulating classroom is a place where no energy is generated. The alchemy of new ideas that may have seemed possible outside the room, may not survive the room itself.
>
> (Davies and Gannon 2009: 135)

This multimodal assemblage did not only function by means of juxtaposition but also through 'in depth' relations, it also incorporated layers of meaning, an aggregate of references and allusions. The entire space was saturated by instances/assemblages pointing to a specific area for dialogue varying from methodological or aesthetic issues, to contentious socio-political topics (Figure 10.4). It could be said that these dialogues were generated around perceived (un)truths.

Badiou (2005) quotes Lacan who 'expressed in his famous aphorism from *Seminar XXIII*: Truth cannot be said "whole". It can only be half-said [*mi-dite*]'(p. 23). He goes on to say: 'The mystery is, strictly speaking, that every poetic truth leaves at its own centre what it does not have the power to bring into presence' (ibid.). Perhaps what the poetic truth does is precisely break down what an incontestable truth is, turning it into an aporia. Enigmatic half-truths can be more affective, provocative and therefore effective in generating thinking and making. 'The Benevolent Trap' is a constellation of truths half told, of allegories rather than contentions. The participants are invited to 'put the pieces together' in a rather Sisyphean task that, nevertheless, entices them to revisit their personal truths.

Creating relational spaces of affect: implications of 'The Benevolent Trap' for future practice

> What might become possible and thinkable if we were to take pedagogy to be sensational? What if as educators, we began to consider pedagogy to be a time and space designed to assemble 'with the bodies [of learners] in a web of inter-relational flows in material ways' …
>
> (Ellsworth 2005: 24)

I will recount a little instance, a moment of intensity within 'The Benevolent Trap' which captures the ambiguity and potentiality of its unfolding. A tiny canvas perched on a window sill (see Figure 10.5) incited in me a constellation of thoughts catalysed through sensation: The depicted figure's gaze was vague; inwards as much as addressing the viewer's own gaze. Matter, colour, contours dissolved, as if the white background of the canvas interpenetrated with the 'inner substance' of the painted figure. The sunlight also seeped through the canvas, intensifying the effect of dissolving, becoming part of it, making it hard to look at. This artwork conveyed the impossibility of self-contained objects or subjects; it alluded to how inner and outer fold into each other.

This painting spoke from a middle point where 'neither inner or outer reality impose itself on the other', (Ellsworth 2005: 55) it spoke from the only place where thought can confront us: 'from a created outside, which in turn opens up space for what is not yet here' (ibid.). Semetsky (2006: 59) explains that what is said and how it is said converge in the 'middle' creating a new idiom, a highly expressive, passionate language, an 'intensive and affective logic of the included middle' (Bosteels 1998: 151, cited by Semetsky 2006). The positioning of the canvas (perched on a windowsill) was a decision which is part of the artwork, the way the little canvas works with its environment makes clear that there are no clear-cut limits between the artwork (canvas) and the installation/environment. It is a performed thought; or in Bourdieu's terms, 'a mode of thought that works by making explicit the work of thought' (1990: 91).

Observation is a movement from sensation to cognition, one based on language which captures the sensuous and contains it in the stratified space of language. However, the visual, the affective, the artistic, is exactly that which is beyond cognition.

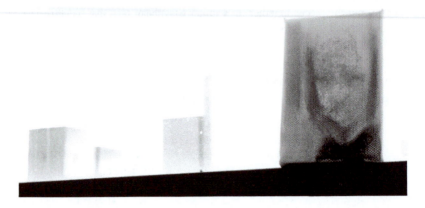

Figure 10.5 Detail from 'The Benevolent Trap', 2010. (Photographer: Panagiotis Dafiotis)

> The very possibility of thought is predicated upon our opportunities and capacities to encounter the limits of thinking and knowing and to engage with what cannot, solely through cognition, be known. Aesthetic practices and experiences provoke precisely such engagements and to the extent that they are provocative of thought, they are crucial to understanding pedagogy.
>
> (Ellsworth 2005: 25)

In order to 'encounter the limits of thought' and keep 'the loop open' to unforeseen possibilities, Ellsworth (2005) promotes the idea of creating places as hubs where affects, relations, encounters circulate and provoke hitherto unforeseeable assemblages of feeling and thinking. The idea of place making as central for an art education rethought and redesigned as a relational form of art is also promoted by Davies and Gannon (2009), marking a turn to new reconceptualisations of the porous relationship between the relational, the aesthetic and the pedagogical.

Affect can foster reflexive thinking on what underpins subjectivity vis-à-vis the encounter with the 'other' (be that a person, an artwork/object, or a 'heterogeneous system' comprised of both). As Addison (2011) puts it in an article exploring affective strategies employed in art education:

> Affect comes on us unannounced. It enters from without (from others, the environment) and does things to us. At the same time it is a force through which we

impact others: our presence, energies and actions attract attention and elicit responses.

(Addison 2011: 365)

Setting the scene for pedagogical exchanges in (or as) classroom spaces, which aim to address 'our images of subjectivity and otherness' might encompass an element of encounter or of witnessing as Zembylas puts it,

> Massumi and Deleuze's attention to affect gestures to the political and ethical consequences that our images of subjectivity and otherness have produced at particular moments in the classroom. We are asked to consider, for example, how teachers and students can create classroom spaces that enable productive critical and pedagogical scenes of witnessing while foregrounding the ungovernability of affects.
>
> (Zembylas 2006: 314)

This environment is both made and a maker, both a window to another world of 'a possible art education' and a window towards this world of given ways of pedagogy, knowledge production and cultural reproduction. It is a created environment, but also an environment which functions as a laboratory for generating other possibilities in art education.

Jewitt (in Edwards *et al.* 2009) explains that the physical space of a classroom is not 'other' to the ideological space, as they are mutually reinforced and conditioned as such. Classrooms are 'complex signs' therefore (p. 101), which convey and foster the pedagogical paradigm which underpins the pedagogical exchanges taking place in them. Acknowledging the potential of these complex signs to condition what happens in them is the first step towards reconceptualising, and redesigning these spaces. As Ellsworth (2005) posits, 'for pedagogy to put us in relation to that outside – for pedagogy to put us in relation to thinking – it must create spaces in which to think without already knowing what we should think (p. 54). For her 'the paradox of designing pedagogy as a hinge to an open future' (ibid.), is related precisely to the unpredictability of the effects of those spaces where the content of education is not determined, where 'systems of reason' move 'beyond their systematicity' (ibid.). But for her, as for me, throwing the baby of 'what could emerge' out with the bathwater of unpredictability is too high a price to pay.

Conclusion: towards a teaching artist practice

Education is not an abstraction, but an activity of subjects who have their own ways of learning, teaching and communicating. Likewise, teaching artists cannot do away with the activities of their making practice. As is the case with visual arts, teaching artists can turn classrooms and art lessons into idiosyncratic and subjective, semiotic 'microcosms', which nevertheless, relate to 'the bigger picture'. Rather than self-referential exercises in style, these microcosms introduce new ways of perceiving, new sensations, new questions and possibilities.

Away from the modernist cult of the essential expressive self, or the Derridean postmodern perception of the subject as a mutation within the semiotic nexus of language, I perceive the subject(ive) as a redemptive in-betweenness. This conceptualisation of subjectivity as something that occupies paradoxically the middle ground between the self and the other perceives subjectivity as a process of becoming (Deleuze and Guattari 1988), based on interactions with others.

> [A]n ethics and politics of affect of the kind inspired by Deleuze can forge a critical politics of affect that involves the explicit mobilization of affect to produce new understandings of social interactions. This is precisely why Deleuze's nonsubjective approach breaks down the self/Other dichotomy and sets in motion a practice of relational politics.
>
> (Zembylas 2006: 312)

What I argue here is that subjectivities are formed in the space between subjects and, all the more, what happens in this in-between space is precisely a stage where subjectivity is performed and reformed. However, this space is not only conceptual or metaphorical, but also physical. The environment in which subjectivities are mutually contaminated is never neutral, it can be laden with affective stimuli or characterised with their near-total absence, which is again an affective condition. As environments interfere with the inter-subjective relations, they become inscribed in these exchanges, they are not mere backgrounds but in a sense, active, subject-like factors which can be in turn reshaped by the very subjects which they influence. In a sense the classroom, the affective mechanisms, and the participants become parts of a seemingly heterogeneous system (Fox in Edwards *et al.* 2009). In this system nevertheless, the limits amongst people as well as between the users of a space and the space itself are porous. New understandings of social interactions and, all the more, subjectivities as precisely constitutive of social interactions, need affect to be mobilised. The development which these interactions and negotiated meanings comprise cannot take place in an emotional vacuum.

> Following a Deleuzian analysis of affects as immanent forces that produce creativity, novelty, and transformation, students' and teachers' bodies may be understood as the plane of immanence for any pedagogy; without affects, there is no pedagogy.
>
> (Zembylas 2006: 312)

This entire research project is a conscious effort to be a grounded, applicable and documented inquiry into alternative methods to inform teaching artists' practices. At the same time it is percolated by deeply personal agendas dictated by unconscious processes. It is 'working in between at least two interpretative registers: the conscious and the unconscious' as Morra (in Holly and Smith 2008) puts it. As Massumi (2002) claims: 'The personal is not intentionally prefigured. It is rhythmically re-fused??? in a way that always brings something new and unexpected into the loop. The loop is always strangely open' (p. 191).

Investing in the ambiguous and the personal is antithetical to promulgating a generalisable model for arts-led research methodology. I can only present this trajectory of installations and the ways they have allowed me to think education by making and, all the more, offering up these spaces to participants who in turn, experience this other way of thinking art education. Instead of a representation of how learning in art education can happen, this is a presentation of how learning did happen through creating, experiencing, and sharing bodily-inscribed sensations, movements, thoughts-in-action.

> If philosophers of education are bilingual, it is not by mixing, intermingling or bridging the languages of the disciplines into a comprehensible discourse which educators can understand and perhaps join; it is by creating an unformed philosophical expression which in pedagogy's encounter with philosophical ideas sustains a field of experimentation, a field that is non-translatable against the barren rationality of representationalism.
>
> (Gregoriou in Semetsky 2008: 107)

These installations present a parallel possibility for an in-between, middle ground where art and education meet to rethink their aims, methods and desires. This enquiry does not happen *in* these environments, but *by* these environments:

> Indeed, naturalistic inquiry is open-ended, it grows like Deleuze's rhizome and is based on 'the logical ... connected with the biological in the process of continuous development' (Dewey 1938: 25). As an active process, 'it does not live in an environment; it lives by means of an environment ... [and] in every *differentiation* of structure the environment expands' (Dewey 1938: 25; italics my emphasis).
>
> (Semetsky 2006: 74)

'The Benevolent Trap' (as well as its predecessors) is a 'prototype' of a model classroom-turned-artwork aimed at facilitating thinking/making in dialogue, a process which concurrently alters its own fabric. It invites a practice involving its own appropriation and development by others. This is its function and intention: to generate ideas, reformulations, and above all, relations as fulcrums for advancement. Were (2010: 267–272) delineates the nature and significance of the prototype as a nexus of relations, ideas and intentions which functions as agent:

> One of the crucial issues raised by prototypes is how they present us with the capacity to generate variation. ... For Gell [1998], artefacts are agents capable of acting in ways analogous to persons through their facility to engender social relations. They are designed with complex intentionalities in mind, so much so that the design of an artefact cannot exist in isolation; rather, Gell argues that an artefact encompasses a set of ideas that are carried through the various possible forms it can take on.
>
> (Were 2010: 267–272)

The temporality of the prototype is ambiguous: it encapsulates the preceding instances of practice, while it points to its own future modifications. In effect it functions as the agent that will bring these advancements about, by providing itself as the platform for their realisation.

'The Benevolent Trap' is not destined to function as an apparatus of capture. Deleuze and Guattari (1988) describe such apparatuses as intricate devices set up by state power in the form of institutions, discourses, establishments to 'bog down', to diminish the mobility of uncontrolled forces, external to the system. 'The Benevolent Trap' is an apparatus set to capture by means of affective, perplexing and uncanny devices. Its sole purpose is to release 'lines of flight', to open art education as art, to the unknowable and uncontrollable future modifications by other teaching artists. The sedimented knowledge of artistic skills functions as the trap's memory as well as a springboard for future advancements. As Were (2010: 267–272) puts it:

> [F]or Gell, [1998] an artefact appears to enchain all possible derivations of itself, of the past and of the future, so we are able to see the totality of forms as a cognitive process, a 'movement of thought, a movement of memory reaching down into the past and a movement of aspiration, probing towards an unrealized, and perhaps unrealizable futurity'.
>
> (Were 2010: 258)

Preziosi (1999: 120–136) explains that according to the given paradigms in art history, artwork is (in what he calls) a pantographic manner, a form of indexical trace, or synecdoche which has a relationship of part to whole, with the larger socio-cultural discourses that condition it. This conception or scheme relegates artworks to a spectral status. The return of the artwork, to appropriate a cliché here, is precisely premised on the rematerialisation of the art piece. That is to say, I conceive the artwork not as a representation of a larger discursive formation (saturated and comprised by language) but as a presentation of what eschews it, what creates lines of flight from it. Namely, the artwork is a presentation of personal spaces, of imagined and materialised possibilities. Using art practice is a method of actualisation, which invests in the potential of art to generate meaning, to redefine meaning and therefore to create knowledge. This practice-led research foregrounds a teaching artist who creates the conditions for relational encounters as facilitator and participant. It presents an itinerary to those who imagine art education in similar ways.

One could say that 'The Benevolent Trap' was incomplete, that it needed the presence of the author (or of a participant) to explain to its visitors what 'this is about'. However, this was part of its function: it was not envisaged as an environment for solitary contemplation, as in front of artwork, but a space that needed (in fact incited) explanations, discussions and dialogue as part of its fabric. Its 'incompleteness' invited the negotiation of meaning through conversations and often physical interventions. This space comprised an instance of practice in which teaching artists' background in visual arts is pivotal for the function of a hybrid art/education.

References

Abbs, P. (2003) *Against the Flow: The Arts, Postmodern Culture and Education*, London: Routledge Falmer.

Addison, N. (2011) 'Moments of Intensity: Affect and the Making and Teaching of Art', *International Journal of Art and Design Education*, 30 (3): 363–378.

Addison, N. and Burgess, L. (2005) 'The Friendly Interventionist: Reflections on the Relationship between Critical Practice and Artist/Teachers in Secondary Schools', in: D. Atkinson and P. Dash (eds) *Social and Critical Practices in Art Education*, London: Trentham Books.

Atkinson, D. (2003) 'Forming Teaching Identities in Initial Teacher Education', in: N. Addison and L. Burgess (eds) *Issues in Art and Design Teaching*, London: Routledge Falmer.

Badiou, A. (2005) *Handbook of Inaesthetics*, Stanford, CA: Stanford University Press.

Baxter, K., López, H.O., Serig, D. and Sullivan G. (2008) 'The Necessity of Studio Art as a Site and Source for Dissertation Research', *International Journal of Art and Design Education*, 27 (1): 4–18.

Bosteels, B. (1998) 'From Text to Territory: Felix Guattari's Cartographies of the Unconscious', in: E. Kaufman and K.J. Heller (eds) *Deleuze and Guattari: New Mappings in Politics, Philosophy, and Culture*, Minneapolis, MN: University of Minnesota Press.

Bourdieu, P. (1977) *Reproduction in Education, Society and Culture*, London: Sage.

Bourdieu, P. (1990) *The Logic of Practice*, Cambridge: Polity Press.

Bourriaud, N. (2002) *Relational Aesthetics*, Trans. S. Pleasance and F. Woods, Dijon: Presses du Réel.

Ceppi, G. and Zini, M. (eds) (1998) *Children, Spaces, Relations: Meta-Project for an Environment for Young Children*, Reggio Emilia, Italy: Reggio Children.

Cole, A.L. and Knowles, J.G. (eds) (2008) *Handbook of the Arts in Qualitative Research*, London: Sage.

Crowther, P. (1993) *Critical Aesthetics and Postmodernism*, New York: Oxford University Press.

Davies, B. and Gannon, S. (eds) (2009) *Pedagogical Encounters*, New York: Peter Lang.

Deleuze, G. (1993) *The Fold: Leibniz and the Baroque*, London: Athlone Press.

Deleuze, G. (2003 [1981]) *Francis Bacon: The Logic of Sensation*, Trans. D.W. Smith, London: Continuum.

Deleuze, G. and Guattari, F. (1988) *A Thousand Plateaus: Capitalism and Schizophrenia*, London: Athlone Press.

Dewey, J. (1938) *Logic: The Theory of Inquiry*, New York: Henry Halt and Company.

Edwards, R., Biesta, G. and Thorpe, M. (eds) (2009) *Rethinking Contexts for Learning and Teaching: Communities, Activities and Networks*, London: Routledge.

Eisner, E. (1974) 'Is the Artist in the School Programme Really Effective?', *Art Education*, 27 (7): 12–19.

Eisner, E. (1998) *The Kind of Schools we Need*, Portsmouth, NH: Heinemann.

Ellsworth, E. (1997) *Teaching Positions: Difference, Pedagogy, and the Power of Address*, New York: Teachers College, Columbia University.

Ellsworth, E. (2005) *Places of Learning: Media Architecture Pedagogy*, New York: Routledge.

Gell, A. (1998) *Art and Agency: An Anthropological Theory*, Oxford: Clarendon Press.

Holly, M.A. and Smith, M. (eds) (2008) *What is Research in the Visual Arts? Obsession, Archive, Encounter*, New Haven, CT: Yale University Press.

Kester, G.H. (2004) *Conversation Pieces: Community and Communication in Modern Art*, Berkeley, CA: University of California Press.

Kress, G. and van Leeuwen, T. (2001) *Multimodal Discourse: The Modes and Media of Contemporary Communication*, London: Arnold.

Macleod, K. and Holdridge, L. (eds) (2006) *Thinking Through Art: Reflections on Art as Research*, New York: Routledge.

Massumi, B. (1992) *A User's Guide to Capitalism and Schizophrenia: Deviations from Deleuze and Guattari*, Cambridge, MA: MIT Press.

Massumi, B. (2002) *Parables for the Virtual: Movement, Affect, Sensation*, Durham, NC: Duke University Press.

Polanyi, M. (1964) *Personal Knowledge*, New York: Harper & Row.

Preziosi, D. (1999) 'The Crystalline Veil and the Phallomorphic Imaginary: Walter Benjamin's Pantographic Riegl', in: A. Coles (ed.) *The Optic of Walter Benjamin*, London: Black Dog Publishing.

Semetsky, I. (2006) *Deleuze, Education and Becoming*, Rotterdam: Sense Publishers.

Semetsky, I. (ed.) (2008) *Nomadic Education: Variations on a Theme by Deleuze and Guattari*, Rotterdam: Sense Publishers.

Sullivan, G. (2005) *Art Practice as Research: Inquiry in the Visual Arts*, Thousand Oaks, CA: Sage.

Sullivan, G. (2008) 'Methodological Dilemmas and the Possibility of Interpretation', *Working Papers in Art and Design*, 5. Online. Available at: http://sitem.herts.ac.uk/artdes_research/papers/wpades/vol5 (accessed 1 May 2010).

Trifonas, P. (ed.) (2000) *Revolutionary Pedagogies*, London: Routledge.

Usher, R. and Edwards, R. (1994) *Postmodernism and Education*, London: Routledge.

Van Alphen, E. (1992) *Francis Bacon and the Loss of Self*, London: Reaktion Books.

Were, G. (2010) 'Editorial', *Visual Communication*, 9 (3): 267–272.

Zembylas, M. (2006) 'Witnessing in the Classroom: The Ethics and Politics of Affect', *Educational Theory*, 56 (3): 305–324. Online. Available at: http://onlinelibrary.wiley.com/doi/10.1111/j.1741-5446.2006.00228.x/pdf (accessed 10 October 2010).

Chapter 11

Art, academe and the language of knowledge

Claire Robins

> Speaking recently with my nine-year-old son's class teacher, an issue of concern that was raised was his persistent habit of drawing – in his literacy book. For the teacher this was not acceptable. She reminded him that he should only produce pictures where they are appropriate, or asked for; although recognising the pleasure he found in this activity, she issued him with a separate book, of unlined paper, to draw in. Like many children of his age, the neat distinction between text and image, apparently frustrates his need to articulate his thoughts.
>
> (Smith: 2007)

In this chapter I pursue the effects for knowledge, pedagogy and learning of practice-led research in art and design education. I examine how postgraduate students of art, design and museology at the Institute of Education, University of London, explore and critically engage with the implications of art as a situated research practice. In particular, I foreground the complexities and antinomies surrounding methodology when students negotiate the practice of making in a studio context that encourages them to analyse their subject identities as teachers/lecturers, students, artists, academics and researchers. The expectation of academe and the position which language (written, spoken and visual) occupies is central to the formation of these identities, negotiations and dialogues. I will demonstrate, through discussion of work produced by students, that the traditional division between engagements with art making as a 'sensory experience' and with reading, writing and research as 'rational activities', presents a false dichotomy that needs to be reappraised in the debates surrounding practice-led research and its potential for pedagogy.

Over the last two decades there have been heated discussions and a plethora of publications about art practice and its relationship to the dominant research culture in mainstream higher education (Candlin 2001; Macleod and Holdridge 2006; Elkins 2008; Mason 2008; Sullivan 2008). In the United Kingdom practice-based doctorates were introduced into art universities (formerly art schools and colleges) in the 1990s; however, the desirability and viability of art as an *assessable* research practice remains a topic for debate. Some deliberations echo those from the 1960s and 1970s when the Coldstream Report paved the way for diplomas in Art and Design (1960) and Bachelor of Arts (1974). These standardised qualifications brought requirements for written/theoretical components, which were seen, by some, to be pressing art too deeply into an academic mould. Other discussions have focused on the integrity of art practice and art education in a knowledge-based economy, which has shifted expectations of how research and knowledge will be used (Pierce 2009; Rogoff 2010). The Bologna Process (1999) (see http://ec.europa.eu/education/policies/educ/bologna/bologna.pdf) has also loomed large in many debates (Roelstraete 2010). Twenty-nine European countries signed up to the Bologna Declaration (1999) with an intention to make European higher education more compatible and comparable. However, its mechanisms for regulating and standardising academic qualifications and its homogenising tendencies can be seen to have little regard for the creative importance of art's ostensibly aberrant *modus operandi*. In contradistinction, promises of legitimacy, recognition and parity for a discipline which has resided in the margins of the higher education framework have been welcomed by many commentators (Frayling 1999; Sullivan 2005) who also hold that an acknowledgment of art's contribution to the field of knowledge is long overdue.

Simultaneously, in older established universities, cautious interest in alternative research paradigms has been quietly burgeoning. Typically, these institutions have held art at a distance; as a subject for historical and theoretical study. Whilst as a practice it has been viewed as a pleasing but unsystematic 'other' to the ostensibly rigorous research concerns of (even the newer) academic disciplines. More specifically, the field of educational research, which for many years has been dominated by social science methodologies (Cohen *et al.* 2011), has witnessed a broadening of approach, not only to acknowledge the influence of multimodality and e-learning on the nature of research but also to reflect a diminution of the certainty implied by dominant modernist meta-narratives. Unsettling the old assurances of knowledge has increasingly led to greater scrutiny of accepted scientific method within and across disciplines (a three-century legacy, of the dual influences of Cartesian logic, and Baconian empiricism) and thereby questioning of its reliance solely on empirical or measurable evidence. When phenomena such as reflexivity and transdisciplinarity and heterogeneity emerge and are theorised into the field of epistemology so too the structure and concept of knowledge changes (Gibbons *et al.* 1994; Holert 2009).

Research and knowledge has to be useful for communities, individuals and situations. Particular circumstance will necessitate different approaches to research and definitions of what counts as knowledge. Wilkins (2011) points to the importance of local knowledge which gives agency to educators and enables practitioner researchers to desist from adopting unquestioningly something that someone else has labelled 'best practice'. This is something that has been argued for some time and, as Eraut (1994) has outlined, also necessitates that universities rethink their role in enabling the research processes of professionals.

> The barriers to practice-centred knowledge creation and development ... are most likely to be overcome if higher education is prepared to extend its role from that of creator and transmitter of generalizable knowledge to that of the enhancing and the knowledge creation capacities of individuals and professional communities.

This would involve acknowledging that much knowledge creation takes place outside the higher education system, but is nevertheless limited by the absence of appropriate support structures and the prevailing action orientation of practical contexts.

(Eraut 1994: 57)

According to Kress (2010), not only is educational research faced with 'the unsettling and negation of canonical forms – of genres, for instance – but also of the means of representation: image is displacing word. Process(es) and practic(es) are the focus of attention'. Practices that embrace visuality and embodiment are becoming ever more germane and potent for bringing into focus and enabling new understandings of particular educational phenomena. The research potential of art practice in education has been predicated on an understanding that such interdisciplinary approaches and mixed methodologies can be creative models for producing new insights (Eisner 1998, 2004; Prentice 2000; Hickman 2007; Holert 2009). Eisner, in particular, opines what he sees as an ironic situation in which 'qualities as fundamental and powerful as those that constitute art have been so neglected in research methodology' (1998: 154). It may be that an intransigent interpretation of both art and methodology are amongst the root causes for this neglect in certain sectors of academe. This is particularly relevant in the more general field of education where art is often interpreted as a practice that bears little resemblance to its contemporary manifestations and concerns (Downing and Watson 2004; Leitch 2006).

In reality, contemporary artists are well placed, as Sullivan (2005) notes, to adopt many patterns 'that dislodge discipline boundaries, media conventions, and political interests, yet still manage to operate within a realm of cultural discourse as creator, critic, theorist, teacher, activist and archivist' (p. 225). Sullivan's observations are increasingly manifest in the profiles of artist educators who choose to engage in Masters and Doctoral level research in art education. Operating from these positions appears seamless and unproblematic in Sullivan's depiction, but in fact many artist educators experience tensions and do not find universal recognition of the benefit of supporting a mix of subject identities. Moreover, the specifics of institutional expectation and authority can lead individuals to feel as if they are being pulled in different directions. Students embarking on research propositions in art education that draw on practice-led approaches often find themselves negotiating a 'dual dialogue', as Biggs (2006a: 191) points out, they must answer to 'two sets of regulatory authority', conforming to the regulatory expectations of methodologies that still dominate academe and to the expectations of the 'art world' (see Danto 1964) where amongst other qualities the poetic, ambiguous, creative, and imaginative are revered.

Accredited continuing professional development (CPD), in the form of Masters and Doctoral programmes that acknowledge and encourage practice-led research, offers a creative and intellectual space where the institutional disjunction between multiple modes of making and meaning making is recognised as a subject for enquiry. In this chapter, I draw in particular on the work of students following the 'Learning and Teaching' module of the Institute of Education's MA in Art and Design Education.

This module, which I lead, invites students to develop innovative approaches to academic research. It is guided by a belief in the importance of subject-specific professional development for investigating issues in art and design pedagogy. Such an approach provides an alternative to the temporal linearity of devising research questions, collecting data and subsequent report writing that might commonly be expected in academe. By situating creative practice as a key component for research it acknowledges the relevance of students' prior knowledge and experience and allows for continuity. One MA student, Marina Castelo-Branco reflects as follows:

> In all subjects across education, there are orders and classifications, which led me to reflect on the way that information is ordered and displayed to convey and transfer knowledge. ... I had to break away from a linear way of thinking; shake things up and then allow the pieces to be re-arranged revealing a new path, structure and way of understanding. ... I had to order, then disorder to see anew and then re-order again.
>
> (Castelo-Branco 2009)

Forsaking a literal, linear form for a series of interdependent, embodied actions, Castelo-Branco follows 'a circular form akin to a hermeneutic process where the issues to be explored and transformed are not necessarily determined prior to the research design but rather emerge from the dialogue between artistic and pedagogic practice' (Prentice 2000: 528). Or it could be imagined as a more organic or rhizomatic trajectory. Deleuze and Guattari (1988) use the term 'rhizome' in contradistinction to 'aborescent' to define different approaches to research and knowledge. The aborescent model as its name suggests follows a vertical linear, tree-like form with binaries and bifurcations. The rhizome, on the other hand, is like the root of an iris; without a clear point of origin, or predictable direction it spreads along a plane mingling with the roots of others that intersect it in an organic way. These particular ways of working allow Castelo-Branco to reflect on the processes of play and the role that pleasure occupies in learning in art and design. She credits the place of practice as essential to her understanding. At the start of the module she categorised and photographed hundreds of marbles from a personal collection (a typically anthropological project), but by the end she had produced a mesmeric film of marbles colliding randomly, shot at a low angle and accompanied by a soundtrack of the collisions played out of sync with the visuals.

> I began recording the sounds that the marbles produce whilst moving across wooden floorboards and their movements. Instead of separating the different kinds and groups of marbles I played with them, colliding them and allowing interaction with each other and different environments.
>
> (Castelo-Branco 2009)

Sound became a compelling element of the study, alongside a desire to bring in the sensation of a viewpoint, achieved by lying on the floor. This was a distinct remove from the distanced overview involved in her initial orderings and documentation of the small glass entities. Knowing and understanding through embodied experience is central to what Castelo-Branco describes. 'My research into learning and teaching in art and design was opened up through engagement with art and design practice. Without having undergone practice based research I would not have arrived at my current line of thinking' (Castelo-Branco 2009).

Learning through practice in art and design can be intense and absorbing when there is little separating cognition from bodily experience. Crowther (1993) elaborates such an interconnectedness of mind and body as a process that allows meaning to be felt. He references Merleau-Ponty's *Phenomenology of Perception* (2002 [1945]) to argue that meaning in symbolic formations becomes stabilised through embodiment. Crowther's point is that even prior to language there is being in the world, feeling, seeing, moving, etc., through which the vectors of difference (as articulated by Derrida whereby 'whether in the order of spoken or written discourse no element can function as a sign without referring to another element which is not simply present' cited in Crowther 1993: 28) are experienced prior to their articulation in language. The body and embodied experiences are, for Merleau-Ponty, what make consciousness possible. Bourdieu's reflexive sociology also draws selectively on Merleau-Ponty, particularly in its refusal to separate out from the discursive what Bourdieu (in Bourdieu and Darbel 1997) terms 'bodily hexis'. The latter 'is political mythology realised, *embodied*, turned into a permanent disposition, a durable way of standing, speaking, walking, and thereby of feeling and thinking' (p. 70). As Waquant describes, 'Bourdieu treats the socialised body as the repository of generative, creative capacity to under-stand, as the bearer of a form of kinetic knowledge' (Bourdieu and Waquant 1992: 20). Encounters leave their trace not so much in the form of mental pictures or memory images but as what Merleau-Ponty refers to as 'carnal formulae', structuring devices encompassing all the sensations and experiences of the subject. How we act, move, speak, and make, draws this sediment of past to present. Merleau-Ponty extends his theory of embodiment to include language, which also acts to sediment 'carnal for-mulae', allowing them to be projected when the things that gave rise to them are no longer present. And, as Danvers elucidates 'the visual/spatial arts constitute other particularly effective ways of projecting carnal formulae (Danvers 2006: 148–149).

When given the opportunity to demonstrate how understanding about learning and teaching in art and design can develop through a critical engagement with art practice, it is noteworthy how many students choose to explore both the authority that is given to the word in education and the sometimes problematic place of language in relation to practice-led research.

In an early description of her thoughts, Jo Evans writes: '[t]he module begins with reading and talking and ends with writing. In between all these words is the making' (Evans 2006). In this initial description making appears to be sandwiched between aural and written communication, but, in fact, Evans's making practice only momen-tarily ceased from interactions and manipulations of word-based texts (Figure 11.1). Like many others, Evans initially makes a distinction, not just between reading/writing and the study/production of objects and images, but between different approaches to working with words. Her reflections are not uncommon, the sensuousness of the word

Figure 11.1 Jo Evans, MA student. (Photographer: Peter Thomas)

and the rationality of making are often passed over by students who have become inured of the attributions that typically accompany modes of acting and explaining.

Starting from an investigation on using her own artwork as a learning resource, Evans began to investigate the influence this work had on the primary school pupils she was teaching. Her concerns were centred on the contextual dynamic of power within the classroom. She was looking for a way to find a balance where students were able to move from applicative modes (repeating her schemata) of use, towards interpretive modes (moving beyond exemplars) (Eraut 1994: 48). In her studio work she began to make reference to models of symbiotic relationships, derived from science and specifically animal and plant biology, in order to find useful metaphors, images and descriptions. In plotting scientific terms and diagrams as a continuum from 'mutualism' to 'parasitism' she began to imaginatively 'draw' out the implications of her own role as a teacher. She writes:

> As I folded and turned this object many connections were drawn in my mind, between my process of making artwork and my process of teaching. Through this activity I began to explore through making: aspects of the teacher/student relationship; of collaboration or influence; and of the role of making in art and design teaching.
>
> (Evans 2006: 4)

The direction that Evan's work took reflects a process taking place between making, reading, talking, teaching, learning and writing and re-making. The language she used as part of her 'making' was similarly embedded in the creative process. It was used in the development of ideas, as much for the pleasure of its 'otherness', its potential for suggestion, poetic association and ambiguity, as for its relation to the immediate rational construction of an educational argument. Towards the end of the module she writes:

> At the start I assumed that I would represent ideas about art and design education through visual means. By the close I have come to understand that it is not simply a case of translating language into image or object, but that in the process of making art, meaning is made that can go beyond what can be constructed and articulated through written or spoken language.
>
> (Evans 2006: 10)

Eisner too suggests that 'not everything knowable can be articulated in propositional form. The limits of our cognition are not defined by the limits of language' (Eisner 2004: 7). He advocates 'lessons' in which education might learn from distinctive forms of thinking that the arts embody. One of these is the inextricable connection between form and content; as Eisner puts it, between 'how something is said and what is said' (p. 6). For example, if you 'Change the cadence in a line of poetry […] you change the poem's meaning' (p. 7). Speaking about his encounter with W.H. Auden's, *Five Songs no V*, Dana Gioia (2007) remarks, as if to confirm Eisner's point, 'we experience the joys of words so intricately arranged that their secret harmonies become tangible. … Auden's work employs pleasure as the most reliable means to enlightenment. Intelligence not detached from emotions'. Gioia expresses his enjoyment of the multi-textuality of poetry, its fun, its musicality, its contradictions and complexity as enabling the meaning to be felt, in ways more intense than mere ideas could generate. 'Sometimes the fun is in the subject itself, more often the pleasure is stitched into the very verbal fabric of the line' (Gioia 2007).

Thea Stallwood, an articulate artist/film-maker and educator, recognises the importance of writing (for example, scripts, statements, blogs, evaluations) but characterises her experiences of the expectations of writing in academe as stultifying – 'my brain floods with conventions of essay writing; the structure, the referencing system, it seems stilted and so too, my arguments'. She goes on to say: 'On the occasions I have 'played' with these conventions I have been recommended to seek help with my written work' (Stallwood 2010).

I should confess at this point that one such recommendation came from me. I am personally implicated in the tensions and mix of subject identities I referred to earlier. Often the work of students that I find most inspiring and illuminating is also the work that must be honed and sometimes contorted to meet the expectations of academe. How to do this without losing the crucial qualities of the work both written and practice-led presents a considerable challenge. Those who work in universities are undoubtedly bound and accountable to the legislative power of their institutions. As Biggs (2006b) remarks: 'we may seek to reform the university system from within but by taking employment within it we must accept … certain conventional limits' (p. 192).

In a similar manner, Stallwood repeats this cycle with her A-level students within a secondary school. Her comments are from a practice-led MA assignment in which she translates her experiences to those of young people studying AS and A2 level Art and design. She suggests that the affinity that school students feel with a practical and creative subject can diminish if they are required to conform to an intransigent interpretation of producing 'material of a critical, analytical nature'. She states that her position is 'not against writing *per se*' but crucially that writing 'in a variety of formats alongside and in conjunction with audio and visual practice' (2011) should be legitimately recognised as able to make a contribution to knowledge. Stallwood's proposal was to trial film-making for producing examination work that demonstrates the critical, analytical nature of students' A-level study. Significantly, concerns at the school were not about the acceptability of the *form* but whether there might be a danger (if the A-level students used language, image and text in fluid, filmic manner) that their work would simply not meet the requirements of the examination.

In education, as mentioned earlier, certain ways of producing knowledge have become dominant; this concerns both method and representation. Subtlety, ambiguity and aesthetic criteria are not generally encouraged or understood in educational research. Therefore, proposals that suggest alternatives tend to be measured against the 'yardstick' of the dominant form. 'In the extreme case, nothing recognisable as knowledge can be produced outside of the socially dominant form' (Gibbons *et al.* 1994: 1–2). Butler (1999) also reminds us that 'learning the rules that govern intelligible speech is an inculcation into normalised language' (p. xix). It is precisely on the slippery ground of normalised language and intelligibility where the caveats for practice-led research take their hold. At worst, the price of not conforming can be 'the loss of intelligibility itself' (ibid.).

Acquiring language designates us, according to Luiz Camnitzer (2009), as consumers first and then producers; the suggestion is that our engagement with reading conditions our approach to writing. In contradistinction, Aranda *et al.* (2011) write that contemporary art education (and here we must assume that they mean undergraduate and postgraduate level, not school art) 'has deeply internalized this problem by taking the inverse for granted – that one writes first, and only later develops a language with which to read what was written'. This comment is certainly open to debate, perpetuating as it does a somewhat romantic notion of artistic production, whereas, in fact, the 'language of art' can be well rehearsed. However, there are some aspects of this claim that seem pertinent to the process of making where it is not uncommon for 'what is yet to be said' to be revealed in manifold form, unfurling within the stages of making and meaning making. In this sense art practice can identify itself as a form of thought. Borrowing from Badiou's (2005) discussions of poetry one could say that 'it is not just the effective existence of thought offered up in the flesh of language [object or image] it is the set of operations whereby this thought comes to think itself' (p. 20).

Cases for and against the possibility of art practice-led research contributing to the wider field of 'knowledge' have similarly been argued along lines of linguistic/non-linguistic possibilities. For research degrees, the case has been made that 'there is, as yet, no evidence that a designed artefact or artwork can be relied on to communicate the meaning of its existence and the rationale for its significance' (de Freitas 2007: 2). Seemingly irrefutable, if an artwork cannot speak it needs to be interpreted and so begin the problems of intelligibility. But de Freitas's perspective on a mute work of art hinges on some presuppositions: first, that there will be an absence of words in art – no spoken or written language; second, that there is an assurance of coherent communication in words but not in any other form. And third, that interpretation and artworks must be mutually exclusive, in other words that a piece of art cannot in itself be a form of interpretation (Robins 2007). These points are all eminently contestable but perhaps more fundamentally, they miss a vital point, which is succinctly put by Gibbons *et al.*: 'cultural producers ... do not have to take a detour to delineate or express meaning. They see it as the essence of their activity. For them the distance between creation and contextualization is minimal' (1994: 108).

The question of how meaning is communicated through the work of art does not yield simple answers. It is for sure that attempts to answer will be as complex and as varied as works of art themselves. Addison writes:

> It could be claimed that the work of art, in distinction from other forms of human communication, is specifically organised as a constellation of aesthetic and semantic invitations and provocations, the primary purpose of which is to affect us ... making and looking at works of art is potentially a transformative event through which an engagement with alterity (the other) motivates us to act differently, whether that difference is cognitive, affective or conative in its effects.
>
> (Addison 2011: 366)

The notion that both making and engaging with art works has transformative potential and affects us in a number of ways could also be extended to forms of language, such as poetry. When Ricoeur (1978) writes about the poet's use of metaphor to call old age 'a withered stalk', he makes the case that the poet conveys for readers, 'a new idea, literally he [*sic*] has produced knowledge' (p. 26). The distinctions between word and image, art and poetry seem less important here than what these forms can do to us, how they affect us and shape our understanding. As Biggs remarks the 'advancement of knowledge' in relation to the arts 'is not subject to objective measurement, it is subject to understanding' (Biggs 2006b). On a more pragmatic note, Kress draws our attention to the way that in contemporary everyday reality, modes of representing and communicating are in fact becoming less and less dominated by writing:

> If two modes – say, image and writing – are available and are being used for representing and communicating, it is most likely that they will be used for distinct purposes: each will be used for that which it does best and is therefore best used for. Two consequences arise: one, each mode carries only a part of the informational load; no mode fully carries all the meaning. Two, each of the modes will be used for specialised tasks, the tasks which are best done with that mode. As a consequence writing is no longer the full carrier of all the meaning or types of meaning.
>
> (Kress 2003: 20–21)

For artists, art historians and cultural theorists Kress's point might appear transparently axiomatic, whereas in certain sectors of educational research such a proposition verges on radical; an example, perhaps where 'turns' towards interdisciplinarity serve to highlight some of the benefits gained from interrogating ingrained differences in different academic fields. How knowledge is gained and disseminated through a range of methodological and presentational forms will continue to be debated.

The decision to use image or word according to their suitability for the task at-hand can also be complicated by an individual's history. Annie-May Roberts, another MA student, had a particular investment in how she was herself constructed through language. As someone with dyslexia she reflected on her own education and the impact of her teachers' inabilities to see beyond language in appraising her academic potential. By using her school reports she explored the authority and weight that words had accrued and the signifying power that mastering them would promise. The reports she selected praised 'practical' abilities but detached these from intellectual aptitude: 'I think we all accept that Annie-May is never going to be a high flyer in the academic world, but she can be pleased with her many talents, such as cookery and art' (from Annie May's final school report 1997). By projecting the report texts onto large-scale drawing paper, Roberts was able to magnify and transcribe the words that had once made a profound impact on her understanding of who she was and might become.

The reports, which chart a struggle with language, are used to question the position of words in art and academe. The tedious act of making large-scale drawings of the words rendered them in Roberts's words a 'half way house' – still legible as text yet also carrying the marks of shading and texture pencil. She remarked on the tedious act of copying that it was 'reminiscent both of activities for dyslexics to improve their handwriting and the use of writing as a punishment in school detention' (Roberts 2008). The linking of the two events through re-enactment did not escape her attention. In this process through a series of performative and embodied actions she was able to critique the categories of identity that are engendered by language: 'The iterability of performativity is a theory of agency, one that can disavow power as the condition of its own possibility' (Butler 1999: xxv). Roberts writes of the 'performative interaction' with these oversize reports as a 'deconstruction rather than a destruction, an unpacking of the power of relationships between subjects' (2008). The scale, context and physicality of the work give it a poignancy that comes from blending absurdity with emotional resonance. Roberts makes a self-conscious parody, a refusal to be defined within such binaries. By using art as the form through which the disavowal is played out, her refusal has creative potential. She cites Raney's views that opportunities to disfigure an official document can be a pleasure and 'an act which enables repossession of control of constitution' (Raney 2002: 7). Scrumpled and discarded around the corridors of the Institute of Education the secrecy and shame that these official documents once induced was made public and traduced (Figure 11.2.

Roberts employs a methodology common to many artists where the development of ideas and material forms is interconnected and organic. The artist develops personal working methods and threads these through at various points with new connections and aspects of experience. The process of 'threading through' gives form to

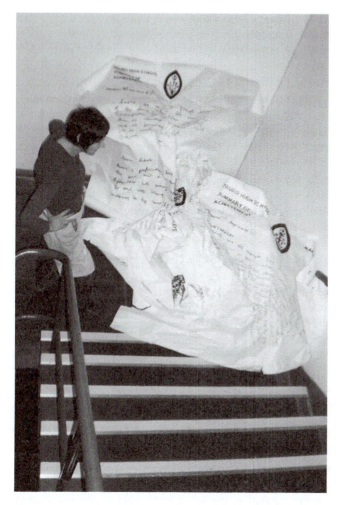

Figure 11.2 Annie-May Roberts, MA student. (Photographer: Peter Thomas)

ideas and concepts and there is an enmeshing or weaving of approaches and methods. Form and content are interconnected as parts of a whole and in this way the practice is essential to conceptual realisations.

Roberts's approach resonates with aspects of Bourdieu's reflexive sociology in which he stresses what is beyond the subjectivised process of self–discovery, by always positioning the individual within the social; the inside within the outside. In the cases that I am discussing, students are similarly concerned with translating and utilising their embodied experiences of making to better understand pedagogic contexts. Their engagement with practice-led research is not undertaken as an end in itself, but rather, between, in relation to, and in conversation with, the practices of

learning and teaching. Such dialogic exchange can act to open up, question and destabilise a dominant discourse. It can propose alternative readings by dislodging fixed
meaning and meta-narrative. Bourdieu sees it as a prerequisite of a reflexive sociology to acknowledge its limits: 'Theoretical knowledge owes a number of its most
essential properties to the fact that the conditions under which it is produced are not
that of practice' (Bourdieu and Wacquant 1992: 70). This is why, as Wacquant states,
reflexive sociology is a science of society that 'must construct theories which contain
within themselves a theory of the gap between theory and practice' (ibid.). In relation
to such an assertion it is significant that Bourdieu has directly championed the work
of two contemporary artists (whose artwork takes a form of research into the practices
of cultural institutions): Hans Haacke, with whom he collaborated for the conversa-
tional publication *Free Exchange* (1995) and Andrea Fraser for whose publication,
Museum Highlights (2005), he wrote an introductory chapter. Both Haacke and Fraser
have had a significant influence on the contemporary and current interconnectedness
between art and museological practices. Both examine the ways in which museums
'naturalise' particular cultural phenomena and their interrelationship with political
and economic networks. Their art practices often take the form of research that bears
a striking resemblance (albeit sometimes parodic) to that conducted by a social scien-
tist, but their modes of dissemination are substantively different, although not always
in appearance. The written reports, statistics and findings expected of the social sci-
entist are sometimes still there, but they are couched in another language, the language of avant-garde art practice which makes use of parodic and ironic strategies to
disrupt dominant meaning. Augmented through the extended vocabularies of avant-
garde approaches to art making, those outcomes of research about the cultural sector
cited above are made manifest through the agency of artworks.

Like the field of cultural studies, art has co-opted the methodologies of other disciplines often for precisely the same reasons: to examine relations of power within its own
domain and within the extended cultural field. This critical turn has been particularly
pronounced in the latter half of the twentieth century when a number of dominant discourses of art were questioned in, and through, artists' recourse to philosophy, anthropology, sociology and psychoanalysis. In each case, it is the 'trespass' of artists into
other fields of knowledge that resulted in, arguably, a more judicious understanding of
art and particularly of its framing technologies. As a corollary, claims have been made
for the 'trespassed field' becoming the beneficiary of new perspectives and methodologies acquired from art. Peter Osborne (1999), for example, holds that philosophy played
an important part for artists who were looking for a tactical strategy for weakening the
formalist stranglehold. He suggests that 'Philosophy was *the means* of this usurpation
of critical power by a new generation of artists; the means by which they could simultaneously address the crisis in the ontology of the artwork (through an art definitional
conception of their practice) and achieve social control over the meaning of their work'
(Osborne 1999: 50). From a different direction, Haacke's engagement with social systems led him to embark on quasi social science audience polls (see Haacke and
Bourdieu (1995). Alternatively, Shelton (2001) and Schneider (1993) have deployed the
tools of anthropology/ethnography, while Jana Graham (2003) those of cultural studies.

Sullivan (2008) aptly points out that an 'ongoing dilemma for practice-based researchers is the difficulty faced in positioning the methodology of studio-based traditions within the language and traditions of research communities in the academy'. Those who explore their own imbrication in cross-disciplinary dialogues do so, not only to attain a better understanding of their professional and personal construction, but also to use this information to move between authorities and instigate change.

Conclusion

The opening epigraph of this chapter illustrates a common enough scenario in which segregation of methodological approach is imposed against the will of a child whose persistent habit of drawing in his literacy book was deemed unacceptable. The instruction is reinforced for a parent to bear witness to the fact that her son was con-travening convention. Pictures are best kept away from words, ordered into the sepa-rate domain of unlined paper and later confined to 'un-ruled' art rooms. Furthermore, pleasurable activities should not be confused with the serious business of learning. Mainstream education progressively iterates divisions to the extent that it becomes hard for most of us to recognise them as such, so inured do we become to the 'order of things'. From the eighteenth century onwards the separation of practice and knowl-edge, and the further division of knowledge and practice into the aborescent branches of autonomous disciplines, has progressively dominated Western epistemology. What started as small fissures, between education and entertainment, amusement and pleas-ure, and furthermore between the emotions and senses and cognitive rationality, widened and deepened, affecting both hierarchies of knowledge and the educational institutions that we have today. Current debates about the value and status of art in education, research and knowledge production are wrapped in these ordering proc-esses. The Cartesian system of binary oppositions from which many of these 'distinc-tions' originate is obdurately persistent, still surfacing in arguments surrounding practice-led approaches to research. Christopher Frayling, for example, states that 'there is still an enormous cachet attached to people in higher education who interpret the world through scholarship and detachment, and not nearly enough attached to people who perform or make things to try and change the world' (Frayling 1999: 55). Whilst this is arguably the case, the reinforcement of dualist categories and binary choices (makers *or* scholars, hands *or* heads) no longer seems the most helpful way of characterising what is actually happening around us in twenty-first century art, epistemology and research activities.

Just as children desire embodied, multimodal ways of engaging with processes of discovery, creation and representation, artists, educators and academics recognise the potential to discern, invent, and articulate ideas and insights through image, text, sound, touch, performance, objects, etc.

In this discussion of the potential benefits in recognising artists' work as a viable form of research I neither propose that all art is a form of research nor set up an opposition between image and word. Rather, I suggest that the embodied practice of art gives rise to new meanings and insights that should not be discounted for their lack of 'fit' in relation to accepted educational research methodologies. Where methodological approaches are combined to optimise knowledge germane to the field of enquiry then they can better serve their purpose for discovering, making and sharing meaning in the world.

References

Addison, N. (2011) 'Moments of Intensity: Affect and the Making and Teaching of Art', *International Journal of Art and Design Education*, 30 (3): 363–378.

Aranda, J., Kuan Wood, B. and Vidokle, A. (2011) Editorial 'Artistic Thinking', *e-flux*, 26, June. Online. Available at: http://www.e-flux.com/journal/editorial—"artistic-thinking"/ (accessed 15 July 2011).

Badiou, A. (2005) *Handbook of Inaesthetics*, Stanford, CA: Stanford University Press.

Biggs, I. (2006a) 'Hybrid Texts and Academic Authority: The Wager in Creative Practice Research', in: K. Macleod and L. Holdridge (eds) *Thinking through Art: Reflections on Art as Research*, New York: Routledge.

Biggs, I. (2006b) 'Art as Research, Doctoral Education, and the Politics of Knowledge', *engage*, 18 (Winter): 6–11.

Bourdieu, P. and Darbel, A. (1997) *The Love of Art: European Museums and their Public Culture*, Cambridge: Polity Press.

Bourdieu, P. and Wacquant, L. (1992) *An Invitation to Reflexive Sociology*, Cambridge: Polity Press.

Butler, J. (1999) *Gender Trouble*, New York: Routledge.

Camnitzer, L. (2009) 'Alphabetization, Part Two: Hegemonic Language and Arbitrary Order', *e-flux*. Online. Available at: http://www.e-flux.com/journal/alphabetization-part-two-hegemonic-language-and-arbitrary-order/ (accessed 30 January 2012).

Candlin, F. (2001) 'A Dual Inheritance: The Politics of Educational Reform and PhDs in Art and Design', *International Journal of Art and Design Education*, 20 (3): 302–310.

Castelo-Branco, M. (2009) *Pushing Marbles: Playing with Order and Disorder*, unpublished MA coursework, London: Institute of Education, University of London.

Cohen, L., Manion, L. and Morrison, K. (2011) *Research Methods in Education*, 7th edn, London: Routledge.

Crowther, P. (1993) *Critical Aesthetics and Postmodernism*, New York: Oxford University Press.

Danto, A.C. (1964) 'The Artworld', *The Journal of Philosophy*, 61 (19): 571–584.

Danvers, J. (2006) *Picturing Mind: Paradox, Indeterminacy and Consciousness in Art and Poetry*, Amsterdam: Rodopi.

de Freitas, N. (2007) 'Activating a Research Context in Art and Design Practice', *International Journal for the Scholarship of Teaching and Learning*, 1 (2). Online. Available at: http://academics.georgiasouthern.edu/ijsotl/v1n2/articles/defreitas/Article_de_Freitas.pdf (accessed 28 January 2012).

Deleuze, G. and Guattari, F. (1988) *A Thousand Plateaus: Capitalism and Schizophrenia*, London: Athlone Press.

Downing, D. and Watson, R. (2004) *School Art. What's in it? Exploring Visual Art in Secondary Schools*, Slough: NFER.

Eisner, E. (1998) *The Kind of Schools We Need*, Portsmouth, NH: Heinemann.

Eisner, E. (2004) 'What Can Education Learn from the Arts about the Practice of Education?', *International Journal of Education & the Arts*, 5 (4). Online. Available at: http://www.ijea.org/v5n4/index.html (accessed 28 January 2012).

Elkins, J. (2008) *Artists with PhDs*, Washington, DC: New Academia Publishing.

Eraut, M. (1994) *Developing Professional Knowledge and Competence*, London: Falmer Press.

Evans, J. (2006) Untitled Coursework, unpublished MA coursework, London: Institute of Education, University of London.

Fraser, A. (2005) *Museum Highlights the Writings of Andrea Fraser*, Cambridge, MA: MIT Press.

Frayling, C. (1999) 'The Flight of the Phoenix', *Royal Society of Arts Journal*, 5490: 49–57.

Gibbons, M., Limoges, C., Nowotny, H., Schwartzman, S., Scott, P. and Trow, M. (1994) *The New Production of Knowledge: The Dynamics of Science Research in Contemporary Societies*, London: Sage.

Gioia, D. (2007) Chief Executive for National Endowment for the Arts speaking on Radio 3, 20 August, 2007.

Graham, J. (2003) 'Museum Acrobatics: Artistic Intervention and the Work of Cultural Studies', *Cultural Studies*, 17 (6): 843–855.

Haacke, H. and Bourdieu, P. (1995) *Free Exchange*, Cambridge: Polity Press.

Hickman, R. (2007) 'Visual Art as a Vehicle for Educational Research', *International Journal of Art and Design Education*, 26 (3): 314–324.

Holert, T. (2009) 'Art in the Knowledge-based Polis', *e-flux*, 3: February 2009. Online. Available at: http://www.e-flux.com/journal/art-in-the-knowledge-based-polis/ (accessed 29 January 2012).

Kress, G. (2003) *Literacy in the New Media Age*, London: Routledge.

Kress, G. (2010) 'The Influence of Multimodality and e-Learning on the Format of Doctoral Theses in Education and Social Science', *ESRC Research Seminar Series*. Online. Available at: http://newdoctorates.blogspot.com/ (accessed 28 January 2012).

Leitch, R. (2006) 'Limitations of Language: Developing Arts-based Creative Narrative in Stories of Teachers' Identities', *Teachers and Teaching*, 12 (5): 549–569.

Macleod, K. and Holdridge, L. (eds) (2006) *Thinking through Art: Reflections on Art as Research*, New York: Routledge.

Mason, R. (2008) 'Problems of Interdisciplinarity: Evidence-based and/or Artist-led Research?', *International Journal of Art and Design Education*, 27 (3): 279–292.

Merleau-Ponty, M. (2002) *Phenomenology of Perception*, London: Routledge.

Osborne, P. (1999) 'Conceptual Art and/as Philosophy', in: M. Newman and J. Bird (eds) *Rewriting Conceptual Art*, London: Reaktion Books.

Pierce, S. (2009) 'Epilogue: Ambivalence and Authority', *Art and Research*, 2 (2). Online. Available at: http://www.artandresearch.org.uk/v2n2/pdfs/pierce.pdf (accessed 29 January 2012).

Prentice, R. (2000) 'The Place of Practical Knowledge in Research in Art and Design Education', *Teaching in Higher Education*, 5 (4), 521–534.

Raney, K. (2002) 'Editorial: Book Art', *engage*, 12 (Summer): 3–7.

Ricoeur, P. (1978) *The Rule of Metaphor: Multi-disciplinary Studies of the Creation of Meaning in Language*, London: Routledge & Kegan Paul.

Roberts, A.M. (2008) *Preoccupied with Language: A Self-positioning Enquiry into Art and Design Education*, unpublished MA coursework, London: Institute of Education, University of London.

Robins, C. (2007) 'How did the Reticent Object become so Obliging? Artists' Interventions as Interpretative Strategies', *engage*, 20 (Summer): 23–28.

Roelstraete, D. (2010) 'Critical Mess: On the Ruins of the Museum's Research Departments', *Mousse magazine*, 26. Online. Available at: http://www.moussemagazine.it/issue.mm?id=32 (accessed 18 December 2010).

Rogoff, I. (guest ed.) (2010) 'Education Actualized', *e-flux*, 14. Online. Available at: http://www.e-flux.com/announcements/issue-14-education-actualized-guest-edited-by-irit-rogoff/ (accessed 30 January 2012).

Schneider, A. (1993) 'The Art Diviners', *Anthropology Today*, 9 (2): 3–9.

Shelton, A. (2001) 'Unsettling the Meaning: Critical Museology, Art and Anthropological Discourses', in: M. Bouquet (ed.) *Academic Anthropology and the Museum*, New York: Berghahn Books.

Smith, S. (2007) *The Ziggurat: The Matter with Text*, unpublished MA coursework, London: Institute of Education, University of London.

Stallwood, T. (2010) *Untitled Coursework*, unpublished PGCE coursework, London: Institute of Education, University of London.

Stallwood, T. (2011) *Unwritten Rule: Proposing an Alternative to Written Critical Studies*, unpublished PGCE coursework, London: Institute of Education, University of London.

Sullivan, G. (2005) *Art Practice as Research: Inquiry in the Visual Arts*, Thousand Oaks, CA: Sage.

Sullivan, G. (2008) 'Methodological Dilemmas and the Possibility of Interpretation', *Working Papers in Art and Design*, 5. Online. Available at: http://sitem.herts.ac.uk/artdes_research/papers/wpades/vol5 (accessed 1 May 2010).

Wilkins, R. (2011) *Research Engagement for School Development*, London: Institute of Education Press.

Part V

Forever changes

Chapter 12

Art education 'as if' for future flourishing

Three analogies between human beings and types of creative grammar

Leslie Cunliffe

Introduction

This chapter is concerned with evaluating the capacity of three different types of creative grammar to service art education 'as if' for 'future flourishing', an emphasis that requires drawing on the claims of wisdom and its corollary of '*generative wisdom*' (Solomon *et al.* 2005). Reconfiguring art education as a form of strategic wisdom requires specifying the conditions for cultivating creativity, knowledge and understanding that is consistent with an ethical vision, a sense of wonder, and a better approach to promoting flourishing on this planet. This aim contrasts with forms of learning, creativity and living that have been in ascendancy in late- and post-modernity, which have emphasised so-called cognitive reliability over ethical responsibility; nihilism, narcissism and narrow desires and pursuits over the promotion of the common good and its corollary of the practice of deep ecology.

Cultivating ethical, epistemic and creative responsibility requires the *as if* process of becoming, so that present circumstances and actions are informed by a meta-level, future tense narrative for living in the world. Dreyfus and Kelly (2011: 220) describe such an approach as necessarily involving acts of 'meta-poiesis', that is, the celebration, acquisition and use of intermediary tools for skilfully revealing things at their best, so that they shine out and by so doing enable us to experience the world in a more affirmative way.

To fully grasp the significance of meta-poiesis for art education, it is important to understand art and culture as operating by what Gombrich (1972) described as the process of 'formula and experience', in which formulae provide the resources that enable creativity, and individual experience the dispositions and traits that promote creativity. By focusing on experience at the expense of formulae, what I shall refer to as 'the dreamer analogy of modern art education' failed to harness knowledge-rich cultural formulae that enable creativity. By promoting the knowledge-lean, surface manipulation of formulae, postmodern art education bypasses the need to acquire the complex, knowledge-rich skills that underpin excellence in human endeavour (Dreyfus and Kelly 2011). In this respect, these two modern paradigms of creativity neglected the importance of deliberate practice for developing conscious competence, which later on might become unconscious competence. This 'as if' process of becoming, given its potential to sustain forward trajectory in creative development, can overcome the premature convergence found in much current art education.

To this end, I draw on the notion of 'intermediary tools' to add nuance to three analogies between creative grammar, persons, art, and art education. These analogies revolve around three types of person: the subversive dreamer as promoted in early modernism; the subversive, ironic joker who emerges with Dada (is recovered in late-modernism with the neo-Dada movement, and dominates postmodern creative practices); and the pre-modern, more universal analogy between creative grammar and the person able to formulate and execute a sustainable life-plan. Although the chapter is predominantly concerned with fine art education, the logic of the argument can be applied across a spectrum of visual art disciplines.

But before enlarging on the way intermediary tools service the three analogies outlined above, I will need to clarify how the word grammar is used in this chapter. The clarification is necessary given art educators are inclined to think of creativity as expressive individualism, as forms of transgression at odds with the association of 'grammar' with correct linguistic conventions. However, grammar can also refer to the way social and cultural practices are structured; as described by Wittgenstein (2001), 'Essence is expressed in grammar ... . Grammar tells us what kind of object anything is. (Theology as grammar.)' (pp. 371 and 373). Vygotsky (1971) made a parallel point about art's essence being grounded in the grammar of practices: 'Art is the social within us, and even if its action is performed by a single individual, it does not mean that its essence is individual' (p. 249).

Intermediary tools and the grammar of practices

In making this argument, I will draw, implicitly and explicitly, on parallel features of five important thinkers: Gombrich on art and culture; Dreyfus on the phenomenology of expertise and the dangers of nihilism; Steiner on the capacity of different creative grammars to inhabit futurity; Vygotsky on cultural psychology as manifested in art and mediated through educational processes; and Wittgenstein on philosophy of mind in culture (Cunliffe 1998, 2003, 2005a,b, 2006, 2007, 2008a,b, 2009, 2010, 2011). Their thinking shares the significance of what Bühler (1934) described as 'intermediary tools' for developing and sustaining meaningful differences in cultural practices. The intermediary tools are two-tiered: first, those known as cognitive resources like language and other sign systems, specific knowledge-domains, and the motor skills, intelligence and dispositions that shape 'material consciousness' in a range of activities that enable cultural participation (Sennett 2008); second those described as cognitive strategies that play an executive role in monitoring how the cognitive resources get used (Cunliffe 2008a). All these embodied psychological tools interact with a range of technology which, in turn, gives feedback to the cognitive repertoires, and are at their best when deployed and monitored in an ethical way, as in virtue philosophy that sees epistemic reliability as a corollary of ethical responsibility (Hursthouse 1999; Zagzebski 1996).

In Gombrich's research (1971, 1972) Bühler's notion of '*intermediary tools*' (in Lepsky 1996: 29) is used to explain the production of visual art as a variable relationship of '*formula and experience*', in which formulae in artistic and cultural practices get appropriated and modified by personal experience. The dialectic of formula and experi-ence enables the process of enculturation (an induction into the values and practices of a person's culture) that, by extension, promotes cultural transformation. Dreyfus (1997, 2001), following Heidegger and Kierkegaard, contrasts the use of intermediary tools associated with the so-called 'detached' thinker with how they are actually used by committed, involved, embodied persons. His analysis incorporates the meaningful dif-ferences that stand out and shine when experts use material consciousness to fashion end products, as opposed to the levelling process of indifference that nihilism generates. In this respect, Dreyfus's phenomenological account of material consciousness parallels Gombrich's organic, trans-personal, coral reef-like notion of creativity in art (1972), and overlaps with Steiner's (2001 [1965]) analysis of the capacity of different creative gram-mars to fashion future flourishing. Steiner's trans-personal approach to creative gram-mar is echoed in Vygotsky's (1978: 73) description of cognitive development as *'intertwining external and internal factors'*. Vygotsky explores the way language and alternative intermediary tools are mediated through educational and other socio-cultural processes, so that the achievement of students as scaffolded by adults is a more accurate reflection of their real ability than what they accomplish alone. Wittgenstein (2001: 11) represented his later philosophy of language as functioning like tools from 'a tool box', that is, as intermediary tools used for different tasks, an analogy derived from Bühler's research into the function of language (Peters *et al.* 2008).

Creative grammar: a cultural comparison

The grammar of practices is taken for granted until different cultural settings reveal discrepancies. Dreyfus (1997: 295) highlights such a discrepancy with this example: 'It is hard to picture a tea ceremony around a Styrofoam cup'. This is because a Japanese tea bowl used in the tea ceremony and a Styrofoam cup embody creative grammars that emerge from radically different understandings of being.

A Styrofoam cup expresses the essence of a technological understanding of being that dominates our time. Its grammar is influenced by thinking of everything in the world, including people, as a resource that has to be flexibly and efficiently used up. The flexibility includes the option of drinking on the move. The efficiency is found in Styrofoam's capacity to insulate, which makes it possible to handle very hot and cold beverages in varied situations. The material structure of Styrofoam allows the cups to be efficiently produced and flexibly disposed. All the flexibility and efficiency is developed for its own sake, not for any deeper purpose in life.

The immediacy of drinking from a Styrofoam cup shows up in its present tense grammar, as the resource is used without regard for the past or for future conse-quences. The way a Styrofoam cup erases the past and truncates the future tense is symptomatic of how, more generally, the technological understanding of being emas-culates past accomplishment and jeopardises future ecological well-being.

In contrast to a Styrofoam cup, the creative grammar embedded in a Japanese tea ceremony bowl articulates the past, present and future tense. The past tense is found in the tradition of ceremonial tea drinking that goes back hundreds of years to its origins in China and Zen Buddhism. The look of each unique Japanese tea bowl is derived from a form of Korean ceramics that is valued in Japan because of its capacity to evoke modesty and simplicity. The present tense grammar of the tea ceremony bowl is articulated in the realisation that all the details of the art form have their significance in making and serving a cup of tea with politeness, graciousness and charm. The future tense perspective is maintained in the way someone aspiring to be a tea master has to commit many years, even a lifetime, to accomplish this aim to include acquiring knowledge of alternative Japanese aesthetic practices, all of which involve overriding the ego to engage with a transcendental understanding of being (Houser and Katsuiko 1992).

This comparison between a Styrofoam cup and a Japanese tea bowl is given to enable the reader to understand how contrasting creative grammar gets articulated by the use of intermediary tools in what Heidegger called a clearing. This is a potential space that a cultural paradigm opens up so that its participants know what to do by distinguishing meaningful differences. Not all cultural paradigms do this. Dreyfus (1997: 301) thinks: 'There can be nihilistic paradigms. Such paradigms ... do not always promote meaningful differences'.

Such a nihilistic clearing was opened up by the technological paradigm of being, as progressively developed throughout modernity. The analogy between creative grammar and the subversive, ironic joker briefly touched on in the introduction mainly applies to the practice of art in the late- and post-modern phase of this cultural paradigm, although the nihilistic grammar and its associated intermediary tools emerge in the early-modern phase with the Dada movement.

By now it should be obvious why Dreyfus thinks it difficult to picture a tea ceremony using a Styrofoam cup, as the grammar of a tea bowl embodies and mediates a totally different understanding of being from that of a Styrofoam cup. The tea bowl promotes meaningful differences; the Styrofoam cup levels them.

Analogies between creative grammar, art and art education

The idea that creative grammar is embedded in art objects (Steiner 2001 [1965]) can be extended to art education; hence the significance of making analogies between types of creative grammar and persons, as both embody and manifest social, historical, cultural practices and ecological processes. Wittgenstein (1997: 23–24) used such analogies when contrasting the '*unruly*' nature of a Beethoven symphony with the '*correct*' character of an architectural feature. The Beethoven symphony is tremendous in the way it '*makes a great impression*', whereas a Georgian door frame is '*well-behaved*'.

Following Wittgenstein, Hagberg (2004) has devised a series of such analogies: a person's moral status and rights is analogous with works of art having artistic integrity (a phenomenon that can be easily misrepresented, violated or debased); a person's sense of wholeness is analogous with a work having internal coherence; a person's capacity to hold values is analogous with a work of art projecting values; a person's ability to make choices is analogous with a work of art being a depository of artistic choices; and, a person's capacity to formulate a life-plan is analogous with works of art revealing strategic intelligence as sustained artistic development.

Hagberg's analogies can illuminate the way different forms of art education have attempted to nurture personhood. For example, the understanding of creativity in early modernism as analogous to a subversive dreamer, in modern art education shows up as self-expression. The focus on inward processes nurtures persons as thought to be divorced from their socio-cultural surroundings, and thus only belonging to nature. The late- and post-modern analogy of creativity with the ironic joker, in postmodern art education gets manifested as subversion. Privileging subversion nurtures persons as socio-cultural artefacts who articulate 'the one-liner work' (Stallabrass 2006: 100). The modern preference for selecting and using subversive creative grammar is at odds with the analogy between creativity and persons that has informed most pre-modern and non-European practices of art, in which the creative grammar is analogous to a person who formulates and carries out a sustainable life-plan.

The logic and capacity of three creative grammars

Steiner (2001 [1965]) takes creative grammar to be 'the articulate organisation of perception, reflection and experience, the nerve structure of consciousness when it communicates with itself and with others' (p. 5). Steiner's creative grammar and the associated intermediary tools is of three types: accretion, omission and nihilism. They operate with different logic and capacities.

Accretion

Accretion builds cloud-like creative grammar from two forms of knowledge, 'knowing that' and 'knowing how', which in turn provide enough organisational depth to allow someone to 'know what to do' (see Figure 12.1). The accretions in the 'top coat' of a creative end product metaphorically covers the 'undercoat', 'primer' and original 'base material'. All these can be evaporated back to the complex, cloud-like deposits of skilful knowledge from where they were condensed. The evaporation process also reveals other, non-present aspects to include the cultural paradigm and moral purpose that informs the selection of cultural grammar, the type of artistic practice, duration and methods of training, the breadth and depth of the creative repertoire, the materials and methods available and used, and the preparation, revision, experimentation that shape the final product.

The relative significance of each one of these aspects of the process of accretion varies according to background and cultural setting, as engaged on a spectrum between formula and experience. The organisational depth of accretion, like the cycle of cloud formation and rain, allows the creative grammar to be deployed and continually reconstructed.

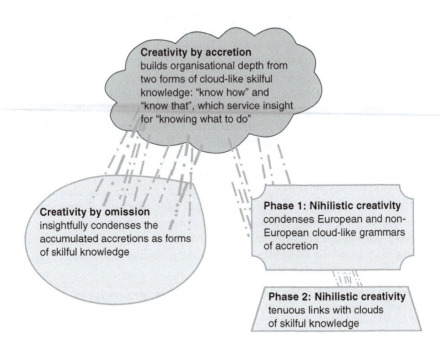

Figure 12.1 The logic and capacity of three creative grammars.

Omission

Creativity by omission is made possible by selectively condensing the cloud-like accretions of skilful knowledge. This form of creativity by omission has been used in non-European and older Western collaborative, ritual practices of art. An excellent example is the Japanese tradition, where omission condenses fullness in an exacting way (Rousmaniere 2007). Some practices of omission are constrained by environmental factors beyond the control of creative agents. The small scale and limited range of materials, say, found in traditional Inuit art is an example.

Nihilism

Nihilistic creative grammar, like the process of omission described above, can also be condensed from the organisational depth established by accretion, which was the case with much of the positive nihilism of early modernism. Nietzsche's positive nihilism was a response to the loss of meaning that afflicted modernity, which he thought could be compensated by adopting the attitude of a superman: a free, creative spirit who aims to realise meaningful differences. Early modernism is replete with such epiphanic creative grammar, a word with etymological roots in *epiphaneia*, meaning a divine or super human manifestation, a showing. In the older Western tradition epiphany was a trans-personal phenomenon associated with Christianity, but in modernity became increasingly understood as a personal, esoteric experience.

The epiphanies of early modernism were made possible by condensing formulae from two traditions: Western creative grammar articulated in the material consciousness of past practices, notably the revival of interest in old Western art as exemplified by, say, Maurice Denis, and in the use of autographic skills as deliberately learned in the ten-year art education of Matisse; and non-European creative grammar as experienced in ethnographic collections and therefore divorced from its original cultural setting and purpose of conveying meaningful differences. For this reason the grammar was misunderstood as free-floating and *primitive* (Cunliffe 2008b; Gombrich 2002; Rubin 1984).

In contrast to the process of omission that serviced the early-modern, positive phase of nihilism, the second, late- and post-modern phase of nihilism abandons the forms of material consciousness condensed from the creative grammar of accretion to focus on more tenuous, conceptual links to the past. This move levelled rather than emphasising meaningful differences (Steiner 2001 [1965]). In other words, the grammatical essence condensed by both early-modern art and the spiritual aims of modern art education were an attempt to overcome the technological understanding of being, while late- and post-modern practices of art and art education broadly accommodate to the technological understanding of being in the form of technological nihilism. To get a better grip on the contrast between these grammars it is necessary to trace the genealogy of the two analogies between creative grammar and subversive persons.

The genealogy of the analogy between creative grammar and the subversive dreamer

The dreamer analogy for creativity as tapping an interior source emerged in the second half of the eighteenth century when Western art changed from practices based on the aesthetics of effects, as influenced by Christian and Platonic shared forms of epiphany and transcendence, to biological aesthetics as immanence. Burke (1759) inaugurated this change, in which reactions to beauty were thought to result from sexual instinct, and moderate sensations of fear experienced as sublime responses to nature which were derived from the drive for self-preservation.

With Romanticism, the role of immanence moved from the beholder's response to nature to the artist's imagination, which was increasingly thought of as a natural reservoir for sincere, self-expression. The concern with inward processes was provoked by the new clearing that the dystopian, technological understanding of being opened up that denied the shared expression of epiphany in the clearing established by the Christian, transcendental understanding of being. The change radically displaced the third-person, shared practice of creativity as analogous with formulating a life-plan with that of the excluded first-person, subversive dreamer (Williams 1965). The individual, visionary calling was an attempt to model, prophetically, an 'as if', re-enchanting, alternative dream to the nightmare reality that had come to prevail (as exemplified by industrialisation). William Blake can be thought the exemplar Romantic artist who combined subversive visionary art with political, cultural and social critique.

primary process thinking
the unconscious

secondary process thinking
the conscious

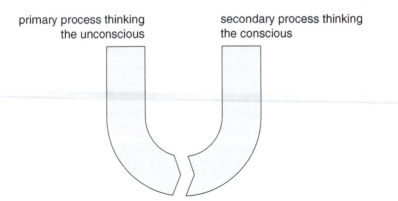

Figure 12.2 The U-curve dichotomy between primary and secondary process thinking.

As the nineteenth century wore on the Romantic dream analogy for creativity steadily fuelled a false dichotomy between ordinary and extraordinary seeing (Gombrich 2002), in which the shared grammar of cultural practices was considered ordinary, and, as such, opposed to the extraordinary possibilities of individual experience. This shift from the socio-cultural practice of art as the aesthetics of effects mediated by a range of intermediary tools, to a less mediated, individual conception of art took an inflationary step when twentieth century artists attempted to articulate something primitive as thought to reside in the 'beast in the basement', unconscious mind (Claxton 2005: 155).

The early-modern preference for the primitive explains why Freud's *Interpretation of Dreams*, published in 1900, resonated with the art world, which already associated creativity with the ineffable. Using Freud's terminology, this further dichotomised secondary process (conscious) thinking with primary process (unconscious) thinking. Weisberg (1999) describes the dichotomy that characterises the dreamer analogy for creativity as the 'tension view', as represented by a broken U-Curve with creativity and primary process thinking at one end, and secondary process thinking stranded at the other (Figure 12.2).

The tension view paradigm, worked out in early modernism as omission by regression, aimed to express a more involuntary, authentic, primitive sensibility (Gombrich 2002) by erasing accumulated accretions of skilful knowledge. The early-modern fixation with primitive sensibility explains why non-naturalistic old Western practices of art, naïve art, and non-European art came to be especially esteemed in modern as opposed to pre-modern times, and why a special emphasis was given to self-expression in child art, as thought to be best nurtured by shielding children from adult practices. More importantly, the focus on primitive sensibility obfuscated the way creativity operates in unconsciously incompetent persons, as opposed to unconsciously competent persons. In this respect, Dreyfus's (2001: 33–49) phenomenological account of unconscious competence, in which more is shown and known than can often be said, is a million miles away from a novice's inability to articulate insight about their own performance.

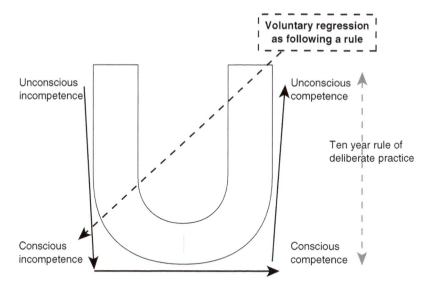

Figure 12.3 U-curve ten-year journey to expert performance and the role of voluntary regression.

The blurring of understanding of the role of competence in the dreamer analogy for creativity can be grasped by understanding the significance of Picasso's response to a flippant question about whether one of his 'child-like' drawings had only taken a couple of minutes, to which he replied that it had required a lifetime. Picasso's answer appropriately identified that the drawing articulated voluntary regression aimed at temporarily refreshing the more sophisticated accretions that formed his unconscious competence. By contrast, the creative grammar manifested in child art or the naïve adult artist Alfred Wallis remains involuntary, given both are incapable of choosing to be unconsciously competent. This is why Picasso's wilful regression would be a meaningless act for a novice, as emptying something out presupposes fullness, hence the insight encapsulated in Picasso's comment about his drawing needing a lifetime.

For this reason the dreamer analogy does a disservice to art and art education, given that it fails to account for Picasso's and every other person's conscious journey towards competency and expertise, which is now known as the ten-year rule of deliberate practice (Chi 2006; Weisberg 2006). Such a journey involves moving from the unconscious incompetence of young children, to the conscious incompetence of older children, on to the conscious competence of adolescents and young adults, in order to realise the unconscious competence found in expert performers who, like Picasso, may choose to voluntarily regress by consciously following a rule (Howell 1982 – see Figure 12.3). The journey of expert performance is a research finding that complements Vygotsky's insight, referred to earlier, about the essence of art being an individual action that is scaffolded by social and cultural intermediary tools. It is also consistent with creativity as accretion.

The dreamer analogy, curriculum design, pedagogy and assessment

The inadequacies of the dreamer analogy for nurturing creativity further explain why curriculum design, pedagogy, and assessment practices in modern forms of art education were poorly conceptualised and inadequately practised. For if creativity is analogous with dreaming, that is, devoid of an intelligible shared reality and a calibrated use of intermediary tools shaped by meta-cognition, this would mean art cannot be deliberately planned, taught or assessed. The subject floats free from justified knowledge, making it impossible to develop complex as opposed to trivial cognitive processes in art education. The resulting practices of curriculum, pedagogy and assessment mirror-image the art educator as dreamer and the corollary of student-centred solipsism (Jones 1997; Madge and Weinberger 1973).

An example of conceptualising assessment practice for art education that inadvertently results in solipsism is found in Curtis *et al.*'s (2000) stress on intuition for assessment, so as to 'take into account qualities which go beyond what is immediately apparent'. In advocating an intuitive practice of assessment Curtis *et al.* fail to distinguish its role when following a rule explicitly formulated for actions from cases where people comply with rules by acting in accordance with them. For intuition to become normative in the practice of assessment, the intuitive judgements would have to be consistent with procedures explicitly formulated for managing actions, which is made possible by acquiring and appropriately using intermediary tools. Harré's (2001) nuanced exegesis of Wittgenstein's philosophy brings this out:

> We can say that a rule is immanent in a practice if the normative character of what is being done comes from simply learning the practice, but a rule could be formulated to express the normative character of the practice. In contrast, a rule is transcendent to a practice if the rule exists in the same symbolic realm as the practice, such as when an actor attends to a rule and uses it as an instruction for performing certain actions, or a teacher deploys a rule to guide the actions of a pupil. A rule may be transcendent to the practice for the trainer but immanent for the learner, if the latter is not taught the practice by being given the rule as an instruction.
>
> (Harré 2001: 155–156)

For Curtis's occult-like notion of intuition to be normative in assessment the intuitive judgements would need to be grounded in procedures explicitly formulated for actions by participants.

Curtis's fetishisation of intuition reflects a continuing preoccupation with the inward processes associated with the asocial, dreamer analogy for creativity, as opposed to any concern to develop a practice of assessment that can lead students out of solipsism by mediating intermediary tools with which to monitor their own performance. This is a better example of implementing Wittgenstein's notion of explicitly formulating rules for action in a practice of education, because "'knowing a rule" is a kind of cognitive metaphor for "being able to do something correctly"' (Harré and

Tissaw 2005: 123). In this respect, GCSE (General Certificate of Secondary Education) assessment objectives or any criteria for success can be employed as intermediary tools to enable students to manage their own actions normatively by learning how to learn to provide calibrated forms of evidence (Cunliffe 2007).

Summary of the analogy between creative grammar and the subversive dreamer

The discussion has shown the analogy between creative grammar and the subversive dreamer deforms the complexity of persons and art. The involuntary nature of dreaming fails to make sense of the conscious process of acquiring intermediary tools. Such embodied, cognitive routines make it possible to solve current complex problems in a fluent way while standing-in-reserve to resource future artistic endeavour in the operation of the 'cognitive unconscious' (Claxton 2005: 210).

Strauss and Quinn (1997) refer to the material consciousness manifested in unconsciously competent persons as well-learned schemas:

> They [schemas] can adapt to new or ambiguous situations with 'regulated impro-visation', to use Bourdieu's term (1977: 11). The reactions … are improvisational because they are created on the spot, but regulated because they are guided by previously learned patterns of associations; they are not improvised out of thin air.
> (Strauss and Quinn 1997: 53–54)

The cross-traffic between conscious and unconscious thought described above is common to all, as can be illustrated by suddenly remembering a name after abandoning the previous effort to do so. The ordinary nature of this cycle of activity needs to be distinguished from the extraordinary content and intensity of thought that divides an expert's act of meta-poiesis from a novice's creative products. For creativity in art to operate effectively, a range of intermediary tools have to be used to synthesise many elements, which the asocial dreamer analogy for creativity fails to explain.

The genealogy of the analogy between creative grammar and the subversive, ironic joker

The significance of the social within us for giving an intelligible account of creativity can be grasped by contrasting the unconscious process of dreaming with that used in joking. In contrast to dreaming, joking is made intelligible by its reliance on shared language and life-world gestures. These allow humour to be crafted, improvised, revised and assessed (Freud cited in Gombrich 1984: 105). The intermediary tools used in a shared, socio-cultural context enable humour to fulfil Wittgenstein's requirement that: 'An inner process stands in need of outward criteria' (2001: 580). The outward criteria that make humour a more suitable analogy for creativity is a corollary of Wittgenstein's wider critique of the Cartesian view of mind as an inner process, and Gombrich's parallel exposure of the expressionist, dreamer analogy of creativity in art as the unmediated representation of an inner world (Gombrich 1971: 56–69, 1972: 304–329). But does the shared socio-cultural context that scaffolds joking make wit a perfect analogical fit for creativity in art and art education?

Answering this question requires making sense of the second part of each of the following conundrums: Why is the early modern analogy of creativity with dreaming wrong, but its use of accretion right for sustaining forward momentum in art education; and, why is the late- and post-modern analogy of creativity with joking appropriate, but its nihilistic grammar (that makes tenuous, conceptual links with accretion) inappropriate for servicing future flourishing in art education?

Foster (1996: 71–96) identifies the inability or unwillingness to engage with inspirational epiphany as a common feature of the neoconservative and post-structuralist strands of postmodernism. The neoconservative strand responded to the erosion of the stock of creative grammar in late-modernism by attempting to recuperate cultural memory. This worked out as the manipulation of 'surface' appearances rather any deeper engagement with the grammar that had been the armature for older creative products. The neoconservative choice of surface over depth turned art and architecture into forms of pastiche, so that 'the typically postmodern image is one which displays its own artificiality, its own pseudo-status, its own representational depthlessness' (Kearney 1988: 3). Pastiche, like doubt's relationship to belief, always leans backwards.

The weakening of creative potency in the neoconservative strand of postmodernism was paralleled in the post-structuralist strand that, following Dada, chose to bypass acquiring and using deep creative grammar in preference for surface subversion. With this move art became analogous to a person capable of frustrating but not fulfilling expectations; a limited disposition that shares pastiche's backward leaning posture. The surface subversion was articulated in post-it, 'one-liner works' (Stallabrass 2006: 100) aimed at deconstructing the cultural memory that the surface grammar of neoconservatism had failed to recuperate. The choice of post-it grammar also eroded the remaining material consciousness deposited in the autographic craft skills used to express previous shared forms of enchantment. The result was to defer on future flourishing in favour of servicing temporary mindsets, a move that ironically parallels the short-term desires that global capitalism promotes (Barber 2007).

Given that this analysis of the inability of postmodern creative grammar to stride forward is correct, it would seem that Fuller's description of postmodernism as forms of anaesthetic art exhibiting 'kenosis' (1986: 14) is appropriate. Kenosis is a theological term used to describe Christ voluntarily emptying himself of his divinity that Fuller applied to postmodernism's voluntary abandonment of the grammar of accretion, which had underwritten art's previous capacity to evoke epiphany.

That such a minimum stock of anaesthetic, surface creative grammar can be maintained without acquiring much material consciousness becomes obvious when a comparison is made between the way intermediary tools are appropriated and used in the life-world with how they are acquired and used in domains of skilful knowledge. In the life-world intermediary tools are acquired through informal learning and experience, which contrasts with the formal training and deliberate practice used by knowledge-rich communities of practice. The 'indirect' method of deliberate practice is the reason why nobody becomes a professor of physics, medical doctor, grandmaster chess player, skilled craftsman, elite sportsperson, professional ballet dancer, by just inhabiting the life-world (Dreyfus 2001; Ericsson *et al*. 2006). The same cannot be said of the intermediary tools needed for being, say, an actor, comedian and, by extension, a postmodern nihilistic artist, which can be acquired by just inhabiting the life-world.

The irony of this state of affairs is that postmodern nihilism, which partly emerged to critique the modernist analogy of creativity with subversive dreaming, ends up sharing its occult-like disassociation of creativity from skilful knowledge (Smith 1990). The lack of organisational depth in postmodern creative grammar means it can only embody a 'negative virtue, a preference for the absence of something' (Steiner 2001 [1965]: 272–273). Postmodern nihilism, like Dada's rocking horse, gives the impression of generating forward momentum while remaining static. This conjuring trick creates special problems for educational processes which have to embrace real forward momentum.

The joker analogy, curriculum design, pedagogy and assessment

Because the subversive joker analogy with creativity is made possible by people sharing and subverting an intelligible reality, it is not surprising that it emerges at roughly the same time as the national curriculum, a greater focus on the efficacy of pedagogical practices, and the initiative known as assessment for learning. These initiatives not only share many of the positive features of the ironic joker analogy with creativity, but also had the potential to recover an alternative discursive, socio-cultural view of the person who inhabits a well-formulated life-plan.

That creativity in art education came to be associated with the subversive joker rather than the pre-modern person's capacity to formulate a life-plan can be illustrated by the way art educators have interpreted the national curriculum and examination syllabi as advocating the backward leaning stance of pastiche and subversion, as revealed in practices that confuse evidence for 'knowing that' with evidence for 'knowing how'. The discrepancy is crystallised in England's GCSE, the art examination for 14–16 year olds (Cunliffe 2005a, b). For example, evidence for understanding the meaning and ritualistic function of, say, the Aboriginal Australian memorial poles in the British Museum is not achieved by looking at, drawing from, or making some kind of pastiche response to them. Discerning their meaning requires possessing the necessary cognitive stock to read their text-analogue code and how this links to the background cultural paradigm and context. Such evidence is provided in the form of language.

To grasp the depth and meaning of a work of art, the presence of the 'top coat' needs to be understood in relationship to its non-present 'undercoat', 'primer' and original 'base material' as found in the cultural paradigm and moral purpose, type of artistic practice, duration and methods of training, the breadth and depth of creative repertoire, the media and methods available and used, and the forms of preparation, revision, and experimentation that shape the material consciousness that fashions the final product.

Gombrich (1973: 108) described the practice of trying to find meaning in art by just looking at it, and, by extension, drawing from it and doing pastiches, as the 'physiognomic fallacy', as explained by Summers (1998): ' ... the meanings we simply see in works of art, although not without their own value, are not historical, and therefore not explanatory. In order to gain such understanding we must actually do history' (p. 134). The meaning gained from looking at a person's face as present in the life-world should not be conflated with knowing about their social and cultural background. Discovering such evidence, and checking its validity, like working in any knowledge-domain, requires training in the appropriate cognitive stock.

The confusion between procedural and declarative knowledge in current art education prevents students from acquiring the cognitive tools that act as metaphors for showing understanding in practice (Harré and Tissaw 2005). In this respect, postmodern art education's version of the physiognomic fallacy continues to deepen rather than address the weakness Harland *et al.* (2000) identified in the provision of arts education in the United Kingdom as:

> The development of critical discrimination and aesthetic judgment-making, especially the capacity to locate these in their social, artistic and cultural contexts; the furthering of thinking skills, or more accurately, a meta-awareness of the intellectual dimensions to artistic processes.
>
> (Harland *et al.* 2000: 566)

The analogy of art education with the subversive joker also excludes students from understanding most of the art that human beings have ever made, as 'an entirely different game is played out in different ages' (Wittgenstein 1997: 23). The ritualistic game of art carried out over the last 30,000 years is not understood by playing the ironic and subversive game of contemporary art. Art as the mastery of autographic craft skills aimed at enchantment will not be understood by using advanced technology.

Furthermore, the backward lean of the joker analogy for creativity is unable to embrace a pedagogy capable of building a world (Cunliffe 2003). This is because joking, like parable's role in narrative, can only subvert an existing world established by myth. In Crossan's words: 'myth proposes, parable disposes' (1988: 47). No one lives outside myth, a principle that also applies to educators who engage with deliberate patterns of learning that, like the narrative purpose of myth in culture, primarily aim to promote solution, not subversion. Teachers have little or no choice to share myth's forward leaning posture. In this respect, pedagogies that conflate subversion with solution make a category error as subversion is always parasitic on any existing attempt at solution, as revealed by the etymology of the word parable, which is found in the Greek verb *paraballo* that means 'to hurl alongside'. Parable, critique, and subversion share the same limited family resemblance of only being able to hurl alongside myth. Their backward leaning stance proves incapable of establishing the forward trajectory that myth provides.

Summary: art education as the subversive joker

The discussion has shown that although the joker analogy has many attributes to facilitate a strong, socio-cultural practice of art education, the logic of its grammar as worked out in postmodernism precludes it from adopting a forward trajectory towards solution. One-liner works, like persons only capable of frustrating expectations, are quickly exhausted, making any future attempt at achieving unexpectedness congeal into entrenched expectedness. The limited capacity of nihilistic grammar not only disqualifies it from sustaining short-term shock but from evoking any other durable response, as Hans Richter (1965), an original member of the Dada movement, has identified in the conundrum of the second time round neo-Dada movement:

> a Cezanne, or a Picasso, or any work of art, could be seen again and again and yet afford new sensations, new emotions, new matter for meditation. ... This is not true of the coal shovel, the bicycle wheel, the urinal. They were not intended by Duchamp to stimulate meditation or artistic emotions, they were intended by Duchamp to shock. ... Such a shock is not repeatable. ...They no longer have any anti-aesthetic or anti-artistic function whatever, only a practical function.
>
> (Richter 1965: 53)

In contrast, the organisational depth built by the creative grammar of accretion sustains unexpectedness in the form of renewable closure, as the 'artistic surprise never wears off' (Gombrich 1987: 214). Its depth of grammar also trumps the capacity of postmodern art to sustain moral outrage, as can be seen by comparing Gericault's *Raft of the Medusa* (1818–1819) or Picasso's *Guernica* (1937) with a Banksy mural. The postmodern analogy of creativity with the subversive joker cashes out in art education as a socially centred person only capable of striking 'puerile' attitudes (Collings 2008).

The analogy between creative grammar and the person capable of formulating and executing a sustainable life-plan

Given that I have already illustrated accretion's capacity to act as an analogy for the person capable of formulating and executing a sustainable life-plan, in this section I want to flesh out this perspective as a curriculum designed for understanding meaningful differences in practices of art, a Vygotskian pedagogy aimed at mediating a range of intermediary tools, and a practice of assessment that promotes the same forward trajectory of art education as found in its curriculum content and pedagogy.

In this respect, the geological process of accretion is a poor metaphorical fit with the accretions that build up in a person's cognitive repertoire. Unlike geological formations, human accretions require an active process carried out by involved moral agents (Dreyfus 2001). A way to conceptualise such a human process of accretion is best captured by the German notion of *Bildung*, a word that describes the multidimensional

Ancient and European Art: before c.1800	Romantic and Early-Modern Art: c.1800 – c1950
Artistic grammar derived from collective effervescence aimed at expressing and conserving a shared, aspirational 'future tense' understanding of being: grammar used for expressing meaningful differences	Artistic grammar that is increasingly generated by the emergence of expressive individualism aimed at overcoming the technological understanding of being: grammar used in Romanticism and the 'positive nihilism' of early modernism as expressed in esoteric epiphanies aimed at realising meaningful differences
Pre-Historic and Non-European Art	**Late- and Post-Modern Art: c.1950 onwards**
Artistic grammar derived from collective effervescence aimed at expressing and conserving a shared, aspirational, 'future tense' understanding of being: grammar used for expressing meaningful differences	Artistic grammar that accommodates to the technological understanding of being, which articulates the overcoming of the desire to overcome nihilism: a grammar that levels meaningful differences

Figure 12.4 A heuristic for curriculum design as types of art practices and the related use of creative grammar as structured by cultural paradigms.

Procedural knowledge: *as revealed in the way visual grammar is used to resolve and realise the end product*

Declarative knowledge: *as revealed in the way verbal grammar articulates third person understanding of text analogue meanings*

Ancient and European Art – before c.1800	Romantic and Early Modern Art – c.1800–1950
Pre-Historic and Non-European Art	**Late- and Post-Modern Art – c.1950 onwards**

Declarative knowledge: *as revealed in the way verbal grammar articulates first person understanding of face-analogue meanings*

Procedural knowledge: *as revealed in the way the creative grammars are used on a spectrum that ranges from formulae to experience and combinations in between, all of which prime and direct preparatory studies and associated working processes in relationship to realising the end product*

Figure 12.5 A heuristic for representing types of visual and verbal grammar used.

The student's desire and ability to engage with:

be meta-cognitive

be broad and
adventurous

acquiring and
using procedural
and declarative
knowledge that is
necessary for completing a
range of complex tasks;
right social-cultural
circumstances;
good mentors

plan a course of action
and be strategic

clarify and seek
understanding

seek and evaluate
reasons

be intellectually careful

Figure 12.6 Socio-cultural conditions for becoming proficient in learning as formed by the process of accretion. The cognitive resources that enable learning are described on the inside of the hexagon; the cognitive and meta-cognitive dispositions that promote learning are on the outside. (Adapted from Tishman *et al.* 1993).

journey of education as formation. Bildung is comprehensive and ambitious: it aims to form knowledgeable, skilful, ethical persons capable of engaging with meta-poiesis and future flourishing.

An art curriculum that reflects the ambition of Bildung would aim to promote meaningful differences in the way artistic grammar has been articulated in four clearings (see Figure 12.4). By understanding the contrasting ways creative grammar has been used in such different cultural paradigms, students would develop forward momentum in their journey of art education as Bildung. Such a journey draws on types of intermediary tools, as further differentiated by how they function on axes of declarative and procedural knowledge (Figure 12.5). At the very least, such an approach to curriculum would avoid conflating knowledge of art in its socio-cultural context with facile acts of pastiche, and thus avoid perpetuating the physiognomic fallacy.

An example to illustrate the approach might be useful here. In fine art education, one such intermediary tool might be a cognitive resource for 'knowing how' to represent, say, three-dimensional space on a two-dimensional surface by consciously learning to use some or all of the seven methods identified by research (Blakemore 1973: 40–45). A supplementary 'knowing that' resource would be acquired and used to articulate a text analogue understanding of the cultural and religious reasons for why artists in fifteenth-century Italy embarked on rediscovering the original Greek invention of perspective, and to give a face-analogue description of how this was achieved in one Renaissance work of art. The process would be further enhanced by using cognitive and meta-cognitive strategies, which would enable students to gradually learn how to plan, monitor, and revise the efficacy of their verbal and non-verbal cognitive resources (see Figure 12.6).

For students to develop and maintain forward trajectory in dealing with complex as opposed to trivial problems in art, they would have to incrementally improve the

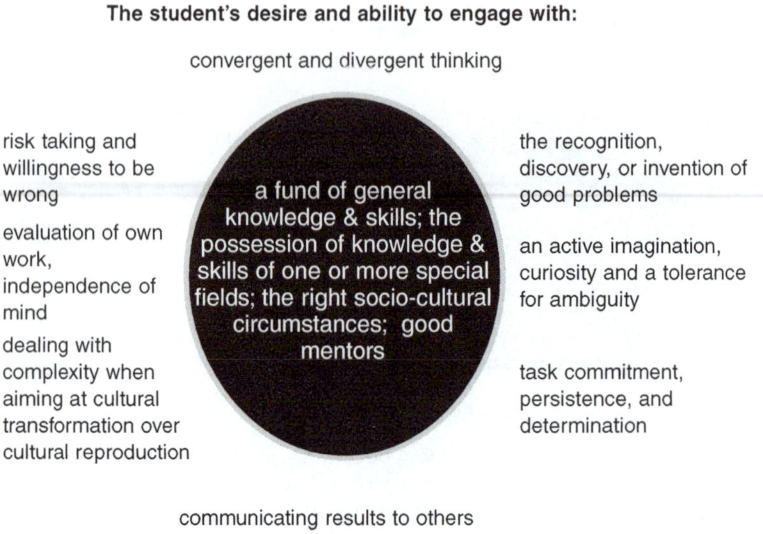

The student's desire and ability to engage with:

convergent and divergent thinking

risk taking and
willingness to be
wrong

evaluation of own
work,
independence of
mind

dealing with
complexity when
aiming at cultural
transformation over
cultural reproduction

a fund of general
knowledge & skills; the
possession of knowledge &
skills of one or more special
fields; the right socio-cultural
circumstances; good
mentors

the recognition,
discovery, or invention of
good problems

an active imagination,
curiosity and a tolerance
for ambiguity

task commitment,
persistence, and
determination

communicating results to others

Figure 12.7 Socio-cultural conditions for realising proficiency in creativity as
formed by the process of accretion. The cognitive resources that
enable creativity are described on the inside of the hexagon; the
cognitive and meta-cognitive dispositions that promote creativity
are on the outside (Nickerson 1999; Ochse 1990; Perkins 1988;
Weisberg 1999).

stock of cognitive resources to 'enable' enculturation, while at the same time developing dispositions and cognitive strategies that 'promote' cultural transformation
(Perkins 1988 – see Figure 12.7).

For pedagogy to sustain the forward stride of solution, it would have to scaffold the
conditions that make it more rather than less likely for students to experience their
present learning as directed to future flourishing. To achieve this aim teachers would
have to adopt a pedagogy that not only mediates the requisite knowledge and skills,
but also the necessary dispositions for developing ethical forms of strategic intelligence (see Figure 12.8).

For assessment practices to embody the same forward trajectory, students would
need to learn how to monitor their use of declarative and procedural forms of knowledge independently. This would require deliberately planning for and using meta-
cognition in the practice of formative, self-assessment, so as to nurture their own feed
forward as opposed to the teacher's feedback (Cunliffe 2009 – see Figure 12.9;
Faultley and Savage 2007).

Understanding learning and creativity as shaped by intermediary tools formed by
the process of accretion makes it easier to see assessment as dealing with three types
of knowledge: procedural knowledge, declarative knowledge, and the knowing what
to do of ethical, self-knowledge (Figure 12.10). In this respect, educational practices
that aim for cognitive reliability miss the point, as reliability is more often than not a

The teacher's ability and desire to:

take students'
suggestions and
questions
seriously

offer students
opportunities to work
with a wide variety of
materials under different
conditions

encourage flexible
thinking

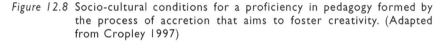
the mediation of a
fund of general
knowledge & skills; the
mediation of knowledge &
skills of one or more special
fields; right sociocultural
circumstances

have a cooperative,
socially integrated style
of teaching

enable students to learn
to cope with frustration
and failure, so that they
have the courage to try
the new and unusual

encourage
students to learn
independently

communicating results to others

Figure 12.8 Socio-cultural conditions for a proficiency in pedagogy formed by the process of accretion that aims to foster creativity. (Adapted from Cropley 1997)

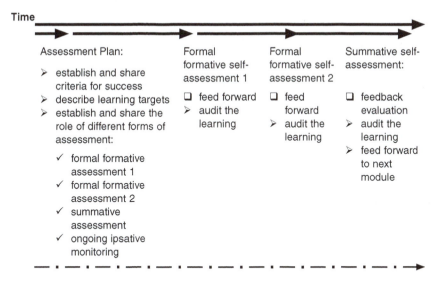

Time

Assessment Plan:

➢ establish and share
criteria for success
➢ describe learning targets
➢ establish and share the
role of different forms of
assessment:

  ✓ formal formative
  assessment 1
  ✓ formal formative
  assessment 2
  ✓ summative
  assessment
  ✓ ongoing ipsative
  monitoring

Formal
formative self-
assessment 1

❑ feed forward
➢ audit the
learning

Formal
formative self-
assessment 2

❑ feed
forward
➢ audit the
learning

Summative self-
assessment:

❑ feedback
evaluation
➢ audit the
learning
➢ feed forward
to next
module

Figure 12.9 An example of using assessment for learning as an analogy with persons who are capable of realising a life-plan.

by-product of ethical responsibility. Therefore, the character traits that are engendered to promote creativity in art education require an ethical gloss, as someone can have excellent forms of 'knowing how' and 'knowing that' but lack the desire to use 'knowing what to do' to realise good, creative ends.

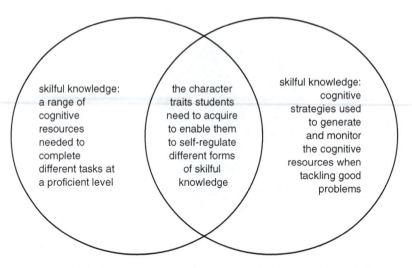

Figure 12.10 The 'knowing what to do' of insightful, ethical knowledge.

Summary: art education as the person who develops and executes a life-plan

A curriculum structured to promote meaningful differences in the way intermediary tools function in various cultural paradigms, along with a Vygotskian pedagogy aimed at mediating such tools, and a practice of assessment as feed forward, proves to be a worthy analogy with a person who formulates and realises a life-plan. Such a life-plan supports the formation of 'as if' solutions by nurturing socio-cultural, ecological persons capable of making nuanced judgements and engaging with 'meta-poiesis' (Dreyfus and Kelly 2011: 212). Discerning and creating meaningful differences not only makes a person more able to resist nihilism but also better attunes them to a relationally responsive ethical way of life.

Conclusion

Only the forward leaning process of creativity by accretion has the potency and logic to build the necessary complex, calibrated range of creative grammar that can stand in reserve to service the future needs of art educators and artists, and, by extension, to embody art with the analogical complexity with which persons engage, most notably their capacity to formulate and exercise a life-plan. In this respect, the creative grammar of accretion represents the high road to sustainable creative flourishing.

References

Barber, B.R. (2007) *Consumed: How Markets Corrupt Children, Infantilize Adults, and Swallow Citizens Whole*, London: W.W. Norton.

Blakemore, C. (1973) 'The Baffled Brain', in: R.L. Gregory and E.H. Gombrich (eds) *Illusion in Nature and Art*, London: Duckworth.

Bühler, K. (1934) *Theory of Language: The Representational Function of Language*, 2nd edn, Trans. D.F. Goodwin, Philadelphia, PA: John Benjamins.

Burke, E. (1759) *A Philosophical Enquiry into the Origins of our Ideas of the Sublime and the Beautiful* [revised edition, 1990], A. Phillips (ed.), Oxford: Oxford University Press.

Chi, M. (2006) 'Two Approaches to the Study of Experts' Characteristics', in: K.A. Ericsson, N. Charness, P.J. Feltovich and R.R. Hoffman (eds) *The Cambridge Handbook to Expert Performance*, Cambridge: Cambridge University Press.

Claxton, G. (2005) *The Wayward Mind: An Intimate History of the Unconscious*, London: Little, Brown.

Collings, M. (2008) 'Banksy's Ideas Have the Value of a Joke', *The Times*, 28 January.

Cropley, A.J. (1997) 'Fostering Creativity in the Classroom: General Principles', in: M. Runco (ed.) *The Creativity Research Handbook, Volume 1*, Cresskill, NJ: Hampton Press.

Crossan, D. (1988) *The Dark Interval: Towards a Theology of Story*, Salem, OR: Polebridge Press.

Cunliffe, L. (1998) 'Gombrich on Art: A Social Constructivist Interpretation of his Work and its Relevance to Education', *Journal of Aesthetic Education*, 32 (4): 61–77.

Cunliffe, L. (2003) 'Connectivity for Showing and Saying across Differences in Art Education', *International Journal of Art and Design Education*, 22 (3): 305–315.

Cunliffe, L. (2005a) 'Forms of Knowledge in Art Education and the Corollary of Authenticity in the Teaching and Assessment of such Forms of Knowledge', *International Journal of Art and Design Education*, 24 (2): 199–208.

Cunliffe, L. (2005b) 'The Problematic Relationship between Knowing How and Knowing that in Secondary Art Education', *Oxford Review of Education*, 31 (4): 547–556.

Cunliffe, L. (2006) 'A Wittgensteinian Approach to Discerning the Meaning of Works of Art in the Practice of Critical and Contextual Studies', *Journal of Aesthetic Education*, 40 (1): 65–78.

Cunliffe, L. (2007) 'Towards a More Complex Description of the Role of Assessment as a Practice for Nurturing Strategic Intelligence', in: T. Pateman (ed.) *Assessment in Art and Design Education*, Bristol: Element Books.

Cunliffe, L. (2008a) 'Using Assessment to Nurture Knowledge-rich Creativity', *Innovations in Education and Teaching International*, 45 (3): 309–317.

Cunliffe, L. (2008b) 'A Case Study of an Extra-curricular School Activity Designed to Promote Learning', *International Journal of Education through Art*, 4 (1): 91–105.

Cunliffe, L. (2009) 'Using Assessment to Cultivate Proficient Creativity and Strategic Intelligence in Art Education', *Measuring Unique Studies Effectively: Creativity and Assessment in Higher Art Education*, (MUSE) Conference, Savannah, GA. Online. Available at: https://education.exeter.ac.uk/staff_details.php?user=lcunliff (accessed 15 July 2011).

Cunliffe, L. (2010) 'Representing and Practising Meaningful Differences in a Well-structured but Complex Art Curriculum', *Journal of Curriculum Studies*, 42 (6): 727–750.

Cunliffe, L. (2011) 'Creative Grammar and Art Education', *Journal of Aesthetic Education*, 45 (3): 1–14.

Curtis, R., Weeden, P. and Winter, J. (2000) 'Measurement, Judgment, Criteria and Expertise: Intuition in Assessment from Three Different Subject Perspectives', in: T. Atkinson and G. Claxton (eds) *The Intuitive Practitioner*, Maidenhead: Open University Press.

Dreyfus, H.L. (1997) 'Heidegger on the Connection between Nihilism, Art, Technology and Politics', in: C. Guignon (ed.) *The Cambridge Companion to Heidegger*, Cambridge: Cambridge University Press.

Dreyfus, H.L. (2001) *On the Internet*, London: Routledge.

Dreyfus, H.L. and Kelly, S.D. (2011) *All Things Shining: Readings in the Western Classics to Find Meaning in a Secular Age*, London: Free Press.

Ericsson, K.A., Charness, N., Feltovich, P.J. and Hoffman, R.R. (eds) (2006) *The Cambridge Handbook to Expert Performance*, Cambridge: Cambridge University Press.

Faultley, M. and Savage, J. (2007) *Creativity in Secondary Education*, Exeter: Learning Matters.

Foster, H. (1996) *The Return of the Real*, Cambridge, MA: MIT Press.

Freud, S. (1991) *Interpretation of Dreams*, London, Penguin.

Fuller, P. (1986) *The Australian Scapegoat: Towards an Antipodean Aesthetic*, Nedlands: University of Western Australia Press.

Gombrich, E.H. (1971) *Meditations on a Hobby Horse and other Essays on the Theory of Art*, 2nd edn, London: Phaidon Press.

Gombrich, E.H. (1972) *Art and Illusion: A Study in the Psychology of Pictorial Representation*, 4th edn, London: Phaidon Press.

Gombrich, E.H. (1984) *Tributes: Interpreters of our Cultural Tradition*, London: Phaidon Press.

Gombrich, E.H. (1987) 'A Theory of Modern Art', in: R. Woodfield (ed.) *Reflections on the History of Art: Views and Reviews*, London: Phaidon Press.

Gombrich, E.H. (2002) *The Preference for the Primitive: Episodes in the History of Western Taste and Art*, London: Phaidon Press.

Hagberg, G.L. (2004) *Art as Language: Wittgenstein, Meaning, and Aesthetic Theory*, London: Cornell University Press.

Harland, J., Kinder, K., Lord P. *et al.* (2000) *Arts Education in Secondary Schools: Effects and Effectiveness*, Slough: NFER.

Harré, R. (2001) 'Norms in Life: Problems in the Representations of Rules', in: D. Bakhurst and S.G. Shanker (eds) *Jerome Bruner: Language, Culture, Self*, London: Sage.

Harré, R. and Tissaw, M. (2005) *Wittgenstein and Psychology: A Practical Guide*, Aldershot: Ashgate.

Houser, P.L. and Katsuiko, M. (1992) *Invitation to Tea Gardens: Kyoto's Culture Enclosed*, Kyoto: Mitsimura Suiko Shoin.

Howell, W.C. (1982) *Conscious Competence Learning Model: Stages of Learning – Unconscious Incompetence to Unconscious Competence*, Online. Available at: http://www.businessballs.com/consciouscompetencelearningmodel.htm (accessed 4 July 2008).

Hursthouse, R. (1999) *On Virtue Ethics*, Oxford: Oxford University Press.

Jones, R.L. (1997) 'Modern and Postmodern: Questioning Contemporary Pedagogy in the Visual Arts', in: J. Hutchens and M. Suggs (eds) *Art Education: Content and Practice in a Postmodern Era*, Reston, VA: National Art Education Association.

Kearney, R. (1988) *The Wake of Imagination*, London: Century Hutchinson.

Lepsky, K. (1996) 'Art and Language: Ernst H. Gombrich and Karl Bühler's Theory of Language', in: R. Woodfield (ed.) *Gombrich on Art and Psychology*, Manchester: Manchester University Press.

Madge, C. and Weinberger, B. (1973) *Art Students Observed*, London: Faber.

Nickerson, R.S. (1999) 'Enhancing Creativity', in: R.J. Sternberg (ed.) *Handbook of Creativity*, Cambridge: Cambridge University Press.

Ochse, R. (1990) *Before the Gates of Excellence: The Determinants of Creative Genius*, Cambridge: Cambridge University Press.

Perkins, D. (1988) 'Creativity and the Quest for a Mechanism', in: R.J. Sternberg and E.E. Smith (eds) *The Psychology of Thought*, Cambridge: Cambridge University Press.

Peters, M., Burbules. N. and Smeyers, P. (2008) *Showing and Doing: Wittgenstein as a Pedagogical Philosopher*, London: Paradigm Publishers.

Richter, H. (1965) *Dada: Art and Anti-art*, London: Thames & Hudson.

Rousmaniere, N. (ed.) (2007) *Crafting Beauty in Modern Japan*, London: British Museum Press.

Rubin, W. (ed.) (1984) *'Primitivism' in 20th Century Art: Affinity of the Tribal and the Modern*, New York: Museum of Modern Art.

Sennett, R. (2008) *The Craftsman*, London: Penguin Books.

Smith, B. (1990) 'Modernism: That is to Say, Geniusism', *Modern Painters*, 3 (2): 56–59.

Solomon, J.L., Marshall, P. and Gardner, H. (2005) 'Crossing Boundaries to Generative Wisdom: An Analysis of Professional Work', in: R.J. Sternberg and J. Jordan (eds) *A Handbook to Wisdom: Psychological Perspectives*, Cambridge: Cambridge University Press.

Stallabrass, J. (2006) *High Art Light: The Rise and Fall of Young British Art*, 2nd edn, London: Verso.

Steiner, R. (2001 [1965]) *The Education of the Child in the Light of Anthroposophy*, London: Rudolf Steiner Press.

Strauss, C. and Quinn, N. (1997) *A Cognitive Theory of Cultural Meaning*, Cambridge: Cambridge University Press.

Summers, D. (1998) '"Form", Nineteenth Century Metaphysics, and the Problem of Art Historical Description', in: D. Preziosi (ed.) *The Art of Art History: A Critical Anthology,* Oxford: Oxford University Press.

Tishman, S., Jay, E. and Perkins, D.N. (1993) 'Teaching Thinking Dispositions: From Transmission to Enculturation', *Theory into Practice*, 32 (Summer): 147–153.

Vygotsky, L.S. (1971) *The Psychology of Art*, Cambridge, MA: MIT Press.

Vygotsky, L.S. (1978) *Mind in Society: The Development of Higher Psychological Processes*, M. Cole, V. John-Steiner, S. Scribner and E. Souberman (eds), Cambridge, MA: MIT Press.

Weisberg, R. (1999) 'Creativity and Knowledge: A Challenge to Theories', in: R.J. Sternberg (ed.) *Handbook of Creativity*, Cambridge: Cambridge University Press.

Weisberg, R. (2006) *Creativity: Understanding Innovation in Problem Solving, Science, Invention, and the Arts*, Hoboken, NJ: John Wiley & Sons.

Williams, R. (1965) *The Long Revolution*, Harmondsworth: Penguin.

Wittgenstein, L. (1997) *Lectures and Conversations on Aesthetics, Psychology and Religious Belief*, 3rd edn, C. Barrett (ed.), Berkley, CA: University of California Press.

Wittgenstein, L. (2001) *Philosophical Investigations*, 3rd edn, G.E.M. Anscombe and R. Rhees (eds), Trans. G.E.M. Anscombe, Oxford: Blackwell.

Zagzebski, L. (1996) *Virtues of the Mind: An Enquiry into the Nature of Virtue and the Ethical Foundations of Knowledge*, Cambridge: Cambridge University Press.

Chapter 13

Learning, truth and self-encounter

The dilemma of contemporary art education

Dennis Atkinson

There are two concerns I want to cover: first, the importance of *real learning* which I propose as a form of self-encounter, or a politics of the self, through which the self and the world are reconfigured. This has implications for the idea of the 'learner-as-subject' where practising and experiencing art (or any other domain) is a process of becoming in which art is experienced as a part of self, a self that evolves in the process of making, doing, seeing, speaking. This self-encounter through art constitutes a formative process/experience for the learner, but his or her participation in this collective enterprise that we call art must also form art itself.

The second concern, I pose as a question: How do real learning and self-encounter impact upon educational projects, pedagogies and learning communities? After all, procrastinations from partisan agendas concerning both the purpose of education and curriculum content may serve some more than others and thereby establish a 'dominant' world of learning and teaching that serves and protects particular interests so as to reduce and regulate learning and teaching to these ends.

The aim of this chapter is to try to marry the notion of real learning and its encounter with some thoughts about a more open educational project and the kinds of pedagogies that might be commensurate, which in turn has implications for how we might reconceive learning communities.

Introduction

Perhaps today we can outline two contrasting projects of education since the introduction of state education in England (and other countries); one that is grounded in economism, the need to design an education system that fuels and sustains economic growth and the ability to compete successfully in market economies, and one that is immersed in a more humanist and communal tradition grounded in the notion of a public good. In recent years under consecutive UK governments the former project has dominated government policy, a key priority being to educate students in those subjects that will service and maintain economic competitiveness. The recently elected coalition government's White Paper entitled *The Importance of Teaching* (DFE 2010) sets out its new agenda for the school education system, teaching quality and the curriculum in England; it begins with a statement from the Prime Minister, David Cameron:

So much of the education debate in this country is backward looking: have standards fallen? Have exams got easier? These debates will continue, but what really matters is how we're doing compared with our international competitors. That is what will define our economic growth and our country's future. The truth is, at the moment we are standing still while others race past.

(DFE 2010:3)

This market-led philosophy not only predicates the purpose of education but also, more compellingly, determines the provision of education; where parents compete for school places, where there are winners and losers, where schools compete with each other, where league tables are ubiquitous, where different funding systems support different kinds of schools. Mortimore (2010) argues that in this market-led project, education comes to be viewed as a private good and thus little attention is given to local communities and communal learning, even though the notion of 'every child matters' (DfES 2004) (no child left behind) is held as a guiding precept.

In the university sector in England crippling cuts to the arts and humanities drive these Faculties further towards a market-led logic that degrades or decreases the communal project of the university as a public good so that university education becomes more clearly defined as a commodity whose form is driven and regulated by the demands and benefits of individual consumers. Knowledge becomes a prized commodity to fuel the cauldrons of competitive markets. In 1984 Lyotard commented, 'knowledge in the form of an informational commodity indispensible to productive power, is already and will continue to be, a major – perhaps the major – stake in the worldwide competition for power' (p. 5). In this economist market-driven scenario, performativity becomes a key concept, driving ranks of targets, performance indicators or specified outcomes. Many in education have come to experience its imperatives through the stranglehold of audit culture, strictly regulating and evaluating the way in which educational institutions function so as to colonise their working discourses and reconfigure education as practice. Here performance is predicated upon rigid and prescriptive criteria of 'performance' which delimit its functioning reality. From the USA Eisner (2002) writes:

What we are now doing is creating an industrial culture in our schools, one whose values are brittle and whose conception of what's important narrow. We flirt with payment by results, we pay practically no attention to the idea that engagement in school can and should provide intrinsic satisfactions, and we exacerbate the importance of extrinsic rewards by creating policies that encourage children to become point collectors. Achievement has triumphed over inquiry. I think our children deserve more.

(Eisner 2002)

Alongside this economist view sits the current drive by the current UK Education Secretary, Michael Gove, to review the National Curriculum and introduce a new English Baccalaureate upon which White (2011) comments with some acidity:

> [Gove's] new English Baccalaureate is virtually a carbon copy of the 1868 Taunton report's curriculum for most 'middle class schools', as they were then called. The new award will be given to all 16-year-olds who have good exam grades in 'English, mathematics, the sciences, a modern or ancient foreign language and a humanity such as history or geography'. Taunton's list is identical, except that it makes both history and geography compulsory. How is it that a curriculum designed for clerks and shopkeepers in Dickens' England is at the cutting edge in 2010?
>
> (White 2011: 27)

This is not the first time in recent decades that government has taken a reactionary stance toward curriculum content arguing for a return to more traditional subject disciplines established over a century ago.

Humanist projects of education can be traced back through time and include the work of Rousseau, Froebel, Montessori, Dewey, Holt, Friere, hooks, Giroux and others (see Steiner 2001 [1965]; Addison 2010). The central purpose of education in such projects, though it varies according to context, can be considered in terms of a public good whereby the intention is to educate all students, whatever their capabilities, interests or predilections, to their full potential under the assumption, in turn, that this will create greater public benefit. Bingham and Biesta (2010) describe three kinds of educational projects grounded within a humanist narrative in their lucid account of Rancière's intervention into the practice of education. These projects are summarised as traditional, progressive and critical (pp. 110–112). Traditional education's purpose, they argue, is to disseminate valued knowledge to students without taking into account how such knowledge relates to the experience and backgrounds of individuals. Progressive education is similarly concerned with the inculcation of valued knowledge but also with how this *can* be made relevant and accessible to individuals. The purpose of critical education is to reveal inequalities in the educational system, curriculum and teaching methods, for example, accessibility and opportunity, resources or cultural bias, in order to argue for more equitable and emancipatory systems and procedures.

This chapter proceeds to outline a further project, which views learning as a pursuit of truth, a political act of *self-encounter* which ruptures existing frameworks of practice and knowledge for both learners and teachers. The polemic is influenced by the philosophical writings of Jacques Rancière and Alain Badiou which are concerned with specific ideas of knowledge, truth, equality, politics and emancipation. It will consider real learning as a political act, as defined by Rancière, or as an event followed by a truth procedure, as described by Badiou – rather than, for example, an incremental process of psychological or sociological development (Vygotsky 1978; Piaget 1996).

In the light of these ideas on politics, event and truth I will consider a pedagogical attitude concordant with an effective pedagogic action. To this end I propose what might be termed pedagogies against the state, or pedagogies of the event, in order to respond to acts of learning that involve leaps of becoming into a new or reconfigured world. Practical exemplification will be taken from contexts of art practices and art in education but the general argument is directed at learning and equality across all human endeavours (see also Atkinson 2011). So I hope readers might be able to link what I am saying to their specific domains of practice and research.

Art practice

Stephen Wright (2008) points to the challenge that many artists are making to more traditional notions of the term 'art' in order to counter policing tendencies which he believes exist even in the world of contemporary practice. I quote:

> Every year, more and more artists are quitting the artworld frame – or looking for and experimenting with viable exit strategies – rather than broadening it further through predatory expeditions into the life-world. And these are some of the most exciting developments in art today, for to leave the frame means sacrificing one's coefficient of artistic visibility – but potentially in exchange for greater corrosiveness toward the dominant semiotic order.
>
> (Wright 2008: online)

I mention this writing from Wright because it raises questions for me concerning the coefficients of pedagogical visibilities, in other words how learners/teachers *appear* as learners and teachers; is there a consensus, a series of normative assumptions, according to which they are conceived as learners and teachers? How might we, if desirable, move beyond such consensus?

The fact that artists today and historically produce work outside of acknowledged frameworks of art and their respective institutional forces so that it is sometimes difficult to conceive as art, raises some pertinent issues relating to recognition, objects and practice. For example, in recent years some artists (Rainer Ganahl, Tino Seghal, Liam Gillick, Irit Rogoff and the projects ACADEMY (2006) and Summit (2007)) are engaging directly with pedagogical practices such as reading groups and seminars, alternative learning sites, and free schools, in their art practice. Their focus it seems is to reconsider sites of learning such as universities, schools, galleries and museums and ask how these sites might be expanded to involve new forms of learning, discussion and debate and so, we might deduce, new forms of competence and new economies of knowledge (its history, evolving technology, social organisation, distribution and management). Such work challenges us to imagine both what art can be but also what learning can be beyond the parameters of reproduction, packaged knowledge, traditional skills and the pragmatic and predictable application of knowledge. Thus what this work is attempting is a radical intervention into traditional sites and economies of institutionalised knowledge and a redistribution of such economies. It also challenges us to consider the idea of community, communal knowledge and communal learning.

A key factor which may become obscured, though not necessarily, in these artistic–pedagogical initiatives concerns the individual's spatio-temporality of learning. It is not the structural therefore with which I am concerned (though this is important), not the notion of core competences, or new curricula, however much they may dissolve and reform, but the idea of events of learning and their implicit subjectifications. These ideas will be unpacked shortly because they are at the heart of what I am trying to say about learning.

In a parallel move to Wright's critique: is there a predominant framework or consensus in art education that persists? Research by Downing and Watson (2004) into secondary school art in England suggests that there is. But can we envisage an art education along different lines that may be more appropriate or responsive to learners and the ways in which they learn? Is it possible or desirable to reconsider sites of learning to stretch our comprehension of what learning can become? Is it possible to do this in the light of the power of institutional formatting and norms? Is it possible or desirable today for educators to sacrifice their coefficient of pedagogic visibility in order to corrode current policing frameworks and establish more productive, equitable or emancipatory spaces for learning? After all not all policing orders are bad or unproductive. Is it desirable to interrogate the predominant frameworks in which teaching and learning are conceived, which construct their coefficient of visibility or their coefficients of competences? Is it possible for institutions, such as schools, universities, galleries, to do and be much more than their current function?

A current advocacy in school art education in the USA concerns visual culture art education (Freedman 2003; Tavin 2003; Duncum 2006), responding to the wider established field of research into visual cultures. This has opened new critical perspectives for the study of the visual in schools by canvassing the need for a critical interrogation of how, for example, visual productions and practices seduce and regulate vision, how visual media precipitate and cultivate desire, and construct identities and subjectivities. In other words, this form of art education attempts to expose the ideological underpinnings of visual products and practices in order to equip learners with the power of discernment. But here, as jagodzinski (2010) cautions with a hint of reprove, the visual becomes captured by an oral eye which tends to prioritise aesthetics and representation, thus occluding the domains of aisthesis and poiesis that are formative in local becomings of art practice.

In summary the generic concern of much contemporary art is a constant interrogation of established ideas of artist, object, performance, spectator, skill, technique and media. It is an art that attempts to break new ground and to push our boundaries of understanding. The challenge to art as we know it means that this term has always been a moveable feast, a signifier with no absolute or final meaning, and this has implications for the term art education and its coefficients of visibility, knowledge and practice.

We can say that contemporary art is concerned with the production of the new which, in some cases, has transformative effects upon practice and understanding. The key point to make is that it is through the temporality of the *art event* and its consequences that new directions and reconfigurations begin to appear. My intention is to make a similar point regarding processes of learning and in order to do this I draw upon the philosophical work of Badiou and Rancière.

Badiou and Rancière

The notion of 'event' lies at the centre of the philosophical work of Badiou and others (Deleuze, Foucault, Bergson, Whitehead, Arendt) and I believe that their explorations of this term have direct relevance for education, teaching and learning. Foucault's work is deeply concerned with events in thought, Deleuze with the dynamic immanence of forces that become actualised and Badiou with the event as a puncturing of established knowledge and subsequent pursuit of truth through which a subject and a reconfigured world emerges. It is with Badiou's work on event and truth that I shall be concerned in offering a third educational project beyond economism and humanisms registered in being. This project is articulated around the notion of becoming, where real learning is conceived as self-encounter, an event that projects a learner into a new or modified ontological state. It is concerned with learning as a process of becoming through local 'lines of flight' (Deleuze and Guattari 1988) or in my terms, local curations of learning. But then I want to move quickly to Rancière in order to consider learning as a political event or act and the emergence of new subjectifications of learning.

Knowledge and truth

> A truth is, first of all, something new, what transmits, what repeats, we shall call knowledge. Distinguishing truth from knowledge is essential.
>
> (Badiou 2005a: 45)

Both Badiou and Rancière have similar but not identical views on knowledge and on truth but they vary in their discussion on how truth emerges. Truth is not concerned with 'being correct' or ideas of adequation. For Badiou truth is linked to the eruption of an event and its generic consequences, it is nothing to do with knowledge or meaning. Truth is not what knowledge produces; on the contrary, 'it is what exceeds, in a given situation, the knowledge that accounts for the situation' (Leclercle 1999: 8). In other words truth is what cannot be conceived in a particular situation according to existing knowledge, 'a truth is a puncturing of such knowledge' (ibid.).

Meanwhile Rancière writes: 'Each one of us describes our own parabola around the truth. No two orbits are alike' (1991: 59). 'Truth exists by itself; it is that which is and not that which is said. Saying depends on man, but the truth does not' (p. 58). In other words, for Rancière truth lies beyond language, it cannot be captured by language, it is eternal.

For Badiou, 'Truths exist as exceptions to what there is' (2009: 4). For him truth is infinite. A key aphorism from his book *Logics of Worlds* appears to have some resonance with Rancière's idea that truth does not depend on man if we read this statement as meaning that 'man' indicates an established knowledge of 'man'. Badiou states, 'There are only bodies and languages, except that there are truths' (ibid.). Truths are *in excess* of established forms of knowledge and practice. We might say then, echoing Badiou, that, 'a truth bores a hole in knowledge' of 'man'.

Truth is infinite but it is taken up by various subject points through time and this also resonates with Rancière's idea above, that we each 'describe our own parabola around truth', which is to suggest that we never attain truth in itself but develop our local relations towards truth. It is therefore possible to verify objects of knowledge but impossible to determine if they are true. This can be acknowledged when we consider, for example, the evolution from Newtonian science grounded in a separation of space and time to the relativity of Einstein's project. In such transformations of knowledge truth acts as a driving force producing new forms of knowledge but truth in itself can never be knowledge.

Another way of conceiving the infinity of truth is by considering it as an unfurling process. For example, the full implications of Galileo's work in mathematics were not 'realised' until years after his passing and the ramifications of Duchamp's use of his readymade objects are still unfurling today. In other words, after the initial event of the break with established practices and forms of knowledge the truth of these examples is concerned with the ongoing unfurling of new worlds and their subjects.

For both philosophers therefore truth is exceptional to established knowledge. For Badiou knowledge is that which constitutes a situation or a 'world' and for Rancière it constitutes part of a 'distribution of the sensible' (police order). Truth is never finally captured or known in itself and in this sense it has no substantial existence (see Badiou 2009: 5). Peter Hallward (2003) writes in his book on Badiou:

> Truth can only be reached through a process that breaks decisively with all established criteria for judging (or interpreting) the validity (or profundity) of opinions (or understandings) … access to truth can be achieved only by going against the grain of the world and against the current of history.
>
> (Hallward 2003: xxiii–xxiv)

The key idea then is that knowledge is part of an existing world whereas truth is that which punctures this world through the force of an event, which I will come to shortly. The way in which knowledge forms in Badiou's account is through what he terms a *count as one*. Without proceeding with a detailed account of the count here, the essential idea is that this is Badiou's term in *Being and Event* for a basic categorising ontological process operating on a pre-ontological multiplicity so as to create a form or a being (Badiou 2005b). Thus a situation consists of a series of counts that determine ontological properties. In *Logics of Worlds* he replaces the term situation for world (Badiou 2009). An event is that process which punctures a collection of counts that make up a particular world and so has the potential to transform this world.

The identification of an object of knowledge is also the assertion of a particular world in which it is conceived as an object. For example, the identification of a learner is possible through a series of established conceptions of what it is to be a learner, or more precisely different degrees of being a learner. Here we are concerned with the idea of *appearing in a world* and what Badiou terms the identity-function which is facilitated by what he terms the transcendental of a world, a rather technical term for its structuring logic (see Badiou 2011: 51–63).

In the context of education we might consider real learning (in contrast to normative learning) as a process in which new objects emerge and new structuring processes develop on the ontological level (new counts as one). Such learning may be recognised according to the transcendental structuring logics through which we recognise learning but equally there may be processes of learning that are not recognised within these prevailing systems of recognition that are constituted by our knowledge formations (Vygotsky 1978; Piaget 1996; Gardner 1983).

So a count as one at the ontological level brings an object into existence within a world whilst simultaneously confirming a world. But there are occasions when the circularity between object and world is disrupted due to the fact that something happens that is difficult to comprehend within the logics of established worlds; something that brings about a reconfiguration of a world and its objects as well as the emergence of a new subject. With reference to major disruptions in politics, art or science, Badiou terms such a disturbance an *event*, a process through which an established order (world) is punctured leading to the development of a truth process that reconstitutes the world. An evental site is the location of change; it is rather like a void in the established order of things out of which a particular truth process evolves to change the order. Badiou writes:

> To be faithful to an event is to move within the situation that this event has supplemented, by *thinking* … the situation 'according to' the event. And this, of course – since the event was excluded by all the regular laws of the situation – compels the subject to invent a new way of being and acting in the situation.
>
> (Badiou 2001: 41–42)

> an event, in affecting a world, always has a local rearrangement of the transcendental of this world as its effect
>
> (Badiou 2009: 222)

> for me, the event is the immanent principle of exceptions to becoming, or [in other words] Truths.
>
> (Badiou 2009: 385, my bracket)

He cites the examples of the Schoenberg event in music, the Cantor event in mathematics, the Galileo event in science and the French revolution as a political event. Though Badiou references major disruptions in their respective fields, I have argued (Atkinson 2011) that it is possible to conceive such events occurring on a more micro level in local events of learning in which learners, for example, the entry into language in early years, new forms of art practice or new forms of mathematics production (see Brown 2011), make leaps into new spaces of learning, create new frameworks of understanding, and emerge as reconfigured subjects within reconfigured worlds. For Badiou the task of education is 'to arrange the forms of knowledge in such a way that some truth may come to pierce a hole in them' (2005c: 9).

The count for one refers to established patterns of conceiving or representing ourselves, others and objects in our worlds; but such counts are subject to change as circumstances change or they may be more severely disrupted within local evental sites.

New 'countings' may confirm an existing world but an evental disruption has the potential to reconfigure a particular world and its transcendental so as to produce a new order of counts. My point is to argue that we can conceive real learning as involving a disruption of a learner's transcendental, his or her structuring logics in a particular field of practice, so as to precipitate the learner into a new ontological state where new orders of counts evolve. These ideas suggest an educational project not determined completely by established knowledge nor established ideas of teaching and learning.

An illustration

A recent exhibition by student teachers displaying their explorations of critical pedagogies through visual practice contained a number of exhibits that manifested what I have termed real learning that effected an ontological and critical displacement. The exhibition is the culmination of a course on critical pedagogies taught by John Johnston and Tara Page at Goldsmiths, University of London. One exhibit consisted quite simply of a three metre by two metre gigantic assessment pro-forma (normally an A4 sheet of paper), a ubiquitous object in secondary schools in England and elsewhere. The student teacher was challenging the audit culture of the school and in doing so questioning his being as a teacher within the current structure of education and assessment. Through this work and its critical manoeuvres and lines of flight the student was *becoming minor* in the Deleuzian sense of challenging the hegemonic form of assessment. This challenge to institutional practice through art involved a profound process of self-encounter or a politics of the self that has led to a reconfiguration of self and world. On another level, of course, the production of this giant artefact laid down a challenge to the student's university tutors who have to assess his work as part of a course on critical pedagogy! The art object here is saying rather impudently, 'go on then … assess me!' Here the artefact in the form of an assessment pro-forma constitutes a point of exception that explodes the existing semiotic and epistemological codes and their respective ontological positions. It creates a void space that has the potential to effect new or different creative processes that are occluded by existing institutional (school) frameworks. The art object is therefore functioning as a political act in that it disturbs both the apparatus of assessment, introducing a potential for reconfiguration, and also the university course which led to its production. It is a political act in the sense that it challenges the world of assessment, its ways of speaking and practising – from an idea of equality its force is to rupture and challenge established technologies and how they produce specific subjectivities. This notion of politics as rupture will be discussed shortly.

Rancière: distribution of the sensible, police, politics and equality

Rancière produces a series of conceptualisations that have some resonance with those I have discussed from Badiou. We might view as equivalent to Badiou's 'world' (or situation) Rancière's notion of the 'distribution of the sensible'. He uses this term to refer to a 'system of divisions and boundaries that define among other things what is visible and audible in a particular aesthetico-political regime' (Rancière 2004: 1). A distribution of the sensible is concerned with organising and legitimating ways of doing, saying and seeing in particular social contexts. With this notion he is seeking to explore the ways in which social communities are formatted; how this formatting regulates and defines social spaces and positions; who is able to participate within this particular formatting and who is not; what parts individuals play according to the format of particular communities. His general emancipatory project is concerned with how such social distributions are disrupted in order to precipitate a reconfiguration of the sensible which would facilitate recognition of individuals or groups previously marginalised or invisible.

Rancière does not follow Badiou's ideas on radical change precipitated by an event in that he does not view such processes of change as a radical rupture with the logics of an existing world order; rather he articulates radical change as the consequence of a confrontation between two worlds in one world, or two logics within one world (see Rancière 1999: 27–30): 'I have tried to conceive heterogenesis through a type of thinking and activity that produces shocks between worlds, but shocks between worlds in the same world: re-distributions, re-compositions, and re-configurations of elements' (Rancière 2010: 212).

His key conceptual tools are the notions of 'police', 'politics' and equality. In a nutshell, politics for Rancière creates a rupture in the established police order in the name of equality. Politics constitutes a form of dissensus through which the invisible or the inaudible (inexistents for Badiou) are able to partake in a reconstituted sharing of the social order.

For Rancière politics is not concerned with the skirmishes of party politics or with parliamentary democracies as we know them in Europe and other parts of the world. Rather it is a process that is fuelled by an issue of equality or a 'wrong' which precipitates action against the existing distribution of the sensible comprised of those established ways of seeing, doing and speaking; those forms of organisation and conduct, values, orders and powers, the distribution of places and roles (see Rancière 1999: 28–29) that together form a community. The distribution of the sensible is closely associated with Rancière's idea of the police:

> The police is thus first an order of bodies that defines the allocation of ways of doing, ways of being, and ways of saying, and see that these bodies are assigned by name to a particular place and task; it is an order of the visible and the sayable that sees that a particular activity is visible and another is not, that this speech is understood as discourse and another is noise.
>
> (Rancière 1999: 29)

And further:

> It is police law, for example, that traditionally turns the workplace into a private space not regulated by the ways of seeing and saying proper to what is called the public domain, where the worker's having a part is strictly defined by the

remuneration of his work. Policing is not so much the 'disciplining' of bodies as a rule governing their appearing, a configuration of occupations and the properties of the spaces where these occupations are distributed.

(ibid.)

These passages have direct implications for reflecting upon spaces of teaching and learning in the sense that we can conceive them according to particular distributions of bodies, tasks, modes of being; where certain activities, discourses and practices are visible and others not so much; where learners and teachers *appear* according to the logics and rules of certain practices and discourses; where particular organisations of space and their properties are established and effect such appearance. For Badiou (2011: 26–32) the notion of appearance is linked closely to existence. Existence registers a 'being-there' in a world which involves degrees of appearing. Existence is not therefore a category of being but of appearing and the degree of appearing is controlled by a transcendental of a world or its dominant structuring logic.

The police order is never total, nor should it be viewed necessarily in negative terms, in that for any social organisation to be such it depends upon structures and orders that afford some sense of functional stability. But there are moments when, within a police configuration which upholds a particular distribution of the sensible, those who have no part or visibility or voice begin to 'speak' or become visible; where once their speech was noise or their visibility obscure. We can witness such events in the worlds of fashion and popular music (see McRobbie 2007) where young designers working on kitchen tables or young musicians force their forms of subcultural capital into existing distributions that effect reconfigurations of their respective cultural and social spaces. This 'antagonistic' process relates to Rancière's articulation of politics:

> Political activity is whatever shifts a body from the place assigned to it or changes a place's destination. It makes visible what had no business being seen, and makes heard a discourse where once there was only place for noise; it makes understood as discourse what was once only heard as noise.
>
> (Rancière 1999: 30)

So for Rancière politics is concerned with a disruption of the general orders and organisations, of the *logos* and *aisthesis* of a particular community or social context by bodies that have no 'say' or status (apart from being marginalised) in such orders. Politics is initiated by a 'wrong', an issue of equality, on behalf of those that have little or no say: 'Politics exists because those who have no right to be counted as speaking beings make themselves of some account' (Rancière 1999: 27). And further: 'Politics occurs when there is a place and a way for two heterogeneous processes to meet. The first is the police process in the sense we have tried to define. The second is the process of equality' (p. 30).

Perhaps we can also view politics in terms of a process of self-encounter through which a new subject emerges through subjectification (a term I will discuss shortly) to a new idea that challenges existing states of being and their embedding worlds;

where something appears to change the relation at a local level between elements in a world and the logics of their distribution in order to produce a reconfigured world.

The idea of equality precipitated by a perception or experience of inequality is therefore that which forms the basis for political action to arise. However, equality is not to be conceived as an end-point, a specified target to achieve but rather in terms of an assumption that needs to be discerned and verified through political action. The idea of verification takes the form of a *subjectification* to the struggle for equality:

> Politics is a matter of subjects or, rather, modes of subjectification. By subjecti- fication I mean the production through a series of actions of a body and a capac- ity for enunciation not previously identifiable within a given field of experience, whose identification is thus part of the reconfiguration of the field of experience.
>
> (Rancière 1999: 35)

For me, the relation between politics and equality resonate with Badiou's event-truth relation in that politics and event both articulate a process of rupture to existing orders, whilst equality and truth indicate the propellant that leads to disruption and change.

The idea of subjectification is entirely appropriate, I would argue, for considering the emergence of learners (teachers) through the process of what I call real learning (see Atkinson 2008, 2011). The subjectification of a learner equals the emergence of a learner *as a learner* following a pathway of inquiry which breaks new ground beyond established parameters of learning. Such learning involves a movement into a new ontological state which, in agreement with Rancière, involves new forms of action and speech not previously made manifest in a 'given field of experience' and this novelty invokes a reconfiguration of this field.

Truth and subjectification in Rancière and Badiou

The relation between truth and subjectification provides an understanding of the sub- ject which is in one sense 'immaterial' in that the subject is not conceived as a sub- stantial entity or as an amalgam of different positions or performances – but as a commitment to the truth of an Idea (Badiou) or the assertion of equality (Rancière). This is not the same understanding of truth as in the relation between truth and knowl- edge presupposed by explanation, whereby the truth of education is to induct students into existing explanatory forms of learning and understanding. To repeat Rancière:

> By *subjectification* I mean the production through a series of actions of a body and a capacity for enunciation not previously identifiable within a given field of experi- ence, whose identification is thus part of the reconfiguration of the field of experience.
>
> (Rancière 1999: 35)

Subjectification therefore is a term that articulates both the emergence of a new subject but equally a reconfigured world. Pedagogical subjectification involves the evolution of real learning and the emergence of a new world for the learner; we might argue as do Bingham and Biesta that subjectification happens not in actuality but in spite of actuality:

> It happens as new speech is forced onto the scene of discourse. This new speech will not have a direct referent in the realm of what is already considered to be true. It is poetic in the sense that poetry exists in spite of, rather than within, what is true. This new speech 'cannot be rationalised in the form of a discourse that separates truth from illusion' (Rancière).
>
> (Bingham and Biesta 2010: 130)

They argue that for Rancière, subjectification is rather like a poetic event, as it reconfigures the field of experience (ibid.). Such events cannot be understood, 'in the realm of what is already considered to be true,' or part of existing knowledge, but rather in the sense of the creation of a new or reconfigured world as can be gleaned in the production of poetic form.

For Badiou subjectification emerges from the consequences of an event, which is not part of a situation nor its epistemic framework. But as Hallward (2003: 145) comments, Badiou's later work on the subject (2009) moves from an instantaneous precipitation to a process happening over time and where an event has the potential to produce different spaces of subjectification, faithful, reactionary and obscure. Truth is dependent upon something new coming into appearance, 'a new body forms in the world that will be the body of truth or a subjectivizable body' (Badiou 2011: 85). Badiou provides a number of examples of subjectivisation in art (Schoenberg, Pollock) in politics (May 1968) in mathematics (Cantor). We can think of real learning as a subjectivisation on a local level which has significant affects on the learner and his or her world of learning in specific subject domains. In the latter, new subjects and their respective worlds emerge by persevering with a line of enquiry without knowing where it is going but which when undertaken eventually changes the horizon of the learner and his or her situation as well as the view of the past situation of the learner. It is the event of learning and a subsequent perseverance with its line of enquiry, its line of flight, which constitutes a becoming subject.

For Rancière subjectification is the process through which a new becoming occurs; in my terms it is the route to real learning as it reconfigures the world of the learner and evokes a self-emancipation into a new ontological state. Subjectification is therefore a *disidentification* (Rancière 1999: 36) which redefines the field of experience '... it is the space where those of no account are counted' (ibid.). I have provided exemplifications of subjectification in learning elsewhere (Atkinson 2011: 7–8 and 38–39) where I describe a young child 'becoming painting' (in the Deleuzian sense) and a young teacher whose practice is transformed when he experiences a radical self-encounter in his teaching that projects him into a new and reconfigured pedagogic space.

How might we then conceive of pedagogical subjectification? It is not difficult to articulate a prototypical conception of a learner in current educational contexts, but the idea of pedagogical subjectification punctures this perception by questioning *who is a learner* and *what is learning*. Furthermore, *what is a school? What is a university?*

It questions the *existence of learning* (see Rancière: 1999: 36, for equivalent interrogations of the terms 'worker', or 'women'). This subjectification opens a gap between current understanding and the real of existence in a particular context: 'Any subjectification is a disidentification, a removal from the naturalness of place' (ibid.). It is a matter of reconfiguring the coordinates between appearance and existence.

Conclusion

A third educational project accruing from these philosophical discussions is one concerned with the notion of real learning, learning as a process of self-encounter, learning as a political act. This cannot sit easily with an economist model where educational priorities are predicated by economic performance and competition. Nor does it suit a more liberal humanist project predicated upon established values and understanding of what it is to be human – simply because real learning, learning as self-encounter or learning as a political act, involves moving beyond such established ideas and values and extending our understanding of what it is to be human. This is what happens in creative practices in fields such as art, science or politics – where the emergence of the new precipitates new becomings at local levels and the emergence of new worlds.

Eight statements for a project towards real learning

How might we therefore envisage or utilise these philosophical ideas from Badiou and Rancière to reconfigure an educational project in contrast to economist or humanist models? What do these ideas advocate for education and learning? I conclude with eight statements for a project of real learning.

1 Knowledge is important for functioning in a world.
2 But knowledge is 'not all' – there are worlds beyond existing knowledge.
3 Events (or politics) may precipitate truths through becoming that expand our comprehension of existence and lead to a configuration of new worlds.
4 This process I call real learning.
5 Appropriate pedagogies (or anti-pedagogies) are required to support and expand real learning.
6 These are pedagogies against the state or pedagogies of the event.
7 Education must involve the acquisition of knowledge but equally the pursuit of truth.
8 Learning can be conceived as a political act of self-encounter.

References

Addison, N. (2010) 'Art and Design in Education: Ruptures and Continuities', in: N. Addison, L. Burgess, J. Steers, and J. Trowell *Understanding Art Education: Engaging Reflexively with Practice*, London: Routledge.

Atkinson, D. (2008) 'Pedagogy against the State', *International Journal of Art and Design Education*, 27 (3): 226–240.

Atkinson, D. (2011) *Art, Equality and Learning: Pedagogies against the State*, Rotterdam: Sense Publishers.

Badiou, A. (2001) *Ethics: An Essay on the Understanding of Evil*, London: Verso.

Badiou, A. (2005a) *Infinite Thought: Truth and the Return of Philosophy*, London: Continuum.

Badiou, A. (2005b) *Being and Event*, London: Continuum.

Badiou, A. (2005c) *Handbook of Inaesthetics*, Stanford, CA: Stanford University Press.

Badiou, A. (2009) *Logics of Worlds*, London: Continuum.

Badiou, A. (2011) *Second Manifesto for Philosophy*, Cambridge: Polity.

Bingham, C. and Biesta, G. (2010) *Jacques Rancière: Education, Truth Emancipation*, London: Continuum.

Brown, T. (2011) *Mathematics Education and Subjectivity: Cultures and Cultural Renewal*, Boston, MA: Springer.

Deleuze, G. and Guattari, F. (1988) *A Thousand Plateaus: Capitalism and Schizophrenia*, London: Athlone Press.

DfE (Department for Education) (2010) *The Importance of Teaching*, London: The Stationery Office.

DfES (Department for Education and Skills) (2004) *Every Child Matters: Change for Children*, London: DfES.

Downing, D. and Watson, R. (2004) *School Art. What's in it? Exploring Visual Art in Secondary Schools*, Slough: NFER.

Duncum, P. (2006) *Visual Culture in the Art Class*, Reston, VA: National Art Education Association.

Eisner, E. (2002) 'What can Education Learn from the Arts about the Practice of Education?', John Dewey Lecture, Stanford, CA: Stanford University.

Freedman, K. (2003) *Teaching Visual Culture: Curriculum, Aesthetics and the Social Life of Art*, New York: Teachers College Press.

Freire, P. (1970) *Pedagogy of the Oppressed*, New York: Continuum.

Gardner, H. (1983) *The Theory of Multiple Intelligences*, New York: Basic Books.

Giroux, H. (1996) *Counternarratives*, London: Routledge.

Hallward, P. (2003) *Badiou: A Subject to Truth*, Minneapolis, MN: University of Minnesota Press.

Holt, N. (2003) 'Representation, Legitimation and Autoethnography: An Autoethnographic Writing Story', *International Journal of Qualitative Methods*, 2 (1): 1–22.

jagodzinski, j. (2010) *Visual Art and Education in an Era of Designer Capitalism*, New York: Palgrave Macmillan.

Leclercle, J.-J. (1999) 'Cantor, Lacan, Mao, Beckett, Meme Combat: The Philosophy of Alain Badiou', *Radical Philosophy*, 93: 6–13.

Lyotard, J.-F. (1984) 'The Postmodern Condition: A Report on Knowledge'. Online. Available at: http://www.marxists.org/reference/subject/philosophy/works/fr/lyotard.htm (accessed 30 November 2011).

McRobbie, A. (2007) *The Los Angelisation of London: Three Short-waves of Young People's Micro-economies of Culture and Creativity in the UK*, Linz, Austria: European Institute for Progressive Cultural Policies.

Mortimore, P. (2010) *Markets Are for Commodities, Not Children*, Keynote Lecture Campaign for State Education Conference, 20 November 2010. Online. Available at: http://www.guardian.co.uk/education/2010/dec/07/fight-gove-education-reforms (accessed 29 January 2012).

Piaget, J. (1996) *Psychology of the Child*, New York: Basic Books.

Rancière, J. (1991) *The Ignorant Schoolmaster: Five Lessons in Intellectual Emancipation*, Stanford, CA: Stanford University Press.

Rancière, J. (1999) *Disagreement: Politics and Philosophy*, Minneapolis, MN: University of Minnesota Press.

Rancière, J. (2004) *The Politics of Aesthetics*, London: Continuum.

Rancière, J. (2010) *Dissensus: On politics and Aesthetics*, London: Continuum.

Steiner, R. (2001 [1965]) *The Education of the Child in the Light of Anthroposophy*, London: Rudolf Steiner Press.

Tavin, K. (2003) 'Wrestling with Angels, Searching for Ghosts: Towards a Critical Pedagogy of Visual Culture', *Studies in Art Education*, 44 (3): 197–213.

Vygotsky, L.S. (1978) *Mind in Society: The Development of Higher Psychological Processes*, M. Cole, V. John-Steiner, S. Scribner and E. Souberman (eds), Cambridge, MA: MIT Press.

White, J. (2011) 'Gove's on the Bac Foot with a White Paper Stuck in 1868', *Times Education Supplement*, 21 January, p. 27.

Wright, S. (2008) 'Be for Real, the Usership Challenge to Expert Culture'. Online. Available at: http://www.artandresearch.org.uk/v2n1/wright.html (accessed 24 July 2008).

Index